Help Me, Somebody!

Help Me, Somebody!

by
Fred C. Lofton

Progressive Baptist Publishing House
850 North Grove Avenue
Elgin, Illinois 60102

Copyright © 1988, by Fred C. Lofton
Published by Progressive National Baptist Convention

Library of Congress Cataloging-in-Publication Data

Lofton, Fred C.
  Help me somebody!

  Bibliography: p.
  1. Jesus Christ—Miracles—Sermons. 2. Spiritual
healing—Sermons. 3. Title. N.T. Luke—Sermons.
4. Baptists—Sermons. 5. Sermons, American. I. Title.
BT366.L58 1988   232.9′55   88-19619
ISBN: 1-55513-964-7

*To all workers in the healing professions,
especially to my colleagues
Chaplain William Young and
Drs. Edwin W. Cocke, Jr., Roger G. Smith,
and Joseph Blythe*

Table of Contents

Preface	9
The Physician in the Jewish World	11
The Physician in the Graeco-Roman World	13
Introduction	15
Help, Jesus, I Am Possessed	19
Please Help Her	31
They Needed His Help	40
He Needs Healing and Help	50
Jesus, Help This Man	63
Jesus, Help My Hand	78
Jesus, This Man Deserves Your Help	85
She Needs My Help	95
I Must Help This Man—Part I	106
I Must Help This Man—Part II	116
This Man Has My Help—Part III	126
This Man Has My Help—Part IV	135
Help, My Daughter Is Dying!	142
Help Me, Somebody!	156
Help Is Needed in the Valley	169
The Helper of the Dumb—Part I	182

The Helper of the Dumb—Part II	188
The Helper Helps the Helpless	195
Is It Legal to Heal and Help on the Sabbath?	204
Jesus, Master, Help Us!	211
Jesus, Son of David, Help Me!	227
The Healer Helps the Earless	246
Epilogue	261
Bibliography	269

Preface

This book is the outgrowth of my interest in the healing ministry of Jesus, whose healing miracles are fascinating to me as well as to those in the healing profession—hospital chaplains and medical doctors. My personal interest in Jesus' ministry of healing led me to preach a series of sermons at our church, Metropolitan Baptist, in Memphis, Tennessee. In these sermons, I sought to probe, analyze, and examine the biblical context for the healings as presented in the Gospel of Luke.

The Gospel of Luke was specifically chosen for two reasons: Luke was a medical doctor, and, according to most authorities, he uses in his gospel a number of medical terms which other writers do not use. As such, we have in Luke's account the observations of a trained medical doctor who undoubtedly was a man of science and also a man of faith. The second reason for this choice is that the Gospel of Luke is known for its universal concern for humanity.

I have sought in this book to present these sermons from an expository point of view and to let the Scriptures speak for themselves. I have also tried to utilize the diagnoses and prognoses of modern medicine concerning each healing event, and thereby point out from a scientific viewpoint what these deliberations might reveal.

The medical diagnoses and prognoses have been given by men of faith as well as men of science. This helps us to relate to the scientific field and also to what we might call "the faith field." Ultimately, the scientist and the minister are practitioners of faith, and there should not exist any conflict between the two, for we both seek to help and provide hope for the people of God as we practice our vocations in the Name of Jesus.

This book should be helpful to all who are interested in the healing arts—preachers, teachers, doctors, psychologists, psychoanalysts, psychiatrists, social workers, and lay people in general who help to share the burden of ministry in our modern world.

A personal word of appreciation goes to Mrs. Vera Clark, who provided skillful assistance during the preparation of this manuscript.

Finally, my thanks is expressed to Mrs. Jeanetta H. Powell for helping to bring this work to completion.

Most of all, I wish to thank my wife Dorothy and the kind people of Metropolitan for the moments we spent away from them in making final plans for this book.

The Physician in
the Jewish World

In the ancient Jewish world, the physician was highly esteemed, as we can see in this tribute to him from the Apocrypha, Ecclus 38:1-8:

> Honour the physician with the honour due to him,
>   according to your need of him,
>   for the Lord created him;
>
> for the healing comes from the Most High,
>   and he will receive a gift from the king.
>
> The skill of the physician lifts up his head,
>   and in the presence of great men he is admired.
>
> The Lord created medicines from the earth,
>   and a sensible man will not despise them.
>
> Was not water made sweet with a tree
>   in order that his power might be known?
>
> And he gave skill to men
>   that he might be glorified in his marvellous works.

By them he heals and takes away pain;
the pharmacist makes of them a compound.

His works will never be finished;
and from him health is upon the face of the earth.[1]

---

1. William Barclay, *Jesus As They Saw Him* (New York: Harper & Row, 1962), p. 201.

The Physician in the Graeco-Roman World

In the Graeco-Roman world, the physician was also held in high regard. The famous Hippocratic oath comes from Greece. A portion of this well-known creed follows:

> The regimen I adopt shall be for the benefit of the patients to the best of my power and judgment, not for their injury or for any wrongful purpose. I will not give a deadly drug to anyone, though it be asked of me, nor will I lead the way in such counsel; and likewise I will not give a woman a pessary to procure abortion. But I will keep my life and art in purity and holiness. Whatsoever house I enter, I will enter for the benefit of the sick, refraining from all voluntary wrong-doing and corruption, especially seduction of male or female, bond or free. Whatsoever things I see or hear concerning the life of men in my attendance of the sick, or even apart from my attendance, which ought not be blabbed abroad, I will keep silence on them, counting such things to be religious secrets.[1]

1. William Barclay, *Jesus As They Saw Him* (New York: Harper & Row, 1962), p. 202.

Introduction

This work is an attempt to illumine the darkened thinking concerning healing and salvation. Because we have tended to compartmentalize the ways in which we approach illness, we have left man with only a partial sense of wellness. This type of thinking has caused a division between faith and science, though both seek to bring wholeness to the human predicament. Jesus, our Great Physician, is shown in the Book of Luke as one who is just as concerned with ministry to physical needs as to those of the spirit.

The Jewish tradition saw man's healing as holistic. The Reformation rejected many of the Catholic practices as non-scriptural. It rejected relic-veneration healing, the sacrament of extreme unction, and pushed exorcism to the fringes of the church.[1] These attitudes greatly contribute to our separation of religion and physical health. We have given the physician all of our ques-

---

1. Lindsey P. Pherigo, *The Great Physician: The Healing Stories in Luke and Their Meaning for Today* (New York: The Education and Cultivation Division of the Women's Division, General Board of Global Ministries, The United Methodist Church, 1983), pp. 14-15.

tions concerning health. And the pastor's business is that of religious questions or spiritual matters. In the words of Paul Tillich, "Theology and medicine lost the intimate connection they originally had, and always should have—for saving the person is healing him."[2]

The miracle healings recorded in Luke show that Jesus never intended any such loss of connection. The sermons in this volume show Jesus as one who saw fragmented man in need of wholeness.

There is a growing consciousness of the need to recover the ancient awareness of the essential unity of the human being in our modern health care field. The Christian medical doctor, the Christian hospital chaplain, and the Christian pastor form a team that has recently formed a trilogy of helpers. With the emergence of psychosomatic medicine, there is an integration of the physical and the non-physical. Mental health, spiritual health, emotional health, and physical health are all addressed in an interrelated way. When any of these aspects are affected by illness, then that illness affects all the others.

The Christian doctor today acknowledges that the ultimate healing belongs to God, although he is an instrument through which that healing is made available. It is a proven fact that the attitude of the healer greatly enhances the healing process. The doctor who has faith in the patient, in himself, and in God is much more likely to have success than one who has no faith.

In helping one come to a state of mind where healing can take place, a wise physician may call upon the Christian hospital chaplain. Emotions like hate, greed, resentment, lust, and envy often are basic ingredients for many illnesses. Ulcers, cardiac conditions, alcoholism, and hypertension frequently result from such emotions.

In the same manner, primary physical illness works to distort and destroy the workings of the mind and therefore affects the care of our being, the soul, or the spirit; and so the cycle begins. The chaplain whose background is heavily steeped in

2. Ibid., p. 15.

Introduction   17

psychology and the behavioral sciences is able to apply this
knowledge in reaching the patient's theological frame of
reference. Jesus' question to the man who had lain beside the
pool for many years was, "Do you really want to be well?" Jesus
sensed that the man was pitying himself, making excuses, and
being evasive. He was unwilling to face the responsibilities of living a normal life, should he be returned to health. This question-
ing, as a means to acceptance of healing, is largely the work of
the Christian hospital chaplain.

Acceptance is a bridge concept between the totality of an individual's response to danger and the particular phenomenon
seen in healing.[3] The chaplain must enter into one's suffering in
order to bring one to acceptance. Without this acceptance, true
healing will be difficult, if not impossible.

The Christian pastor, who is the undershepherd of the flock,
plays a very important role in the healing process. Because he is
much more familiar with the person than all of the others, he
brings a dimension of spirituality that comes from one in whom
trust is imputed. Like Jesus, he is familiar with many things about
the person that give that added confidence. There seems to be
less conflict in terms of what is necessary for healing when the
Christian pastor is present.

All three helpers, through the guidance of the Holy Spirit,
make healing a reality when faith and acceptance are present.
The Christian medical doctor brings his part of the puzzle. The
Christian hospital chaplain brings his contribution. And the
Christian pastor brings to bear his influence on the holistic ap-
proach to man's healing.

The sermons that follow will show Jesus as the Great Physician and how humanity's brokenness was made whole by his
presence.

                              —William M. Young
                              Staff Chaplain, Methodist Hospital
                              Memphis, Tennessee

3. Claude A. Frazier, *Healing and Religious Faith* (Philadelphia: Pilgrim Press,
   1974), p. 99.

Help, Jesus, I Am Possessed

Jesus casts out an unclean spirit
Luke 4:31-37

Patient/Diagnosis:
A man who had the spirit of an unclean demon

Doctor:
Jesus of Nazareth

Cure:
"[Jesus said], Hold thy peace, and come out of him. And when the devil had thrown him in the midst, he came out of him, and hurt him not."

Comments:
The ancient world believed that the air was thickly populated with evil spirits which sought entry into men. Often they did enter a man through food or drink. All illness was caused by them. The Egyptians believed there were 36 different parts of the human body and any of them could be entered and controlled by one of these evil spirits. There were spirits of deafness, of dumbness, of fever; spirits which

took a man's sanity and wits away; spirits of lying and of deceit and of uncleanness. It was such a spirit that Jesus exorcised here.

William Barclay
The Gospel of Luke, p. 50

I doubt that modern medicine would confirm the existence of demons. My understanding is that certain cults practice demonology today; certainly their activities are less than scientific.

I would want to think that Jesus' reputation as the Son of God, a healer of any disease or affliction, certainly placed him in the best position to act as a psychiatrist and to encourage and cure of any psychogenic problems which may have been perceived as miracles.

My interpretation of a miracle . . . the result of events that take place that are not understood in the light of knowledge existing at the time the event takes place.

Dr. Edwin W. Cocke, Jr.
Specialist in diseases of the ear,
nose, neck, and throat
Memphis, Tennessee

We live in a day when the healing ministry of Jesus is being studied by those engaged in all areas of the helping professions. This is especially true of ministers and doctors who have a faith commitment to Jesus as Lord.

The healing ministry of Jesus is most controversial. Even in his day, his divine acts of healing provoked the admiration and respect of some and the criticism of others. Those mighty deeds of Jesus opened wide the vistas of human thought and have continued to stimulate man's thinking to the present day. They are, without doubt, beyond our mental capacity to understand. However, we must remember that what is incomprehensible to us may be perfectly rational to God. What is irrational depends

Help, Jesus, I Am Possessed   21

upon the vantage point. Man's vantage point is limited; God's vantage point is unlimited.

The healing acts of Jesus went beyond every ordinary incident of healing and restoration ever performed in the history of religion. They were like the miracles of Moses in Egypt. Because they were extraordinary, they provoked positive as well as negative responses from those who were personally helped and from their loved ones. The negative responses came from those who opposed Jesus and his works of mercy. They came from those who felt that Jesus was usurping the prerogatives of God. It was their belief that God worked only through those who controlled the religious establishment of their time. They could not believe that God would perform his mighty acts through someone outside of their esteemed religious aristocracy. Certainly God would not work through a lowly Galilean.

The Synoptic writers bear powerful witness to the healing ministry of Jesus. Each in his own way presents to the reader of these valuable documents healing events which took place during the early life of Jesus. None, however, deals with the healings of Jesus with as much compassion and sympathy as does the writer of the Gospel of Luke. Luke's emphasis can also be seen in the Book of Acts.

In this sermon we want to look at the healings of Jesus as recorded by Luke, the only Gentile gospel writer and the only medical doctor in the group who sought to write a portion of the history of Jesus and the beginnings of the early Christian movement.

Because of his own faith commitment, Luke was not ashamed or embarrassed to attest to the fact that Jesus performed divine acts of healing. Moreover, he gives accounts of healings by the apostles in the Book of Acts. We should bear this in mind. Faith in Jesus as a divine helper and healer need not distort our view as rational beings with limited knowledge and wisdom. Luke's faith commitment did not prevent him from believing in Jesus as divine healer and helper. He was one of the best trained men of his day who had faith in Jesus and in the

22   HELP ME, SOMEBODY!

miraculous healings of the apostles.

That Luke was very well-trained is shown in the medical terms and phrases found throughout the writings of the "beloved physician" (Col. 4:14).

William Kirk Hobart, in his interesting book, *The Medical Language of St. Luke*, sheds some additional light on this man's knowledge and training:

> The purpose of this work is to show, from an examination of the language employed in the Third Gospel and the Acts of the Apostles, that both are the works of a person well-acquainted with the language of the Greek medical schools—a fact which, if established, will strongly confirm the belief that the writer of both was the same person and was the person to whom they have been traditionally assigned by the Church (a), who is mentioned by St. Paul (Colossians 4:14) as "Luke, the Beloved Physician"—an identity which some have doubted or denied.[1]

Let us look at Luke 4:23: "And he said unto them, Ye will surely say unto me this proverb, Physician, heal thyself." Here Luke uses the term *heal*. Because he uses the term more frequently than do the other gospel writers, we can assume that he saw Jesus as a divine healer more so than the others did.

At the very beginning of his ministry, Jesus read a portion of Scripture from Isaiah which seems to support the contention that he saw himself as a divine healer and helper of people:

> The Spirit of the Lord is upon me, because he hath anointed me to preach the gospel to the poor; he hath sent me to heal the brokenhearted, to preach deliverance to the captives, and recovering of sight to

---

1. William Kirk Hobart, *The Medical Language of St. Luke* (Grand Rapids, MI: Baker Book House, 1954), p. xxix.

Help, Jesus, I Am Possessed   23

the blind, to set at liberty them that are bruised, to
preach the acceptable year of the Lord (Luke 4:18,
19).

The first public act of healing done by Jesus, according to
Luke, was in Capernaum, a city of Galilee and home of Simon
Peter. Simon was later to become one of the most faithful of the
disciples of Jesus. Matthew and Mark also report this incident. It
was here that Jesus launched one of the most spectacular works
of healing and helping ever recorded in history.

Capernaum was located on the northwestern shore of the
Sea of Galilee. At that time it was an important toll station of the
trade route from Ptolemais to Damascus and a port for maritime
trade with Philip's tetrarchy and the Decapolis. It was therefore
strategically located as a center for Jesus' Galilean ministry.[2]

Jesus, we should note, did not simply come to a city and do
nothing. He came and taught on the sabbath days. His was more
than merely an example of someone who came to preach. The
preacher was also the teacher. Jesus did not come only to heal
the minds and bodies of men and women. He came to give
them an intellectual foundation which would guide and direct
their lives. He was the educator sent from heaven to advance
heaven's wisdom and heaven's knowledge. Faith and reason
must go hand in hand. There can be no divorce between a
man's head and a man's heart. They both have value in God's
sight. Man functions as a whole.

This has been one of the besetting sins of modern society.
But perhaps it started long before our time. One of the ancient
fathers of the church known as Tertullian, said, "What has
Athens to do with Jerusalem?" Athens, he explained, stood for
the mental development of man and Jerusalem, for his mystical
and mysterious nature. Thus he divorced faith and reason. Not
so with Jesus. Jesus saw that the two must go together, for faith

2. *The Interpreter's Bible*, Vol. VIII, Luke—John (Nashville: Abingdon Press, 1952),
p. 96.

and reason are but different sides of the same coin.

So Jesus came teaching in the synagogue. He taught with such authority that the leaders and the people were astonished at his doctrine. Jesus taught with a perception and sincerity that his hearers had never before experienced as they listened to the scribes and other doctors of the law. Luke says "his word was with power."

There is power in the words he used. They had power because they were divine communications which came from God. God's Word has always been powerful. It was powerful in the Old Testament, and it still had that power in the life and times of Jesus. In Isaiah 55:11, the prophet speaks about the Word of God: "So shall my word be that goeth forth out of my mouth: it shall not return unto me void, but it shall accomplish that which I please, and it shall prosper in the thing whereto I sent it."

The Word that Jesus spoke was the Word of God. God had given him the authority to use His Word and that Word was sustained by God. There was to be no failure with Jesus. He had divine power and divine authority supporting him each step of the way. He could not fail! He did not fail!

This power in His Word was not only to be seen in his teaching ministry but also in his healing ministry. There was no weakness in him when it came to relieving the suffering of men and women. Jesus had been equipped to deal with life's manifold problems.

In that very synagogue there was a man with a problem. Luke records it thus, "And in the synagogue there was a man, which had a spirit of an unclean devil, and cried out with a loud voice."

The biblical tradition gives some evidence that there was widespread belief in demon possession. In 1 Samuel 16:23 we find, "And it came to pass, when the evil spirit from God was upon Saul, that David took an harp, and played with his hand: so Saul was refreshed, and was well, and the evil spirit departed from him."

Help, Jesus, I Am Possessed   25

However, most students of the Bible believe that widespread belief in demonic possession which caused disease did not flourish in Judaism until much later. They believed that it was the direct result of coming into contact with the Babylonians and Persians.

Nevertheless, the man that Jesus met in the synagogue had a mental or nervous disorder which prevented him from functioning effectively in society.

It is interesting to note that this man was in the synagogue, a fact which might suggest that this was the place where those with similar illnesses went in times of deep distress.

Maybe some folks don't come to church because they believe the unclean demons have left them alone. They have been cleansed and don't feel inclined to worry the Father for additional relief and cleansing.

This man who needed help was found in the synagogue. Not only was he in the synagogue, but his problem was there with him. This is always the case. We bring our problems with us to the temple. We cannot leave them and then go back and pick them up. They are with us night and day. They hound us, even in the most sacred confines of our houses of worship and instruction. Godet has said:

> This period was a time when it could be generally conceded, moral and social evil had reached their highest point of development. Since that age the power of these destructive spirits of evil has been, if not destroyed, at least restrained by the influence—greater perhaps than men choose to acknowledge—of the Master's religion or by the direct command of the Master himself.[3]

The man who was possessed—when he saw Jesus—cried out

3. H. D. M. Spence and Joseph S. Exell, eds., *The Pulpit Commentary*, Vol. 16, Mark and Luke (Grand Rapids, MI: Wm. B. Eerdmans Publishing Company, 1962), p. 92.

with a loud voice, "Let us alone; what have we to do with thee, thou Jesus of Nazareth? Art thou come to destroy us? I know thee who thou art; the Holy One of God."

That this man was sick beyond his control is seen in the fact that it was not so much the real man who spoke as it was the devil or demon which controlled or possessed him. So instead of the devil saying, "Let me alone," he had the man say, "Let us alone." The devil so controlled him that he made the man say what he wanted said. The demon did not want this man free from the illness for which he was responsible. He wanted to control him and eventually destroy him. "Let us alone."

When Satan has us under his control he does not want anything to disturb the relationship which has been established in the soul of a suffering child of God. He wants exclusive control of the individual, so that he will become twofold, more a child of hell than a son of heaven.

Those who are demonic in nature are never satisfied with being disturbed. They want to be left alone. This is true of all forms of demons. And demons assume many forms. For instance—

The demon of materialism says, "Leave me alone!"
The demon of racism says, "Leave me alone!"
The demon of rape says, "Leave me alone!"
The demon of alcoholism says, "Leave me alone!"
The demon of stealing says, "Leave me alone!"
The demon of cocaine says, "Leave me alone!"
The demon of nicotine says, "Leave me alone!"
The demon of war says, "Leave me alone!"
The demon of greed says, "Leave me alone!"
The demon of hate says, "Leave me alone!"
The demon of laziness says, "Leave me alone!"
The demon of gluttony says, "Leave me alone!"
The demons are on the loose. They say, "Leave us alone!"

They are on the loose, and they were on the loose in the life of this man. "What have we to do with thee?" The demon did not allow the man to speak for himself. The demon took charge and spoke for both of them.

Help, Jesus, I Am Possessed

Many times in the life of the possessed it is not the person who speaks but the possessor of him who is possessed. It is not the alcoholic who speaks but the alcohol. It is not the dope addict who acts but the dope he takes. It is not the cigarette smoker who speaks but the nicotine that he inhales. These demons invade our beings and force us to become their unwilling tools.

The demons are more shrewd and more knowledgeable than we are. They know what is right and who is right. They called Jesus by name: "Let us alone; what have we to do with thee, thou Jesus of Nazareth!" The demoniac called Jesus by his given name and stated that he was from Nazareth, which seems to suggest that evil has its own way of knowing about those who heal and help more than we who need to be healed and helped. His information apparently was founded on academic knowledge, while ours is based on faith.

We have to walk by faith and not by sight. Because we walk by faith, our healings might be limited because our faith is sometimes weak. "O ye of little faith," said Jesus of his disciples when the storm was raging on the sea.

Then the man and the demon in him collectively say to Jesus, the healer and the helper, "Art thou come to destroy us?" This is a tacit acknowledgement that Jesus had the capacity to destroy the evil demon. The same dread appears in the case of the Gadarene demoniac in Luke 8:31: "And they besought him that he would not command them to go out into the deep." It was the belief in that day and time that evil spirits dreaded being driven into the deep, where such spirits await the judgment. Any doom seemed to those lost ones preferable to that "abyss" or bottomless pit to which Jesus might send them.

Yes, Jesus came to destroy the kingdom of Satan! He started the process, and the process is still going on. The full and complete destruction of Satan's kingdom is assured in the blessed call and life of Jesus. Our task is to continue to pray and abide in his love. Then Satan and his host of demons can do us no harm. They know that Jesus is able to defeat them. They recognize that Jesus is able to keep us from falling and to present us faultless before the presence of his glory. This is why they said to him, "Art thou come to destroy us?"

Art thou come to destroy the demonic forces we have let loose in this world? Art thou come to stop our tormenting of the sons of men? Art thou come to replace us with God's grace and mercy? Art thou come to show men and women that they need not live as they have lived in the past? Art thou come? Art thou come? Art thou come?

Then look at the next line where they say to Jesus, "I know thee who thou art; the Holy One of God." I know thee! The demon recognized that Jesus was more than just another man. He recognized that Jesus had powers which only God's Son could have. He knew that Jesus was not just another holy man sent from God, but that Jesus was *the* holy man, in whom dwelleth the fullness of the whole Godhead bodily. "I know thee! I know that you are the Holy One of God!"

"The Holy One of God" is a messianic title. In John 6:68-69 Peter makes the same assertion when the disciples left Jesus because of his most difficult saying: "Lord, to whom shall we go? thou hast the words of eternal life. And we believe and are sure that thou art that Christ, the Son of the living God."

How ironic! The devil was willing to confess him as holy and divine, and so many of us humans are not willing to give glory and honor to his majestic name. Jesus is holy. Jesus is righteous. Jesus is good. Jesus is love. Jesus is grace. Jesus is mercy. Jesus is kindness. Jesus is forgiving. Jesus is peaceful. Jesus is tolerant. Jesus is glorious. Jesus is everything good that we can think and say about him. Peter was right when he asked, "Lord, to whom shall we go?" and answered, "Thou hast the words of eternal life."

Peter is saying what the church seeks to say to those who will not confess Jesus as Lord. The Lord Jesus has the word of power and authority. The Lord Jesus has the word and the authority to deal with our problems. He has the key in his hand. He has the power in his hand. He can deal with our possessions. He can deal with our demons. He can straighten out lives that

Help, Jesus, I Am Possessed

have been distorted by the satanic forces of hell. He came that we might have life and have it more abundantly. Jesus is able to save us. Jesus can claim us from the ash heap of this world's junk piles. Yes, he can! I know he can!

Because he has that power and that authority, he spoke with divine authority to the devil in this man. He said with divine authority, "Hold thy peace, and come out of him." Jesus rebuked the demon. As a last resort, the demon sought to injure the name and reputation of Jesus by bearing testimony to his holy and divine name and holy character. Someone has wisely said, "There are some people from whom it is not desirable to hold certificates or receive testimonials."

The demon did not want the fellowship of Jesus, and Jesus did not want the fellowship of the demon. They operated in two diverse worlds. One world was constructive and the other destructive. The demon wanted to possess the man, but Jesus wanted the man to possess himself—and willingly do the will of God. Jesus wanted to save him. Satan sought to destroy him. Jesus wanted to lift him. Satan wanted to bring him down.

Jesus made the demon close his mouth. He did not want to have fellowship with demons. He did want to save the man. So Jesus drove the demon back to that world of destruction and chaos from whence he came. He then departed to the realm of evil which Paul refers to in Ephesians 6:12—

> For we wrestle not against flesh and blood, but against principalities, against powers, against the rulers of the darkness of this world, against spiritual wickedness in high places.

This demon struck at the helpless victim. He threw the man in the midst of the gathering there in the synagogue. He was stricken in the very presence of Jesus. The demon inside him tried one last time to defeat Jesus in the presence of all the people. But thanks be to God, Jesus was too much for the demon.

The demon can strike, but that is all he can do. In attacking the man, he simultaneously attacked Jesus, and Jesus had power to deal with the demon. Jesus exorcised the demon, but he did not hurt the man. Jesus is able to save us from the demons of our lives. Jesus is able to deliver us. He can deal with our most desperate ills and ailments. Satan knows this. This is why he tries to keep us hooked in his grip. As long as we are hooked, Satan controls, us, but when Jesus comes, the satanic power is defeated.

I am glad about that fact, that I have somebody who can deal with the demon in me. He can make the demon leave me alone and give me a new lease on life. Every now and then I can feel the demons of this world attacking me and the work I am trying to do for the Master. But I experience an indefinable power and authority working with me and on my behalf, saying, "Leave him alone! Leave him alone! Leave him alone! He is bought and sealed in the precious blood of the Lamb of God, and I will never leave him nor forsake him!"

Please Help Her

Jesus heals Peter's mother-in-law
Luke 4:38-39

Patient/Diagnosis:
Peter's mother-in-law who was ill with a high fever

Doctor:
Jesus of Nazareth

Cure:
"And he stood over her, and rebuked the fever; and it left her."

Comments:
Fever: Greek *pyretos*, "fiery heat." A generic term which covers various ailments, all of them suggesting the presence of a high temperature. Luke describes Peter's wife's mother as having "a great fever," indicating that he recognized degrees of fever and, probably, that he saw the grave prognosis indicated by the severity of the fever which Matthew (8:14) and Mark (1:30) did not.

The Illustrated Bible Dictionary, p. 618

Fever, in biblical and modern days, usually indicates an infection of some type. Most infections last several days or more. The chance of a coincidental, spontaneous remission of the fever seems remote. Therefore, it is highly likely that Jesus did influence the course of an infection without the availability of modern antibiotics.

Dr. Joseph Blythe
Pulmonary specialist
Memphis, Tennessee

In this chapter, we want to pick up the thread which runs through the Gospels—the thread of the healing ministry of Jesus. It is there in all three of the Gospels known as the Synoptics. It can also be seen in the Gospel of John. Moreover, Luke records in the Book of Acts those mighty deeds of healing done by the apostles of Jesus. He had promised and given the mighty power with which to accomplish mighty things.

So we come with firm faith in our Lord's capacity to heal and to help. This was one of the hallmarks of his ministry. He himself said, "He hath sent me to heal the brokenhearted, to preach deliverance to the captives, and recovering of sight to the blind."

We do not agree with those who take the position that Jesus was here referring to spiritual rather than physical healing. It is unrealistic to separate man's physical and spiritual being. The Savior of Man must deal with the whole man, and this is what he was able and willing to do. He was both helper and healer. Therefore we want to follow Luke as he recorded the second incident of Jesus' healing of a suffering, helpless child of God.

Luke says, "And the fame of him went out into every place of the country round about." This happened after the healing of the man in the synagogue at Capernaum. Jesus had driven a devil out of the man. The fame of Jesus was carried from one community to another. People were most impressed with this new and different religious teacher, who taught with power and authority, and healed with power and authority. This rare combination of healing and teaching caused Jesus' fame to spread throughout the Capernaum region and was the beginning of holistic ministry for the people who walked in darkness.

The stage was now set for the next miracle recorded by Luke. "And he arose out of the synagogue. . . ." The prior miracle took place in the synagogue. It is very important for us to look at this place called "the synagogue." Its origin is unknown, but it is believed to have been started in Babylon when the Jews were in exile. The name is derived from the Greek word *proseuche*, which means "place of prayer," "a Jewish religious community," or "a gathering of people."

There were four functions of the synagogue in the history of the Jews: (1) It was a "little sanctuary" where people living nearby gathered for worship and instruction. (2) It was a place where both adults and children learned the law and received instruction concerning God's will for their daily lives. (3) It was a social center, where community problems were discussed and solved, where legal transactions of interest to the congregation were posted, where funerals were held, and alms received. (4) It was a place of trial and punishment, and in times of political unrest, an opinion-making center.[1]

Jesus, says Luke, "arose out of the synagogue, and entered into Simon's house." The record is clear that Simon Peter was married at this time and that his mother-in-law shared his home. That Peter was an unusual man may be seen by the fact that he allowed his wife's mother to live with him, a fact that might have impressed Jesus with the potential in Simon. His was the kind of tenderness and compassion that Jesus needed and sought in his men. Seeing that Simon had the makings of a solid disciple, the Great Physician decided to build on this rock-like man.

Simon's house must have been the kind of home that gladly welcomed Jesus. Simon had seen him in action in the synagogue

---

1. Madeleine S. Miller and J. Lane Miller, *Harper's Bible Dictionary* (New York: Harper & Row, 1961), p. 717.

and had sought to have this new kind of teacher and healer come to his home to make his initial house call.

"Come to my house and help my mother-in-law. Come to my house and perform a miracle there. Come to my house and enjoy the fellowship of a fisherman from the Sea of Galilee. Come to my house, Teacher and Healer. There is room in my house for you." You must invite Jesus in, for he does not come where he is not welcome. "Behold, I stand at the door and knock." Jesus will stand there until we open the door. He will not intrude or invade our private domain without our permission.

It was interesting to note that when I asked some of my parishioners about having cottage prayer meetings in their homes, only a few responded. Could this be indicative of a kind of spiritual individualism which has engulfed the church? We should never be adrift from the fellowship of the congregation of God, for we are meant to be a "called-out fellowship," a fellowship that relates to Him and others in sweet communion.

At Simon Peter's house, Jesus observed an unusual closeness, intimacy, and friendship. In that home Simon's mother-in-law found protection and security from the storms of life. Undoubtedly her husband was dead, and as a widow she was living with her daughter and son-in-law. This in itself said a great deal about the character of Simon. We may speculate that he had opened his home to his mother-in-law when life became burdensome and difficult for her.

The mother-in-law might very well have remembered the words of the psalmist, "Now also when I am old and grey-headed, O God, forsake me not." She knew that God had been with her in her youth; now she was asking God for His protection in her old age. This is a common fear of the old. They fear that they will be forgotten. They fear that they will be left alone. They fear that at some future hour trouble will come, and there will be no one to fight life's battles for them. They fear that life will be unkind to them and that those around them will not love and care for them. Some of their fears are real and some of them are imaginary. This is old age. This is, or will be, your old age, and this is my old age, unless someone who loves us will assure us of a secure future. So Simon's mother-in-law had a right to say, "Now also when I am old and greyheaded, O God, forsake me not."

This also says something about Peter's wife. She was the kind of daughter who wanted to take care of her mother. Her mother meant something dear to her. She was willing to pay the price to see that her mother had a roof over her head, nutritious food to eat, adequate clothing, and a haven from the stresses and storms of life. She was the kind of daughter who might have heard her mother sing in youthful years:

When I'm growing old and feeble, Stand by me,
When I'm growing old and feeble, Stand by me,
When my life becomes a burden,
   and I'm nearing chilly Jordan,
O Thou Lily of the Valley, Stand by me!

Both Simon and his wife had decided to be the answer to her prayer request. They became "the lily of the valley" for a dear one who was growing old and feeble.

What about you? Have you decided to become that "lily of the valley" for anyone? In the Name of Jesus, become a "lily" for someone now, for we all need a sweet lily in our lives. We don't know when we will be stricken by illness, insecurity, fear, and helplessness. So we all need a "lily" in life's pilgrimage.

When Jesus entered the house, he found Simon's mother-in-law sick. Luke says, "And Simon's wife's mother was taken with a great fever." Galen states that fevers in that day were distinguished by doctors as "great" or "slight." Today, the terms are "high" and "low." Nevertheless, the great fever she had was abnormal and could lead to serious illness. It prevented her from performing her regular household chores. It lessened the sense of purpose and meaning and belonging in her life.

Many older Americans today live as though there is little purpose or direction in their lives. This is a sickening malady that accompanies old age. Perhaps the most effective and humanitarian remedy is the growing trend of building and maintaining senior citizen facilities which offer protection and support for those who are in the golden age of life.

This woman needed more than one lily in her life. Now she needed someone who could deal with this great fever that had afflicted her. She needed a doctor with healing power.

There is a difference between treating and healing. Doctors treat their patients, but only God can heal them. We should understand this fact. Perhaps more of us would be helped if we only believed in the Source of healing and help.

The people believed that Jesus could heal this woman, for they had seen him perform a miracle in the synagogue shortly before he entered her home. They had witnessed the miraculous powers at work in him, and so they resorted to him for her relief. The Word is very clear about this: "They besought him for her." They petitioned Jesus on her behalf. They asked Jesus to heal her. They pleaded with him to heal her.

We too have to ask. And we must remember the proper manner when we ask. We must not demand; we must ask. And we must ask in humility and in faith. Jesus taught his disciples to ask and promised that what they asked for would be given them.

It could be that we are not healed because we do not ask in the right frame of mind. Our minds need to be conscious of the Source of power and filled with extreme confidence and faith and hope. We may ask amiss. We believe, and we don't believe. We have our doubts and uncertainties. "He that cometh to God must believe that he is, and that he is a rewarder of them that diligently seek him."

Please note that *they* besought him for her. This was the collective faith of a group who interceded on behalf of one of their members. The woman was not present in the synagogue. She had not witnessed the healing miracle there, but the group had; and so they made a specific request for a repeat performance.

Individual prayer is necessary and effective, but when the

group prays, there is a response from God also. That is, if the group has prayed in the Name of Jesus.

The group was at prayer when Peter was arrested. In answer to their prayers, God sent an angel to bring Peter out of jail. At midnight Paul and Silas prayed in a Philippian jail, and again God acted. Peter, John, and the other disciples prayed when they were arrested. When they were released and had returned to the group, the Book of Acts reports, "And when they had prayed, the place was shaken where they were assembled together; and they were all filled with the Holy Ghost, and they spake the word of God with boldness."

The next verse gives us a clue to the writer's concerns as to what method of healing was used. None of the other writers do this. "And he stood over her." Please bear in mind that Luke is concerned about both the mode and the person who employed it.

Jesus approached the sick woman and stood over her. The doctor desired a close look at his patient. He needed to know exactly what her condition was. This was the only way he could arrive at an accurate diagnosis.

Jesus did the natural thing: He stood over her. He stood over her because he was the God over her and over her condition. He was the God-man with the answer to her problem. He was the God-man with healing in his hands. He was the God-man who was sent to relieve her fever-wracked body. He was the God-man who was a general practitioner but who also was capable of specializing.

When Jesus stands over us, we are abiding under the shadow of the Almighty. God was with him. God was in him. God was working through him. When Jesus stands, someone stands who can and will act in the name of God. God is not a helpless God. He is still in control of all the forces of illness and disease in this world. There is no illness, no disease too great, too strong, too devastating, too untameable for our God to deal with.

Standing over her, Jesus, says Luke, "rebuked the fever."

Jesus saw the fever as a personal agent. It seems as if he saw the fever as being caused by a real agent that had life and existence. Therefore, he spoke to the fever-causing agent as one would speak to a person. To *rebuke* means to *reprove, reprimand, censure, upbraid,* or *beat back.* Jesus spoke a word of censure and upbraided the fever.

I would love to have Jesus standing over me, more than any other doctor I know. In him is the power of God to heal and to help the least of the children of this earth. He does not charge an office fee to relieve suffering and pain. O that Jesus were with us today! O that Jesus would make his rounds in the hospitals and nursing homes and free men and women from the high cost of getting well and staying well! Jesus, we need thee! Jesus, we desire thee! Come, Lord Jesus!

Whenever Jesus stands over a sick life, something happens, because he is the source of unlimited power to heal and help. I tell you the truth. When Jesus stands, somebody is standing who can bring joy and restore health. When Jesus stands over us, something gives way to his very presence.

You may recall an incident in Matthew's Gospel when Jesus was making his final journey into Jerusalem. Two blind men sitting on the roadside cried out to him, "Have mercy on us, O Lord, thou Son of David." Matthew records that Jesus stood still, called them and asked what they would have him do. They answered, "Lord, that our eyes may be opened." The same Jesus who stood still then, acts in the name of mercy and compassion today. He "touched their eyes: and immediately their eyes received sight, and they followed him."

When Jesus stands, somebody is standing. And when he stands in the life of a child of God, something miraculous happens.

I would rather have a standing Jesus in my life than a sitting philosopher. I would rather have a standing Jesus over me than a renowned chemist. I would rather have a standing Jesus over me than a nationally-known heart specialist. I would rather have a standing Jesus in my life than the most brilliant surgeon. I would rather have a standing Jesus in my life and over my life than all the doctors at Mayo Clinic. I would rather have Jesus than silver and gold. For when my Jesus stands, God acts through him and things happen to me in my most dire circumstance. I would rather have Jesus, I tell you.

When Jesus spoke, the fever left the suffering woman. The power in his speech is greater than the power in a surgeon's sensitive hands. The power in his speech surpasses the pronouncements of the most gifted psychiatrist. The power in his word is greater than the skill of the most highly acclaimed neurologist.

Most doctors tell us that when a high temperature subsides, it weakens us and saps our strength. We have to regain our strength gradually. But consider what Jesus did for this woman: The fever left her at the word of Jesus and "immediately she arose and ministered unto them."

Immediately she got up and prepared the sabbath dinner. Immediately she got up and cleaned the house. Immediately she prepared food for her guests. Immediately she extended her usual hospitality to them. Immediately she became filled with new life because she had come into contact with a new source of energy, authority, and power that was on the loose in her community.

God's living Son was in that house. God's eternal Son was there. God's Messiah was there. God's Blessed One was there. God's Alpha and Omega was there. God's light from on high was there. God's mercy was there. God's grace was there. God's forgiveness was there. God was there, I tell you. The God who lives was there. The God who gave us life was there. The God who deals with life and sustains life was there. God was there. The living Jesus was able to bring living life to dying life.

Because Jesus was there, Simon's mother-in-law had a tomorrow. You and I have a tomorrow as long as Jesus is here, there, and everywhere. Thank God he lives! Because he lives, I can face tomorrow. Yes, I can and you can! Let us face it together.

They Needed His Help

Jesus heals many sick and demon-possessed people
Luke 4:40-41

Patient/Diagnosis:
   The sick with various diseases; demons in many

Doctor:
   Jesus of Nazareth

Cure:
   ". . . he laid his hands on every one of them, and healed
   them. And devils also came out of many, crying out, and
   saying, Thou art Christ the Son of God. And he rebuking
   them suffered them not to speak."

Comments:
   The wisespread Oriental belief in demonic possession as the
   cause of disease is scarcely to be found in the Old Testament, but it flourished in late Judaism under Babylonian and
   Persian influence. It pervades the gospel tradition. There is
   . . . an observable tendency on the part of the evangelists to
   heighten and embellish the reputation that Jesus had in their

sources as a healer and exorcist. Nevertheless even in his own lifetime it is clear that Jesus was widely known as a healer, particularly of what we should now describe as mental and nervous diseases.

S. MacLean Gilmour, Exegete
The Interpreter's Bible, Vol. VIII, p. 96

In this sermon we will consider another passage of Scripture, where we find Jesus performing what we refer to as *miracles*, those deeds which transcend the ordinary understanding of the average mind. Miracles, then and now, are beyond the comprehension of the average man. The people who followed Jesus were amazed at the things he was able to do, for they knew that he had no formal training in medicine or religion. Like them, we are baffled, and some are prone to try to discredit the Lord Jesus' healing miracles.

However, if we accept him as the Saviour of the world, we must also accept his capacity to heal and to help in every conceivable way. In faith, then, we come to another example of his miraculous powers as recorded in the Gospel of Luke.

Let us forever keep in mind the truth he proclaimed to the disciples of John who came to him with John's question: "Art thou he that should come? or look we for another?" Jesus reply was:

Go your way, and tell John what things ye have seen and heard; how that the blind see, the lame walk, the lepers are cleansed, the deaf hear, the dead are raised, to the poor the gospel is preached. And blessed is he, whosoever shall not be offended in me (Luke 7:22-23).

We must not be disturbed by what our Lord did. We must believe and accept his miracles as mighty deeds done by the Father through His Son, who was the channel for this unique and mysterious power.

42   HELP ME, SOMEBODY!

Jesus was extraordinary, and thus he could and did do extraordinary things. He once said of himself, "The Spirit of the Lord is upon me." When more of the Spirit of the Lord is upon us, we too can do extraordinary things.

It appears that Jesus remained in the house of Simon Peter. There is no indication that he left there after healing Simon's mother-in-law. The record also implies that the house then became a community hospital with no other doctors—only Jesus—helping and healing in his unique manner.

Apparently the news of this latest miracle had been noised abroad by some who had witnessed it. When the news was spread that Jesus had performed another miracle in Simon Peter's home, things began to happen in the little community of Capernaum. The villagers responded as most of us would have done if we knew that there was a healer in town who healed without a fee: they besought Jesus.

Luke proceeds, "Now when the sun was setting." Note that there is no break between the healing incident and the next clause—my reason for feeling that Jesus remained at the house until sundown.

It seems that Jesus enjoyed the fellowship of the meal and the small gathering in Simon's house. He may have continued performing miracles after the meal had ended. At any rate, the next clause indicates that Jesus commenced healing and helping those who were brought to him. "All they that had any sick with divers diseases brought them unto him."

Luke does not say *they* brought them, but *all they*. The emphasis here seems to be that a great host of people were brought by townspeople who had those who were sick and afflicted. He could have merely said *all*; that would have been sufficient. He could have said *they*, and that would have been adequate. Instead, he says *all they*.

Mark, in his gospel, says, "And at even, when the sun did set, they brought unto him all that were diseased, and them that were possessed with devils" (1:32).

Both writers take great pains to emphasize the word *all*. This

They Needed His Help   43

is consistent with the great invitation extended by our Lord in
Matthew's gospel, "Come unto me, *all* ye that labour and are
heavy laden, and I will give you rest." Jesus extended the healing and helping hand to *all*, not merely to *some*. He still extends
this power of God in him to all. The "all-ness" to "us-ness" is the
presence of "God-ness" in him.

So John, when he came to understand the dimension of love
in Jesus, could state with sure conviction: "God so loved the
world, that he gave his only begotten Son, that whosoever
believeth in him should not perish, but have everlasting life."

The word *all* was used by Jesus on many occasions. In the
Sermon on the Mount he said, "For verily I say unto you, Till
heaven and earth pass, one jot or one tittle shall in no wise pass
from the law, till *all* be fulfilled." In Matthew 11:27, "*All* things
are delivered unto me of my Father." Elsewhere, "With God *all*
things are possible."

When the lawyer sought to put him to the test, Jesus said,
"Thou shalt love the Lord thy God with *all* thy heart . . . and with
all thy mind." And in his next statement, Jesus sealed the
lawyer's lips forever: "And the second is like unto it, Thou shalt
love thy neighbor as thyself. On these two commandments hang
all the law and the prophets."

All they, the next phrase, is also instructive. *They* denotes
more than one. This pronoun stands as a symbol of those weary
relatives—aunts, mothers, cousins—who sit by helplessly watching their loved ones waste away when there is no cure for them.
This group has a covenant with misery. They know misery, for
they have stood by when illness ravaged the bodies of those
they loved, admired, and adored. Their common covenant with
misery binds them together with cords of agony and anguish. In
their lonely hours, they long for someone who can comfort,
heal, and help.

They came with their loved ones who were victims of all
kinds of diseases. They brought those who thought they were
sick, and those who knew they were sick. Some were blind,
lame, paralyzed, leprous, cancerous, arthritic, psychotic. Some

were afflicted with tumors, heart trouble, kidney trouble, allergies, hay fever, bleeding, alcoholism, and other destructive additions. Some were overweight and some were underweight. Some had high blood pressure; some had low blood pressure.

They brought them from the east and from the west. They brought them from the north, and they brought them from the south. They brought their sick, and they brought their lame. They brought their deaf, and they brought their dumb. They brought the living, and they brought the dying. They brought them to Jesus, for in him was life!

They brought them unto Jesus after they heard that he was healing and helping at Simon's house, which had been turned into heaven's hospital on earth. God's healing capacity was at work. Jesus had once said, "I must work the works of him that sent me." This was part of the work of God. Again, he said: "I must work . . . while it is day: the night cometh, when no man can work." It was still day, and Jesus continued to work—to help and to heal. As a divine healer, he was committed to the healing ministry of God while it was yet day.

There are not many instances of Jesus in his role as healer and helper at night. Night usually found him busily refueling himself through prayer and meditation for the next day's work. Aware that his power and energy would be depleted by his busy schedule of healing and helping during the day, at night our Lord sought those close encounters with his Father—communication which would provide him with the necessary divine energy and divine power for the following day.

Perhaps this is the meaning of the analogy he gave in John's gospel (15:1) concerning the vine and the branches. There he said, "I am the true vine, and my Father is the husbandman." Every experienced farmer knows that there is a direct relationship between the cultivation of a vine and the fruits of that vine. Jesus knew that to be productive he had to have an intimate relationship with the husbandman, his Father, your God and my God.

Likewise, if we would be productive and effective, we also

must seek continuous, close encounters with Jesus and our God. Jesus says to us, "I am the vine, ye are the branches: He that abideth in me, and I in him, the same bringeth forth much fruit: for without me ye can do nothing" (John 15:5).

Jesus also said to his disciples of that day and to us of this day, "If ye abide in me, and my words abide in you, ye shall ask what ye will, and it shall be done unto you. Herein is my Father glorified, that ye bear much fruit; so shall ye be my disciples" (John 15:7-8).

Jesus could bear fruit because he stayed close to the source of power. He was power and also the source of power. He was life, and life begets life. He was healing, and the Healer heals. He was the Helper, and the Helper helps. So the people discerned that this was no ordinary man in their midst. When they brought their sick to him, Jesus responded with a personal touch of infinite compassion. "And he laid his hands on every one of them." Please note the methodology. Sometimes Jesus spoke the word of power. In this instance, he used his hands to effectuate the cure.

Traditionally, the hands have been used to confer a blessing (Gen. 48:17; Lev. 9:22, 23; Mark 10:16). The hands have also been used to symbolize the transmission of guilt (Lev. 1:4; 8:14; 16:21, 22). Our Lord could heal by his word. He could heal by his touch. He could heal by an act of his will—close at hand or at some distance away.

The fact that Jesus laid his holy hands on them and made them whole should not surprise us. We are those who believe in the holy nature, the holy purpose, the holy plan, and the holy promise of God. This was just a fulfillment of all that God had planned for those who believe in the light which shines in darkness. The darkness of man's doubts and uncertainties will not put out that holy light.

All of life is under the lordship of Jesus Christ, his rule and reign having been transferred to him by his Father. He was charged to use it for the good of life. "I am come that they might have life, and that they might have it more abundantly."

This was the beginning of that vast and mysterious unfolding of God's graciousness to "us-ward." "In him was life; and the life was the light of men." It was your life and my life. It was your strength and my strength. It was your salvation and my salvation. It was your way back to the Father's house, and it was my way back to the Father's house.

The hands of Jesus are imbued with divine healing power. The hands of Jesus possess divine helping power. The hands of Jesus possess mysterious and cosmic power from God on high. His hands give him that unique authority and power to touch the bodies and minds of God's children in lowly and lonely places.

He brings hope to those bound by the satanic forces and evil influences which are a part of this world. Jesus broke through the patterns of the wicked forces which prevent the children of God from enjoying the abundant life. He is our healer and helper; and in his hands are those blessed powers which transform life from the jangling discord of anguish and agony into the sweet melody of hope, recovery, and renewal.

We should pay attention to the fact that Jesus laid his hands on every one of them. This shows the extent of his love and the love of God. No one was excluded from the healing grace which flowed through those holy hands.

The people came as a throng, but Jesus took time to deal with each one of those helpless and hopeless ones individually. He did not rush them through a fast-paced assembly line as today's industries send parts through a fast-paced assembly line. His concern and care was for the whole group of them. He was committed to the total community of the sick. He did what he was called to do: to seek out and save the broken in spirit and body and mind. Those who are whole do not need a physician, only those who are sick.

Not only was Jesus a general practitioner, but he also had the single-minded competence of a specialist. He excelled in cases which rendered other specialists powerless. He did what no other physician or power of his time or ours can do.

A family practitoner once told me that generally he could

see about 25 to 30 patients a day. He said he did not want to run his patients through an assembly line. He wanted them to feel that they were getting the best medical care possible. Thus, he spent unhurried time with each patient in order to do a thorough job.

Like Jesus, he administered his own personal touch. But unlike Jesus, this practitioner informed some of his patients that they would need to return in two weeks. When Jesus completed his healing tasks, his patients did not have to return at all. They did not need to go to a pharmacist to get a prescription filled. Jesus wrote the prescription, and Jesus filled the prescription. Jesus was the question, and he was the answer to the question. He was the problem and the solution to the problem. He was the diagnosis and prognosis, the cause and the cure. He was and is God's holy practitioner on a mission of restoration and reformation for sick bodies and sick minds. *He healed them all.*

Please note that Jesus performed the role of general practitioner and also the role of practicing psychiatrist at the same time. He possessed the gift to play any role that would lift suffering humanity. In the next verse Luke records that "devils also came out of many, crying out, and saying, Thou art Christ, the Son of God." The very presence of Jesus dispelled demons from the bodies of those who were brought into that house. The satanic forces could not survive in the presence of one so divinely equipped with God's power and God's might. Evil cannot long stand in the presence of goodness. "The ungodly are not so: but are like the chaff which the wind driveth away" (Ps. 1:4). Holy goodness wants nothing to do with unholy evil. They cannot co-exist.

One scholar has stated that the exaltation of the demons at this time was indirectly an involuntary admiration of Jesus as the Son of God. The demons knew who he was and tried in their devilish way to pay homage to his nature and mission. But Jesus needed no praise from the lips of those destructive creatures who were destined for eternal damnation.

Jesus knew that everything God had created would sing his

praise. He said to the religious leaders who sought to silence his disciples on the day of his royal entry into Jerusalem, "If these should hold their peace, the stones would immediately cry out."

God has made all things in their time to praise His Son and give glory to the Father. This was perhaps the inspiration of the psalmist when he wrote, "The heavens declare the glory of God; and the firmament sheweth his handiwork."

Not needing their testimony and witness, our Great Preacher and Physician rebuked these devils and suffered them not to speak. He did not permit them to rant and rave about who he was. That was not their responsibility. Ironically, that responsibility belonged to another order of beings who were sick and afflicted by the selfsame forces which sought to identify him as Christ, the Son of God. Jesus recognized the conflict existing between him and them, and the battle was on.

Jesus saw no need to let them preempt the mission before it began. They would not and should not disrupt the plan of God. These same forces had done that to Adam; but Jesus, the second Adam, would not fall prey. He could not fail, and he did not fail.

So the Great Preacher and Physician kept healing and helping all night long. In fourteen hours he turned that humble house into an institution of mercy and love. Here was God's Son in action, seeking to save those who were sick and those who were lost.

I am glad that Jesus did not make any demands upon those who came for a holy dose of grace. He raised no questions as to their belief or lack of belief. He simply responded with compassion and love and mercy, and laid his holy hands on their broken bodies until daybreak. He looked beyond their faults and saw their needs.

This was your Preacher and your Physician. This was my Preacher and my Physician, ignoring our faults and responding to our needs. What amazing love, grace, mercy, compassion, and forgiveness!

They Needed His Help

Jesus Will Forever Reign!

While we deliberate, he reigns.
While we decide wisely, he reigns.
While we decide foolishly, he reigns.
We serve him humbly, royally he reigns.
We serve him self-assertively, he reigns.
When we rebel and seek to withhold our service,
    he reigns.

—William Temple

He Needs Healing and Help

Jesus cleanses a leper
Luke 5:12-15

Patient/Diagnosis:
A man full of leprosy

Doctor:
Jesus of Nazareth

Cure:
"And [Jesus] put forth his hand, and touched him, saying, I will: be thou clean. And immediately the leprosy departed from him."

Comments:
My understanding is that there may have been two varieties of leprosy: one or more severe forms that resulted in a loss of limb, and another that may have been only a dermatitis. More currently it is known as "Hansen's Disease," and in some instances may be curable with administration of one of the mycin drugs.

He Needs Healing and Help

Dr. Edwin W. Cocke, Jr.
Specialist in diseases of the ear,
nose, neck, and throat
Memphis, Tennessee

Leprosy was nothing short of a living death, a corruption of all the humors, a poisoning of the very springs of life; a dissolution little by little of the whole body, so that one limb after another actually fell away. The disease, moreover, was incurable by the art and skill of man—not that the leper might not return to health, for, however rare such cures might be, they are contemplated as possible in the Levitical law.

C. R. Trench
The Miracles of Our Lord

In this sermon we move with the Galilean Physician to another healing incident, the exact location of which is not given. Luke says only that it was in "a certain city." From the record we do know that Jesus had decided to leave Capernaum. In verse 42 of the preceding chapter the people pleaded with him to remain there with them. But he explained, "I must preach the kingdom of God to other cities also: for therefore am I sent."

Jesus was conscious of the fact that his mission was not to be local in nature. He had been sent by God to *all* cities and towns and villages along the journey. This included foreign cities and towns and villages. His mission was to be broadly based. Certainly, his healing ministry was not to be exclusive, but inclusive. This is why he read the prophecy in the synagogue in Nazareth:

The Spirit of the Lord is upon me,
because he hath anointed me to preach the gospel
to the poor;

he hath sent me to heal the brokenhearted,
to preach deliverance to the captives,
and recovering of sight to the blind,
to set at liberty them that are bruised,
to preach the acceptable year of the Lord
   (Luke 4:18, 19).

The first thing we should note is that Luke expresses the fact that Jesus was conscious of time. "And it came to pass." This is the way Luke seeks to express the fact that a certain amount of time had elapsed before this event took place.

Jesus, as you recall, stayed in the house of Simon Peter all night. He was there healing and helping as only the Physician from heaven could do. There is every possibility that Jesus healed and helped those who were brought to him all night. When day came he went into a desert place, and people followed him there. People will follow him who has the solution to their physical, mental, and spiritual needs. They were so impressed with Jesus that they wanted him to settle down as a kind of village physician.

Our Lord would not submit to their request and went on to other villages and towns in the vicinity of Galilee. As Jesus moved from place to place, he came to the Sea of Galilee. There he saw some boats and entered one of them and taught the people. It seems as though Simon had been fishing and had caught nothing. Jesus gave him and the other fishermen instructions about where they might catch some fish. Peter and the others did as Jesus suggested and subsequently caught more than their nets could hold.

After this miracle of the fishes, Jesus extended a call to Peter and his brother. Then he extended the call to James and John, saying to them, "Fear not; from henceforth thou shalt catch men."

We don't know how much time had elapsed, but certainly there was some time before this next event took place.

Luke then says, "When he was in a certain city." As I have

He Needs Healing and Help

said, this city is not known, but we do know that he was still in the area of Galilee. He was still close to the town of Capernaum. The name of the city is not too important. The fact is that Jesus felt that this city should be included in his healing and helping ministry. The Son of God knew that every city had its sick and impotent, that there was need in all the towns, cities, and villages where the sons and daughters of God reside.

Jesus knew the needs of the city. He knew they needed his help. Yet we know that there were cities which did not welcome Jesus. There were places which asked Jesus to leave. This is true of our society. There are cities that want nothing to do with Jesus. There are homes that want nothing to do with Jesus. There are groups and nations that want nothing to do with Jesus. They do not want Jesus!

The presence of Jesus is too disturbing for most of us. We think we can do without his presence and power. Nevertheless, Jesus keeps coming. He keeps coming to our towns and cities and villages. He keeps extending to us his grace and love and mercy and forgiveness. He wants to be used. He wants to heal and to help. Though we refuse, still he knocks. "Behold, I stand at the door and knock."

What a sad and needless commentary! We have offered to us infinite love, and we ignore and disdain that gracious offer.

The cities are full of people with all kinds of problems and difficulties. This is especially true of those who are sick—mentally, physically, and spiritually. Our urban areas are centers of misery, poverty, pain, and sorrow. On every hand we see the deep and harried furrows of men and women burdened down with the pain of misery and the misery of pain.

The climate of agony fills our cities, and men and women are looking for anyone who can relieve the burdens of bodies wracked with pain. This is particularly true of the poor. Someone has said, "If you want a large following, discover a way to heal the bodies of men and women at no cost."

Our Lord and our Savior had this solution. He had this unique power. He could heal and help. He was sent into the world for this cause. This was his claim: "For the Son of man is come to seek and to save that which was lost." Also he said, "I am come that they might have life." The life he gave and gives is healthy. It is healthy now and forevermore. He grants us the wholeness of our being. He grants us the fullness of his being. It is his will that we become what he is. Ultimately, it is his desire that we have a painless existence; this is the meaning of those words given to John on the island of Patmos:

> And I heard a great voice out of heaven saying, Behold, the tabernacle of God is with men, and he will dwell with them, and they shall be his people, and God himself shall be with them, and be their God.
> And God shall wipe away all tears from their eyes; and there shall be no more death, neither sorrow, nor crying, neither shall there be any more pain: for the former things are passed away (Rev. 21:3, 4).

That is the long goal. Until then, we have to depend on the gift of healing given to holy men, trained and untrained. Jesus would be classified as one who was not trained. Yet our Lord had the gift of healing. He was the healer and helper of his day. This is why people came to him from distant places. They had heard about the preacher-physician. They wanted to be made whole and healthy. They wanted a new lease on life. They wanted a brighter tomorrow. They came to Jesus. They came for wholeness.

One of those who came, according to Luke 5:12, was a man who had the dread disease known as leprosy. Dr. William Barclay states that there were two kinds of leprosy in Palestine at the time.

> There was one which was rather like a very bad skin disease, and it was the less serious of the two. There was one in which the disease, starting from a small

He Needs Healing and Help   55

spot, ate away the flesh until the wretched sufferer was left with only the stump of a hand or a leg. It was literally a living death![1]

This disease would head the list of the most frightening and devastating illnesses one could have. In Leviticus 13 and 14 we find rituals and regulations pertaining to it. Perhaps the most terrible thing about it was the isolation it brought about. The leper was to cry, "Unclean! Unclean!" wherever he went. He was to dwell alone; "without the camp shall his habitation be" (Lev. 13:46). He was banished from the society of men and exiled from his home. The victim suffered physiologically as well as psychologically. You will recall that Miriam, too, was set outside the camp for seven days because of leprosy.

Dr. A. B. MacDonald, in an article on the leper colony in Itu of which he was in charge, wrote:

The leper is sick in mind as well as body. For some reason there is an attitude to leprosy different from the attitude to any other disfiguring disease. It is associated with shame and horror, and carries, in some mysterious way, a sense of guilt, although innocently acquired like most contagious troubles. Shunned and despised, frequently do lepers consider taking their own lives and some do.[2]

The leper, says Barclay, was hated by others until he came to hate himself. This was the kind of man that approached Jesus. He was isolated, despised, exiled from home, and sick in body and mind. He sought Jesus. He sought Jesus, the Preacher-Physician.

Yet there is something we should pay close attention to

1. William Barclay, *The Gospel of Luke* (Philadelphia: Westminster Press, 1975), p. 58.
2. *Ibid.*

about this incident. First, the law stipulated that the leper, in his isolation, was to cry, "Unclean! Unclean!" when he approached anyone. This is not here recorded. So we wonder, did Jesus and the crowd come upon the leper suddenly, not allowing him time to warn them? Did the man, in his eagerness, disregard the law and approach the crowd anyway? There is a third possibility. This is a fact which is only given by Luke. Two words are left out of Luke's account, *kai idou*. The words *plarns lepras* seem to imply that this was an advanced case. The man's face and hands would be covered with ulcers and sores, so that everyone could see that the hideous disease was at a very advanced stage. Maybe this accounts for the man's venturing into the multitude, and for their not fleeing at his approach, for a strange provision of the law stated: "If a leprosy break out abroad in the skin, and the leprosy cover all the skin of him that hath the plague from his head even to his foot, . . . then the priest . . . shall pronounce him clean that hath the plague (Lev. 13:12, 13).

At any rate, the man was full of leprosy. It had covered his body but was not the kind which ate away the limbs. As such, the man could approach Jesus and the people without too much hesitation. Nonetheless, he came to Jesus and fell on his face. This is an indication of the humility with which this man approached Jesus.

Please note carefully that Jesus did not tell the man to stand on his feet as Paul did in the Book of Acts. There was more than just another holy man present. This was more than just a great prophet who was passing by. This was Jesus. This was Jesus Christ. This was the Lord Jesus Christ. This was he who was called Priest, Prophet, and King. He was due homage, and this man in agony paid that kind of homage to him.

It might be that in our prayer life we don't bow low enough. As such, we don't have the power and authority which God grants to those who recognize who He is and what He requires of those who would come to Him in prayer. We must remember that Jesus in Gethsemane bowed low and in the dirt. In that intense hour of prayer God heard His Son. He answered with new

He Needs Healing and Help   57

power for the journey ahead. An angel appeared in that garden and gave to Jesus the needed divine energy to move forward. God knew that the future for Jesus was greater than the agony of the moment. So He sent him help and power to move into that future.

The man fell on his face and petitioned Jesus. He asked Jesus to help him. He besought Jesus that he would do for him what no other doctor had been able to do. He wanted relief from the misery of the hated disease, leprosy. Jesus had said we are to ask: "Ask, and it shall be given you." The man humbly and reverently petitioned the Son of God for mental and bodily relief. He said to Jesus, "Lord, if thou wilt, thou canst make me clean."

That word *Lord* has great significance. Some would say that it did not apply to Jesus until after his resurrection from the grave. Others say that it was used of Jesus during his life and ministry. It comes from the Greek word *kurios*. Properly an adjective signifying having power or authority, it is used as a noun, variously translated in the New Testament *Lord, Master, Owner,* and *Sir*—a title of wide significance.

I would contend that Jesus was conscious of this title before his resurrection; and even more so, after his resurrection, did the church realize what Jesus was saying.

It is still true that holy men are sometimes greater after their deaths than during their lives. In Matt. 7:21-22 Jesus assumes this title: "Not every one that saith unto me, Lord, Lord, shall enter into the kingdom of heaven; but he that doeth the will of my Father which is in heaven. Many will say to me in that day, Lord, Lord, have we not prophesied in thy name? and in thy name have cast out devils? and in thy name done many wonderful works?"

I don't know how the man arrived at this position. It could be that the news had spread about the miracles in the other towns, and he made a logical deduction that only the Lord could heal him. He had been declared a leper, and he knew that only an act of God could cure that loathesome disease. "Lord," he said, "if thou wilt," which was like saying, "Lord, if you will."

The man appealed directly to the will of Jesus. Somehow he knew that a willing Jesus was and could be a blessing to his pathetic but sincere prayer. He went directly to the center of Jesus' being. "Is it in your will that I be made whole?" Some doctors don't will that their patients be whole. They prefer to have them come back time and time again. This is especially true for those who are able to pay, and pay on time. The man had no money and no visible means of support, so there was no chance he could keep coming back for costly treatments. Medicare and Medicaid were not available then. He needed an instant act of healing and wholeness.

Jesus had said himself, "I have come that they might have life, and that they might have it more abundantly." He had also said, "The Son of man is come to seek and to save that which was lost." Our Lord had stated, "The Son of man came not to be ministered unto, but to minister, and to give his life a ransom for many." Jesus had also said during his ministry, "Even so the Son quickeneth whom he will." Finally, our Lord Jesus Christ spoke these words of life and hope: "Even so it is not the will of your Father which is in heaven, that one of these little ones should perish."

It is not the will of God that we perish. It is not the intent of God that we be sick. It is not the intent of God that we be broken in body and mind and spirit. It is not the intent of God that our lives be filled with pain and more pain and more pain. It is not the intent of God that our days be filled with agony and anguish. It is not the intent of God that we moan and groan day in and day out. It is not the intent of God that life be surrounded with suffering and sorrow. It is not the intent of God that we experience nothing but evil days and wicked nights. It is not His intent. But this is true.

The pain of purification must sometimes follow the joy of peace. This man wanted the joy of peace. He said to Jesus, "Thou canst make me clean." He shifts from the will of Jesus to the *canst-ness* of Jesus. He knew that *willingness* preceded *canst-ness*.

He Needs Healing and Help

A person *can* and *will not*. But the reverse is impossible: no one *wills* and *cannot*.

"If thou wilt, thou canst make me clean." Make me clean! Make me healthy! Make me sound again! Make me well! Heal me! Help me! I have seen enough of the darkness in life. I have known enough of the misery. I have known what it is to live alone. I have known what it is to live in isolation. I have known what it is like to be pushed out of my home. I have known what it is like to be an exile from home. I have known what it is like to be forced away from cordial society. I have known the loneliness of the nights and endlessness of the days. I have known! I have known!

Jesus heard his plea. He heard his cry. He heard the prayer request. God hears the humble child's first prayer. This might have been the first time that this man had prayed in a long time. He was confronting the man of prayer, the man of our pleas and needs, the man Christ Jesus, the Savior of sinners, the healer of the sick and the lame, the helper of those who are down and out. He was from above but came below to lift us from the depths of pain. He came to give us peace which comes through the pain of suffering and sorrow.

I am so glad he came. I am thankful that he came. I rejoice that he came. I glory in the fact that he came. You ought to be glad that he came. He is the healer for all and the helper for all. All that he asks is that we love him with our whole soul, mind, body, and strength. We are to give ourselves into his hands. That is what this man did. "Lord, if thou wilt, thou canst make me clean."

The willingness of the man to place his life in the hands of Jesus was demonstrated by the fact that he called him "Lord." This acknowledgement led to the Master's actions which followed.

Jesus put forth his hand. Note that it says that he put forth his hand. This is suggestive of the fact that while the man had a bad case, Jesus did not need both hands. It might have been a mild case because the man nowhere cried, "Unclean! Unclean!"

60   HELP ME, SOMEBODY!

Had it been a bad case or a severe case, the man would have been compelled by the Levitical law to cry, "Unclean! Unclean!" Being a mild case, Jesus just put forth one hand. That one hand was enough to do the job. He did not need both hands on this occasion. There are times when one hand will do the job. Nevertheless, I would rather have the one hand of Jesus working for me than two hands of the devil working against me. There is more power in his one hand than there is in both hands of the devil.

Jesus then moved forward with his one hand to help and heal the man. Luke reports that he "touched him." This method is different from the method he used on a prior occasion. There he placed his holy hands on the people and healed every one of them. Here Jesus just touched the man. The touch of Jesus is more therapeutic than that of all the doctors in town. The curative powers in his hand transcended the normal medical powers of his day and time and our day and time. He was blessed by God to be a blessing. He was commissioned by God to do the work of God. It is the work of God to bring to the bodies and minds and spirits of men and women health and wholeness.

Those who were and are touched by Jesus are immediately transferred from the realm of misery to the realm of utter delight. They are lifted from the quagmires of pain to the lofty heights of health and wholeness. They are freed from the pits of anguish to the solemn avenues of sheer joy and happiness. Those who are touched by Jesus are motivated to have faith in the impossible possibility. Jesus has the touch which no one else can duplicate. His touch is the touch of God. By his touch we are healed. We are healed for the new experience of wholeness.

Jesus answered the man's request by saying, "I will: be thou clean." He said to the man that he had rightly discerned that it was in Christ's will that healing took place. "You must first get to my will. You must first touch the heart of my being. You must make the appeal directly to the inner man. It is the will of man which determines his actions. You have rightly stated the case. If

He Needs Healing and Help   61

I did not so will your wholeness, you would not and could not get well. But I so will that you get well. I want you to be whole. I want you to be clean. I will that you live life at another level. I want to bring joy into your life. I want to restore you to community life and living. I want you to have more life—that life which transcends the loneliness of your present existence. I will that you be made well. I quickeneth whom I will! I will that you be whole."

Jesus is for our wholeness. He is for our health. He is for our salvation. He will break the written law to enforce the higher law. It was an infraction of the written law to touch a leper. He would have to withdraw into the wilderness alone if he touched a leper. Jesus did not care about the written law which prevented him from being compassionate and bearing the misery and sorrow of the sons and daughters of men who are to be the sons and daughters of God. Jesus broke the ceremonial law at the demand of a higher law—the law whose source is divine compassion and in whose agent is the power to heal and help.

And once again there is an immediate instance of the miracle-working power of Jesus demonstrated. Luke says, "And immediately the leprosy departed from him." The foul leprosy could not pollute the pure hands of Jesus. Infinite purity can always deal with infinite impurity. The powers of impurity are not greater than the powers of purity. The impure powers are great, but they are not greater than the pure power of God. This is why Jesus could say, "For this cause came I into the world." This is also why Paul warns us to put on the whole armor of God. He said, "We wrestle not against flesh and blood, but against principalities, against powers, against the rulers of the darkness of this world, against spiritual wickedness in high places."

Jesus told the man, "Go, and shew thyself to the priest, and offer for thy cleansing, according as Moses commanded, for a testimony unto them." Jesus also instructed the man to tell no one.

An offering, cleansing, would have to be made by the officiating priest in the temple at Jerusalem. Jesus did not break with the tradition of his people. He also did not want the news at that time to be spread abroad. Jesus would not and did not like a lot of publicity concerning what he did for the kingdom. The time for that would be in the future. But for the moment, he just wanted to help and to heal.

Nevertheless, great works of healing and helping cannot be placed under a bushel. The news will travel far and wide. That is just what happened, according to Luke.

Verse 15 states, "But so much the more went there a fame abroad of him: and great multitudes came together to hear, and to be healed by him of their infirmities."

The leper went on his way, singing in his heart, "Yes, God is real." He did not know how many others could sing the song, but he knew that he could sing that song. "Yes, God is real." I don't know about you, but I have learned to sing that song with new meaning since I have come to really love and know more about Jesus our Lord and our Savior. God is more real to me now than when I was younger. He walks with me and talks with me more and tells me to hang in there and hold on.

He is real! He is real! He is real in my soul! Yes, God is real! Amen and amen.

Jesus, Help This Man

Jesus heals and forgives a paralytic
Luke 5:16-26

Patient/Diagnosis:
A man which was taken with a palsy

Doctor:
Jesus of Nazareth

Cure:
Jesus said, "Man, thy sins are forgiven thee. . . . Arise, and take up thy couch, and go into thine house."

Comments:
The man was presumably at least a paraplegic, since he was in bed and unable to walk. In those days this could have been due to birth defect or previous trauma, or to an adult injury or spinal infection. In any event, damage to the spinal cord is usually permanent, making a spontaneous remission very unlikely.

Dr. Joseph Blythe
Pulmonary specialist
Memphis, Tennessee

In this sermon we pick up the healing ministry of Jesus in the 16th verse of Luke, chapter 5. Our grand Preacher-Physician is once more ready for his merciful ministry of healing and helping the lost sons and daughters of God. In the 16th verse, Jesus retired to the wilderness. There, in that wild and desolate place of stillness and quietness, Jesus prayed. This was the necessary procedure used by our Lord to refuel, retool, re-equip and reempower himself for the tasks of healing and helping that lay ahead. Jesus knew that he needed to remain in constant contact with his Father in glory. For from the Father came the power and the authority to heal the bodies and minds and souls of men. In fact, the Father was in him in a mighty and mysterious way. He possessed the power of God.

Luke proceeds, "And it came to pass on a certain day." This is Luke's way of letting us know that the actual day of this event was not recorded at that time. So he had to conjecture as to when it happened. The important thing is that it did happen. We should not let ourselves get bogged down having to know the exact day when things happened. Luke bears witness to the fact that the incidents did occur.

He then goes on to say, "as he was teaching, . . . there were Pharisees and doctors of the law sitting by." Jesus was not just a healer; he was also a preacher and teacher. Biblical scholarship supports the contention that the name *preacher* was not given to Jesus in the Gospels, yet forty-five times in the Gospels Jesus was called a *teacher*. He sometimes called himself a teacher; at other times he was called a teacher by his followers, such as Mary and Nicodemus; and still at other times his enemies—the Pharisees and Sadducees—called him *teacher*.

Jesus was regularly engaged in teaching. We find him teaching in the synagogues, at the temple, by the seashore, in houses, wherever he found himself. Teaching was his business, and he was constantly engaged in it. He was not a professional teacher, in the sense that he had received special preparation for it, but rather he was a self-appointed or "God-sent" teacher.

Jesus not only taught the crowds, but he also trained a group of teachers who were to continue his work when he departed. Especially was this true in the latter part of his ministry. Thus he became a "teacher of teachers," preparing others to carry on his work. This was accomplished by personal instruction as well as by the example of his life and the activities he entrusted to his followers.

Our Lord also commissioned his followers to teach. When he was ready to leave the earth, he gave them this parting command: "Go ye therefore, and teach all nations, baptizing them in the name of the Father, and of the Son, and of the Holy Ghost: Teaching them to observe all things whatsoever I have commanded you: and, lo, I am with you alway, even unto the end of the world" (Matt. 28:19, 20). This Great Commission seems to require the teaching function for its realization.

Jesus was most often spoken of as a teacher, rather than as a herald (*kerux*). The Greek word used to refer to teaching is *didaskalos*. This is seen in Matthew 4:23, 5:2, 7:29 and 9:35. It is used of *things* taught in the Gospels and Acts, of *persons* and *things* taught (Matt. 15:9; 22:16; Acts 15:35; 13:11), and of both *persons* and *things* (John 14:26; Rev. 2:14, 20).

We should teach because Jesus taught. The primitive church taught; the disciples taught; Paul taught. The church fathers—Augustine, Clement, Calvin, Luther, Barth, and Brunner—taught. M. L. King, Jr. taught, and so did P. J. Jackson, T. J. Searcy, A. Brown, A. M. Townsend and S. A. Owen. Therefore, we must teach.

If we do not teach, we face the following consequences: We will not be "churchly" nor Christlike. Our church will be crowded with passengers—not pilgrims. Our congregations will be open game for cultic groups. There can be no authentic worship. The sheep will find it impossible to pick up the homiletical meanderings of the shepherd. We will not be able to pass on to our children the great content of the faith in an orderly and systematic manner.

Jesus was constantly confronted with the presence of

Pharisees and doctors of the law, who were the official teachers of that day. The next verse states, "There were Pharisees and doctors of the law sitting by, which were come out of every town of Galilee, and Judea, and Jerusalem." These teachers did not come to listen and to learn. They came to criticize and refute the teachings of Jesus. They could not possibly receive instruction from one who had not been trained in the rabbinical schools. Jesus had not been certified and validated as a teacher in Israel. So they did not listen to learn, but only to condemn.

It should be noted that they gathered from all sections of the country. The fame of Jesus had spread from one end of the country to the other. Those in Galilee had sent for those who were the leaders in Judea and Jerusalem. They wanted the doctors of the law to hear and examine the strange new teachings of this peasant carpenter from Nazareth. What they heard and what they saw was not to their liking. In time they would help to plot his destruction and death. But they could not stop his movement, for his movement was from God. God's momentum cannot be stopped by man's puny pendulum.

At this point, Luke says something which is peculiar to his writing: "And the power of the Lord was present to heal them." Luke recalls that this was a part of the mission of Jesus. He said so from the very beginning of his ministry. When Jesus stood in the synagogue and read from the document known as Isaiah, he quoted from those memorable words of that great prophet: "He hath sent me to heal the brokenhearted."

Nothing can break one's heart like sickness, disease, and constant pain, misery, and agony. Jesus came to help those whose hearts had been broken by some terrible sickness of mind, body, and soul. He has the power to heal and help in a most unusual way. He was sent to minister to the God-forsaken, the God-abandoned, and the God-rejected. To all those who walk under the darkness of heavy loads, Jesus came with healing in his wings. It was in his hands. It was in his spittle. It was in his words. It was in the hem of his holy garments, and it was in his holy and precious blood. He had the power to heal and help. It

Jesus, Help This Man

was God-given and God-empowered and God-endowed. Now back to the drama of the biblical text: "Behold, men brought on a bed a man which was taken with a palsy." This is most interesting. Please note that *men*, not *a man* brought him in, a statement which implies that the man had concerned friends who exemplified genuine Christian living. Life is togetherness. We do not and cannot exist alone. We all need one another: you need me, and I need you. We dare not try to live unto ourselves. If we do, there will come a day when we will need someone, and if we are sick, as this man was, not just anyone will do. We need support and assistance from friends who are kind, sympathetic, empathetic, and committed to our welfare.

I would refer to the four men carrying the sick man as "the universe-at-large." That is, as they surrounded the man in four directions, I think of the omnipresence of God. On the east, He is there! On the west, He is there! On the north and on the south, He is also there! Our God is everywhere, and is concerned about us all. He has concern for our President, and He has concern for leaders of countries that we consider adversaries. He has concern for you, and He has concern for me. His eye is on the sparrow.

The afflicted man on the bed might symbolize man as an individual—individual in his misery, in his anguish, in his agony, in his pain, in his helplessness. And fortunately for this man, his friends thought that Jesus was a cosmic healer, so they sought him for their earthly friend. They brought him to Jesus. They brought him to a house where healing was underway in the name of God Almighty.

You, too, ought to bring someone to Jesus. You ought to bring your loved ones who are lost. You ought to bring strangers who are lost. You ought to bring sons and daughters, husbands and wives, anyone who is not in the household of faith to the Preacher—Physician from Nazareth.

Luke continues with the idea that the four friends sought means to bring the sick man into the house. It is so stated in verse 19. Could this mean that they had tried to get him to Jesus before he went into the house? Or does this mean that they had tried to get him in the door and had failed because his bed was too wide, or that they sought to get him in the window which was too narrow? Nevertheless, they were determined to get him to Jesus.

I would to God that more of us had that kind of evangelistic fervor. If we were determined to get men and women to Jesus, our enthusiasm would be contagious, and we could set this city on fire. But most of us are satisfied with mild and lukewarm zeal and zest. We have enthusiasm for everything but the winning of souls for Jesus. When they do come, there is very little joy. We are unmoved and unmotivated. Yet my Bible tells me that there is rejoicing in heaven over one sinner who comes to Jesus. Heaven is moved, and heaven is motivated to rejoice and rejoice whenever another child of God comes home from the far country. It is time to rejoice when Satan misses another soul he thought he had. Let no one fool you—Satan is real and still in business.

The men were not content merely to bring the man to where a crowd had gathered. They brought him in and sought to lay him at the feet of Jesus. At the feet of Jesus men and women can find the healing and help they need and yearn for. There is help and healing at his blessed feet. The lower we are in the sight of Jesus, the better he can deal with our maladies and illnesses. The more desperate our case, the more sympathetic Jesus is with our condition. Jesus will come to us in our quiet moments of desperation. He wants us to come into his presence, meek, humble, lowly.

> All to Jesus I surrender,
> All to him I freely give.
> I will ever love and serve him
> In his presence daily live.

And I say,

All to Jesus I surrender,
Humbly at his feet I bow;
Worldly pleasures all forsaken,
Take me, Jesus, take me now.

All to Jesus I surrender,
Lord, I give myself to Thee;
Fill me with thy love and power,
Let thy blessing fall on me.
—J. W. Van Deventer

Jesus is for the homeless, the helpless, and the hopeless. He is for the abandoned, the rejected, and the isolated. He is for the despised, the defeated, and the denied. Jesus is for the sick and the lost. He came that they might have life and have it more abundantly. This is Jesus, your Jesus and my Jesus.

Our writer then moved to another level of the story. The men were seeking help for this man. This one particular man knew only desolation and despondency. They had brought him with great hopes and lofty expectations.

"And when they could not find by what way they might bring him in because of the multitude," his friends or his relatives, or just plain helpful men, sought to get him into the house, where Jesus had set up another temporary hospital, so that he might receive the blessing and benediction of God that only Jesus had the authority and power to give.

They could not get him through the door. They could not get him through the window. The front entrance was blocked. The back entrance was blocked. The house was filled with those who needed healing and those who sought healing and those who brought others for healing. This was the place where the healing arts were put into practice for the good of all in that community who came with faith and hope and love to the man called Jesus, who was inside the house reclaiming lives and restoring limbs and giving hope to those who had lost all hope of becoming well and whole again.

When those four men saw that they could not get into the house in the usual manner, they would not let that stop them. Nothing must stop us from getting to Jesus. They used their imaginations to get this man to Jesus. They were determined not to fail their friend. Or maybe the pathetic cries of the man on the bed forced them to exhaust every means possible. "Get me to Jesus! Please get me to Jesus! I believe that he can help me! Get me to Jesus! They tell me that he has help and healing for the least of God's children."

"Get me to Jesus! He does not charge one single dime! Get me to Jesus! I don't have Medicare or Medicaid. Get me to Jesus! I have not worked in many years! Get me to Jesus! My way has been hard and my nights dark! Get me to Jesus! Jesus is in that house. Get me to Jesus! Help me get to Jesus! I don't care how you manage, but get me to Jesus!"

You and I must exhaust every means to get our loved ones to Jesus. We must use our minds and hearts and souls and spirits creatively to force them, if necessary, to come and see Jesus. Jesus has the answer. Jesus has the answer for the world today. Yes! Jesus has the answer. We are to be as conscientious as the paralyzed man's friends were. They were not to be denied. They would get this man to Jesus. And so they devised a means for getting this man to Jesus. They decided to go another way. If one way will not get you there, then create another way, but at any cost *get to Jesus!* Take your burdens to the Lord and leave them there.

Luke says, "They went upon the housetop." They went up before they could let him down. One has to go up to Jesus. But we must always keep in mind that he came down from his lofty throne in glory to be with us. This is why he is called Emmanuel, "God with us."

Paul says of Jesus:

> Let this mind be in you, which was also in Christ Jesus: Who, being in the form of God, thought it not robbery to be equal with God: But made himself of

no reputation, and took upon him the form of a servant, and was made in the likeness of men:

And being found in fashion as a man, he humbled himself and became obedient unto death, even the death of the cross (Phil. 2:5-8).

They inverted the process of how we normally come to Jesus. They went up in order to come down. Normally, we must go down in order to come up. We must first look down before we can look up. Nonetheless, their faith drove them to a desperate thing. They sought to get to Jesus by any means necessary. They climbed up to the top of the house and started tearing up the roof of the house to get this sick man to Jesus.

Can you not see those four men and that sick man filled with one thought in mind: Get to Jesus! They knew that if they could only come before his presence, things would happen to help restore this man to wholeness and wellness. They were big in expectation and hope.

Once they got on top of the house, they proceeded to tear away the tile and brushes which covered it. There seemed to be no protest from the owner of the house. The man was more important than the house. Property values must give way to human values. This is always foremost in the mind of Jesus and of those who come to know him as Lord and Savior.

As the four men tore up the roof, they were saying in their minds and hearts, "Jesus can help this man." Another one could be heard saying, "Jesus must help this man!" Still another one could be heard saying, "Jesus will help this man!" Finally, the fourth man said, "For this cause came Jesus into the world!"

While they were tearing up the roof, they might have started to sing a hymn softly to themselves, "What a friend we have in Jesus!" The man on the couch might have started to sing, "Just as I am without one plea, but that thy blood was shed for me."

When you carry someone to Jesus, you must have faith, and the one you carry must also have faith. Faith in Jesus had been produced by what he had done. People had heard and seen him in action. They had heard about this young physician in town. They had knowledge concerning the miracles already performed. This knowledge provoked faith, hope, and love. In each heart that heard about Jesus, a divine spark had been kindled. Those of humble hearts have the capacity to possess great faith. Jesus had taught, "Blessed are the meek: for they shall inherit the earth." Jesus had also said, "Blessed are the poor in spirit: for theirs is the kingdom of heaven."

When the men finally completed the task of tearing up the roof, they proceeded to lower their friend through the ceiling and into the house. Luke says it beautifully: "And let him down through the tiling with his couch into the midst before Jesus."

The man and his couch were placed directly in front of Jesus. Not behind Jesus. Not on the right side of Jesus. Not on the left side of Jesus, but directly in front of Jesus. They wanted to make sure that Jesus saw their friend. They wanted Jesus to know that they had brought him there and that his case was desperate. They had used desperate means and had taken desperate actions to get to Jesus. They did not want Jesus to miss this paralyzed man. They wanted him whole. They wanted him healthy. They wanted this man helped. They wanted this man healed. They wanted this man made into a new being. They wanted Jesus to operate on their friend.

Thank goodness for Jesus! They brought him to the right doctor. The power of healing was with him. He had the gift for healing which had been given to him by his Father. As it was from the Father, so it was also in the Father. What the Father had, the Son had; and what the Son had, the Father had. They placed the man in front of Jesus.

By so doing, they made this man's case top priority. They placed him at the head of the long line of people in that house. They wanted something done for the man immediately. It is interesting that the people who were there first did not complain. Neither did Jesus take exception to the fact that they had done this. Jesus must have been aware of the fact that this man's case was severe and critical. So Jesus placed him in intensive care. He who was an outpatient became an inpatient. He did not have Medicare, but he was about to receive Jesus' care.

Our Lord responded with concern and care for this man. "And when he saw their faith, he said unto him, Man, thy sins are forgiven thee."

"He saw their faith." This would include the four men who brought the man to Jesus as well as the man who was brought. They all had expressed faith by their collective actions of trying to get to Jesus. The four men expressed faith by climbing the roof, tearing up the roof, and letting the man down in the midst. The poor crippled man who was paralyzed did not protest and did not give up when he learned that the entranceways were blocked. He went along with the decision and waited for the response of Jesus.

One could argue that Jesus responded because of the faith of the four men who brought the man to him.

In several other instances Jesus responded to requests for healings because of the faith of a third party. Jesus explained to the father of the epileptic boy that healing was possible for anyone who had faith, and the man cried out, "Lord, I believe; help thou mine unbelief" (Mark 9:24). We see this in the healing of the court official's son (John 4:47-53) and the centurion's servant (Matt. 8:5-13).

"Man," said Jesus to the sick man in front of him, "thy sins are forgiven thee." This was the solution to the man's problem, the forgiveness of his sins. In some distant past the man had lived a reckless and dangerous life. This lifestyle had brought on the illness. Jesus' acute vision penetrated to the root of the man's ill health: he needed to have his sins forgiven. He needed to be free from his deep sense of guilt and shame. Jesus had the answer. Jesus had the solution to his moral pollution. Jesus is also the answer for the world today.

In verse 21 the scribes and Pharisees took offense to the words of Jesus, believing that only God had the authority and power to forgive sins. Jesus' declaration did not pass with favor in their eyes. They accused him of blasphemy and asked, "Who can forgive sins, but God alone?"

Had they been willing to listen and learn, they would have seen the power of God at work in Jesus, and they could have deduced from observation that God was at work in Jesus in a mighty way.

But they were not willing to listen and learn. So they plotted against the Lord's Messiah.

Then Jesus knew that they would not and could not believe in him. He perceived their thoughts and said, "What reason ye in your hearts?" He was actually saying to them, "Why do you thus reason this way in your minds? Don't you know and understand that God can work in many and strange ways? Don't limit God to the past history of the race. God yet speaks in our own history and time."

So Jesus raised a question with them, "Whether is easier, to say, Thy sins be forgiven thee; or to say, Rise up and walk?" This is a very interesting question, and the challenge here is a very practical one. Is it easier to say, "Thy sins are forgiven," because no one can prove that they are not forgiven? This is because we are taught to believe that only God can forgive sins. The claim to heal with a word or a command can be easily and quickly tested or verified. But Jesus moved to another level in this case. He did not want to use the word of healing as evidence. He went on, in the next verse, to identify himself with the title "Son of man." "But that ye may know that the Son of man hath power upon earth to forgive sins, (he said unto the sick of the palsy,) I say unto thee, Arise, and take up thy couch, and go into thine house."

The phrase "Son of man" was not acceptable to the Jews. They could not believe that their Messiah was weak and capable of suffering. They were unable to accept this title, but this was the very reason Jesus used it. "It expressed his Messiahship definitely enough for his purpose: but it expressed it in that veiled and suggestive way which characterized the whole of his teaching on his own person. At the same time, it conveyed to those who had ears to hear the whole secret of the Incarnation.

Jesus, Help This Man 75

That which the Jews shrank from and ignored he rather placed in the forefront of his mission."[1]

So Jesus commanded the man to "Arise, and take up thy couch, and go into thine house." Arise, lift your burden-bearer, and go home with it! The couch had been a place of rest and relaxation for the man. He had grown accustomed to it. It had also become a burden and a heavy duty for the man. Now Jesus gives him the opportunity to return the favor and become a bearer of that which had been his source of helplessness and hopelessness and lifelessness.

The man obeyed the command of Jesus. To obey is better than sacrifice. The verse says of this sick son of God: "And immediately he rose up before them. . . ." He got up from the bed before them. He rose up from the couch beneath him. From his prone position, he lifted himself at the word of Jesus and stood upright. In the presence of witnesses, he demonstrated the power to overcome his helplessness and forlornness.

The man, says the passage, "took up that whereon he lay." He who had been a burden was now given a burden. Jesus immediately put the man to work. He did not tell his friends to take the couch away. He told the man to take the couch away.

Maybe the reason we have so many problems with our children and our neighbors is that they want us to lift the burden and then to carry it. They want us to do for them what they should do for themselves. Maybe in our efforts to help our children we actually cripple them for life. We carry the burdens of life too long for them. We don't let them assume responsibility for carrying heavy loads soon enough. I think that we ought to learn some lessons from Jesus. He told us to take up our crosses, deny ourselves, and follow him. It is only by following him with our burdens that we find the key to his cosmic companionship. "Lo, I am with you alway, even unto the end of the world."

---

1. Rev. Alfred Plummer, *The International Critical Commentary—The Gospel According to St. Luke* (Edinburgh: T & T Clark, Ltd., 1975), p. 157.

Then our passage goes on to say of this one who had been freed that he "departed to his own house, glorifying God." This man reacted to his healing like the lame man that Peter and John healed at the gate of the temple as recorded in the Book of Acts. Verse 8 of the third chapter says, "And he leaping up stood, and walked, and entered with them into the temple, walking, and leaping, and praising God."

I believe that this glorious feeling is expressed by David in Psalm 103:

> Bless the Lord, O my soul: and all that is within me, bless his holy name.
> Bless the Lord, O my soul, and forget not all his benefits:
> Who forgiveth all thine iniquities; who healeth all thy diseases.

It is the Lord who heals us. The Lord said to the Israelites: "I will put none of these diseases upon thee, which I have brought upon the Egyptians: for I am the Lord that healeth thee" (Ex. 15:26). The Lord's Healer had acted in the life of this man. The man responded with gratitude and thanksgiving. He glorified the God of healing, redemption, and release with all his might and power. Jesus had shown him the God of health, wholeness, and wholesomeness.

To glorify God means to magnify, to extol, to praise Him. To glorify God means to acknowledge Him as to His being, attributes, and acts. The man saw in Jesus the very presence of God. He saw the merciful goodness of God in Jesus. He saw the blessedness of God in Jesus. He saw the wholeness of God in Jesus. He saw the power of God in Jesus. He saw the wholesomeness of God in Jesus. He saw the divine might of God in Jesus. He saw God in Jesus. He gave vent to all those years of pain and misery and agony by praising God. "Praise God! Praise God! Praise God! Praise God!" he said as he went home.

"Praise God! Praise God!" He lifted his bed and sang,

"Praise God!" He walked out the door and shouted, "Praise God!" He walked down the steps, "Praise God!" He turned homeward, "Praise God!" He opened the gate to his house, "Praise God!" He knocked on his door, "Praise God!" Praise God! Praise God! Praise God for all His goodness!

Praise God from whom all blessings flow;
Praise him, all creatures here below;
Praise him above, ye heavenly hosts;
Praise Father, Son and Holy Ghost! Amen.

Jesus, Help My Hand

Jesus heals a man with a withered hand
Luke 6:6-11

Patient/Diagnosis:
    A man whose right hand was withered

Doctor:
    Jesus of Nazareth

Cure:
    "And [he] said to the man which had the withered hand,
    Rise up, and stand forth. . . . Stretch forth thy hand. And he
    did so: and his hand was restored whole as the other."

Comments:
    Greek *xeros*, dry, withered, denotes a hand in which the
    muscles are paralyzed and shrunken, leaving the affected
    limb shorter and thinner than normal—a chronic condition in
    biblical times regarded as incurable. Some identify with a
    late complication of infantile paralysis (poliomyelitis).

                    The Illustrated Bible Dictionary, p. 620
                    D. H. Trapnell, Consultant Radiologist
                    Westminster Hospital, London

We have to hold to God's hand, for all other hands are suspect. They cannot see us through the storms and stresses of life, but God can. And he or she who knows that God can, keeps a hand in God's hand.

The passage of Scripture which will form the basis of the Word for this sermon is found in the sixth chapter of Luke. As we journey with this medical doctor, let us consider verses 6 through 11:

> And it came to pass also on another sabbath, that he entered into the synagogue and taught: and there was a man whose right hand was withered.
>
> And the scribes and Pharisees watched him, whether he would heal on the sabbath day; that they might find an accusation against him.
>
> But he knew their thoughts, and said to the man which had the withered hand, Rise up, and stand forth in the midst. And he arose and stood forth.
>
> Then said Jesus unto them, I will ask you one thing; Is it lawful on the sabbath days to do good, or to do evil? to save life, or to destroy it?
>
> And looking round about upon them all, he said unto the man, Stretch forth thy hand. And he did so: and his hand was restored whole as the other.
>
> And they were filled with madness; and communed one with another what they might do to Jesus.

Jesus, help my hand! Have you ever thought about the blessings you have—to be fortunate enough to have two hands, two feet, two eyes, two ears, one mouth, one nose, one head? One could go on naming the various parts of the human anatomy, but have you ever thought how awful it would be to live life with just one hand, or to have a hand that has lost its usefulness, its capacity to function effectively and efficiently?

As I pondered over this passage of Scripture, I tied one hand behind me—my right hand, and sat around for an hour, trying to function with the other, my left hand. I could not function too well. I could not do things with any degree of efficiency until I untied my right hand. This was true because I am right-handed. Had I been left-handed, I might have been able to function, but I tried it this way because the right hand is what Luke picks up on in this passage, which lends credence to the belief that Luke was a doctor. Only a doctor would have perhaps noticed this kind of detail.

There are three outstanding characters here: Jesus, the man with the withered hand—his right hand, mind you, and the Pharisees.

Jesus is in the synagogue teaching the people, as he constantly did. He was teaching them the profound truths of God, his Father. He was trying to illuminate the darkness of their minds, trying to stimulate their creativity to grasp eternal truths, as the human mind can do if it keeps itself receptive to the eternal truths of God. If one walks with God and talks with God, God illuminates the darkness. That's why I think Jesus said, "You are the light of the world." Light shines. Light illuminates. Light creates the capacity to see beyond the immediate surroundings.

He was there teaching in the synagogue. And Luke says, "There was a man whose right hand was withered." His *right hand*—Luke emphasizes this. He emphasizes this because, first of all, he is a doctor, and a doctor ought to know what is wrong with his patient. He ought to know what part of the body is troubling his patient. A good doctor might ask, "Does it hurt here? or over there? Just tell me, where is the pain? Is this the spot?"

There is a lost document called *The Gospel According to the Hebrews*, which some scholars believe was at one time part of Matthew's gospel. At any rate, in this gospel we are told that this man had at one time been a stone mason, or what we would today call a brick mason. Somehow, in the process of his workday he had injured his hand; and as a result of that injury, his hand became paralyzed. He had lost the use of it, and it had withered up. His right hand was withered. He had no means of livelihood, no way of earning his bread, no way to support his family.

Jesus, Help My Hand

There was no welfare system, no community service agencies in that day. The synagogue provided some forms and means, but for the most part, the Hebrews' gospel says that this once self-supporting man was reduced to the status of a beggar. He ran into the synagogue on that day and pleaded with Jesus, "Jesus, help my hand! I don't want to beg for my bread. I don't like the shame and humiliation that goes along with begging. Help my hand!"

Now that's not like many people I know, folks who love to beg. They reflect the begging age in which we live. They are afflicted with beg-itis. Many of them don't want to work, and if they do work, they want the top jobs, which reminds me of a fellow who went to a factory, asking for a job. The man in charge asked him, "What can you do?" He replied, "Most anything." Then came the question, "What job do you want?" to which the man answered, "I want *your* job!" And some of us are just like that. If we must work, we want only the top job; we're not prepared or willing to take anything less.

This man, who wanted to work, came into the synagogue and said to Jesus, "Jesus, help my hand!" And while he was begging Jesus to help, the Word says, "The scribes and Pharisees watched him, whether he would heal on the sabbath day; that they might find an accusation against him."

But they were not watching him directly. "They were looking at Jesus narrowly," says one writer. They were looking at him out of the corner of their eyes.

A lady once told me, "I've been watchin' you." I didn't know she'd been watching me. Then she added, "You ain't like they say you are." Thanks be to God she hadn't seen too much!

Now they were watching Jesus, not because they wanted to become a part of what he was about. They were watching Jesus to accuse him, to ultimately plot his destruction!

Isn't it strange how structured religion many times will organize itself and use its power to destroy those who seek to do the will of God? They were watching Jesus, and they didn't say a word. And the next verse says, "But [Jesus] knew their thoughts, and said to the man which had the withered hand, Rise up, and stand forth in the midst."

O, Jesus knows our every thought. We don't have to say a word. They didn't say a word. They just stood there, looking. And Jesus read their thoughts. It is said that the early Puritans used to put on the doors of their houses these words, "Thou, God, seest me," to remind them that God was always watching them. And God *does* see us. God *does* read our thoughts. God knows our thinking. God knows where we live. God knows where we work. He knows what bed we sleep in and what side of the bed we sleep on. My God is an all-seeing God. My God is an all-knowing God.

Jesus read their thoughts as they stood there, looking mean, looking nasty, looking cruel, looking bad and mad! Just when Jesus was about to make somebody glad, here they were, assembled in their pious righteousness and august dignity and ecclesiastical garb, conspiring to see how they could condemn the Son of God. But—as was his custom—Jesus went about his Father's business.

The man said to Jesus, "Jesus, my hand! I want it well, Jesus! I want it whole! I want you to do something for my hand, Jesus! Please, Jesus, I'd like to go to work. I'd like to be on the job Monday morning. I have a wife and some children. I don't like to beg, Jesus! I don't like to stand at the gates of the city, asking folks to drop me a dime or a quarter. I don't like to ride on anybody's back, Jesus. I'm a man! I want to stand on my own two feet and work for my living. I want to do things with my right hand again, Jesus. I was a good stone mason. I was no apprentice. I had an accident, a freak accident, which caused me to lose the use of this right hand, Jesus. Can you do anything for it?"

And Jesus will hear you when you pray. Jesus will hear you when you really mean business. When you act in faith, hope, and love, Jesus will surely hear you!

Jesus then looked at the man's withered hand and directed him to come forward. One writer's interpretation says, "Stand in front of me." At any rate, the man got up and obeyed. He stood

Jesus, Help My Hand

in the midst, as he had been told to do. "Obedience is better than sacrifice." It's always better to obey Jesus than to obey the folks out there.

The man got up and stood forth in the midst. And then Jesus—whom we often portray as easy, meek, and mild—looked at those pious folks, those respected dignitaries, and said, "I will ask you one thing: Is it lawful on the sabbath days to do good, or to do evil? to save life, or to destroy it?" When you corner a person who doesn't want to answer your question, he just clams up. But the question is still there, still there to haunt him.

Jesus said, in essence, "I know it's the sabbath." They had just rebuked Jesus for working on the sabbath; and here Jesus was again, healing on the sabbath. They were very angry because the Ten Commandments had taught them that the sabbath was to be kept holy. But the Pharisees, the fathers of the faith, had misconstrued that commandment and made it an unholy day by trying to keep it holy. They had tried to define what was work. They criticized Jesus for plucking grain on the sabbath. They ran to the rulebook, and found that it didn't answer their question. But it did say something about rubbing the grains in your hand. So they decided that Jesus and his disciples were rubbing the grains and therefore violating the sacred law. Actually, the Pharisees were splitting hairs, concocting all kinds of rules and regulations to fit their own selfish purposes.

Jesus continued to question them. "Don't you know that the Son of man is Lord of the sabbath? I am the owner of the sabbath. I am the master of the sabbath. I am the creator of the sabbath. And furthermore, I *am* the sabbath. Is it lawful, then, to do good on the sabbath, or to do evil?"

We've built up a whole host of negatives around religion: Don't do this, and don't do that! We emphasize the *don'ts* in our religion, when we ought to concentrate on the *do's*. Jesus made it clear that to do good on the sabbath is always acceptable and right. "Is it lawful to save life on the sabbath?" "Yes," said Jesus. "Man was not made for the sabbath. The sabbath was made for man. Yes, honor the sabbath. Try to keep it holy, and do not withhold any act of mercy, any act of love, any act of goodwill. Use the sabbath for God!"

Turning to the man with the withered hand, Jesus said, "Stretch forth thy hand."

O, I imagine that man had tried to do that a thousand times. When we have an ailment, we try to hurry it well. We do everything humanly possible to hasten recovery. But I have discovered that you can't hurry the body's healing process. The body takes its own time in getting well. We have to learn to wait. Remember the prophetic words of Isaiah, "They that wait upon the Lord shall renew their strength; they shall mount up with wings as eagles; they shall run, and not be weary; and they shall walk, and not faint."

That man with the withered hand had been waiting a long time. When Jesus told him to stretch forth his hand, he did not hesitate for a single moment. The Word says that he stretched forth his right hand, and immediately that hand became well.

"Your hand, man, is well!"

At the command of Jesus there is an instantaneous response, and with that response is the moment of healing. And in the act of healing is the moment of salvation. And in the moment of salvation is the moment of deliverance. And in the moment of deliverance is the moment of wholeness.

"Glory to God!" says the man. "My hand! My hand! My hand is whole! My hand is well! Thank you, Jesus! I can lay stones again. I can report to the foreman tomorrow!"

What have you done—since Christ made you whole—for the kingdom?

What have you done since Christ commanded that you be well?

This is the mission of Jesus: to make us whole and to make us well. I can hear that man saying to Jesus through the vistas of time, "I dedicate this hand to you, Jesus. Take my hand, lead me on, let me stand. There may be some more storms and stresses in my life, but from this moment on, Jesus, I'm in your hand!"

Jesus, This Man Deserves Your Help

Jesus heals the centurion's servant
Luke 7:1-10

Patient/Diagnosis:
A certain centurion's servant who was sick and ready to die

Doctor:
Jesus of Nazareth

Cure:
"And they that were sent, returning to the house, found the servant whole that had been sick."

Comments:
As a physician, I take these verses literally. We can tell that a patient is about to die when the respirations become very shallow and irregular, the pulse weak and irregular, the skin develops a dusky blue appearance and is cold and clammy, he sweats profusely and is not responsive. A patient in this condition is called *moribund*. Unless this patient receives intense resuscitative measures, the prognosis is imminently terminal.

Roger G. Smith, M.D.
Internal Medicine
Memphis, Tennessee

Once more we come to another story of Jesus' ministry of healing as recorded by Dr. Luke. Luke, being the only trained doctor in the group of early disciples, gives us some very interesting insights into the miracles of healing wrought by Jesus. His accounts are more detailed than are those of the other gospel writers. This may be expected because, as a physician, Luke was trained to pay close attention to details.

Luke places this incident against a background of the teaching ministry of Jesus, which was concluded in the passage immediately preceding this one. He opens this record by saying, "Now when he had ended all his sayings in the audience of the people, he entered into Capernaum."

Capernaum was the headquarters for the ministry of Jesus in Galilee. It was the home of most of his disciples and stood at the center of the fishing villages on the Sea of Galilee. It was here that Jesus performed his first healing miracle.

Most scholars say that it was a busy little seaport during Jesus' lifetime. It was located on the northwest shore of the Sea of Galilee, about two and one-half miles west of the entrance of the Jordan. The Capernaum harbor was lively with fishing craft, and its stout stone quays crowded with men packing fish for shipment. It was apparently a Roman military post and the place from whose tax collector's booth Jesus called Matthew (Levi) to discipleship (Matt. 9:9). Because of the many "mighty works" accomplished there, Jesus used this center for his busy Galilean ministry. Thus Capernaum, rather than Nazareth, was called "his own city" (Matt. 9:1)[1].

1. Madeleine S. Miller and J. Lane Miller, Harper's Bible Dictionary (New York: Harper & Row, 1961), p. 91.

Jesus, This Man Deserves Your Help   87

Just as Jesus entered this busy fishing village, a centurion (Roman commander of one hundred men) sent for Jesus to come and heal his servant. The name of the centurion is not given. Luke states in verse 2, "And a certain centurion's servant, who was dear unto him, was sick, and ready to die."

This centurion was a man of some learning and culture. He was also a man of some religious sympathies. Obviously he had a kind heart and had been very generous toward those under his authority.

This particular centurion had a servant who was very valuable to him and who was now close to death. Luke says that the servant was very dear to him. We don't know whether this attachment was emotional or economic. It may have been both. We do know that even the most ruthless slave master has the potential for compassion toward those who have been able to withstand cruelty. This was demonstrated in Alex Haley's *Roots*. It has been repeated in some of the Southern folklore which has been handed down to us. Moreover, it has been seen in our own New Testament how many of those who occupied Palestine came under sway of Jewish piety and ethics; and later Christians so witnessed with their lives and living that saints were later found in Caesar's household. Lowliness, meekness, and humility have converting power.

Nevertheless, the servant was at the point of death. The man needed help. Fortunately, Jesus was nearby and was able to help. Therefore, this master did something which was quite unusual for a Roman officer. Luke makes the case very clear: "And when he heard of Jesus. . . ." Please notice the fact that he had heard about Jesus. Jesus had done some amazing things in and around Nazareth and Capernaum. His mighty deeds had caught the attention of the masses of men and women.

If you want news to spread, share it with the masses. They are many, and they love to tell of events which are extraordinary and astounding. Moreover, they seem to be more "faith-oriented" than "worldly-oriented." They have to depend on God for everything, and they expect more from God. Their dependency on God is primary and not secondary. Maybe this is why God sent Jesus to humble people—to emphasize the simplicity of faith that seeks God anywhere and at any time. The humble masses must say daily with the psalmist:

I will lift up mine eyes unto the hills,
from whence cometh my help.
My help cometh from the Lord,
which made heaven and earth (Ps. 121:1, 2).

Or they might sing with the hymnist:

My faith looks up to Thee
Thou Lamb of Calvary.
        —Ray Palmer

In addition to that, the masses love to tell about one of their own who makes good in the world. They take a great deal of pride honoring someone from their ranks who distinguishes himself in this hard and cruel world. For this world does not look with favor upon those who are born in the ghettoes of this earth. People do not expect anything worthy to come from the ghettoes and slums. Even some of Jesus' own followers raised the question, "Can any good thing come out of Nazareth?" Can anything worthwhile come from that place and that kind of stock?

The problem with that kind of thinking is that it does not take time to check with God Almighty. It is "worldly wisdom" and not "godly wisdom."

So the people eagerly repeated the good news which had come into their midst by the bearer of the good news whose name was Jesus. By word of mouth they told the stories of his humble and mighty deeds. They repeated these stories far and wide. There was no way for the Roman officer to have missed hearing about the Healer from Nazareth. God's story will be told.

Jesus, This Man Deserves Your Help

So the officer did what any desperate person would have done: he sent for Jesus. He did not summon a trained Roman doctor or a renowned Jewish specialist. He sent for a doctor trained in heaven. He sent for God's mighty Healer, Jesus the blessed Son of God, who came with healing in his very being.

Oh, I love the way Luke states it: "He (the centurion) sent unto him the elders of the Jews, beseeching him that he would come and heal his servant." The man did not go himself; instead he sent the Jewish elders to Jesus to intercede for him, to ask that he would help both him and his servant. This is an indication of the man's humility. This humility was also demonstrated a little later in the text. The centurion did not feel himself worthy to approach this holy Man sent from God. He felt it more appropriate that those of his own race, those who knew about his works of charity, should approach Jesus on his behalf.

It is always good to have someone who knows about our work to intercede for us. It is not good to sound our own trumpets. If we have done good works, let our works speak for us. And we ought to do works of charity, for charity makes the heart cheerful, and, more significantly, it delights God and the one who receives the blessing as well.

This is another reason that the common people loved Jesus. He did so many good works for them and in their midst. He was not greedy for gain and power and prestige. When the Jews sought to stone him, according to the Gospel of John, Jesus said to them, "Many good works have I shewed you from my Father; for which of those works do ye stone me?" The Jews then said to Jesus, "For a good work we stone thee not; but for blasphemy; and because that thou, being a man, makest thyself God." Jesus then countered that argument with one of the most profound statements in the Bible: "Is it not written in your law, I said, Ye are gods? If he called them gods, unto whom the word of God came, and the scripture cannot be broken; Say ye of him, whom the Father hath sanctified, and sent into the world, Thou blasphemest; because I said, I am the Son of God? If I do not the works of my Father, believe me not. But if I do, though ye believe not me, believe the works: that ye may know, and believe, that the Father is in me, and I in him'' (John 10:32-38).

So the centurion had the elders of the Jews carry his request to Jesus. They had witnessed the works of Jesus and had been impressed with his teaching, healing, and preaching.

In verse 4 they came to Jesus with the request. It is always good to take the requests of others to Jesus. This is especially true if the petitioner is as interested and concerned as this centurion was. He was interested in the people and in his post of duty. He sought to make the people aware that all Romans in positions of authority were not callous and selfish. He sought to be a good citizen of Rome and also a good citizen of the world.

The Jews held this Roman soldier in high regard. They told Jesus, ''that he was worthy.'' In other words, they wanted Jesus to know that the man merited and deserved his help and healing power.

In a sense this might have been true. For the Jews listed some worthwhile accomplishments which would make us think highly of this man too. In the next verse they explained, ''For he loveth our nation, and he hath built us a synagogue.'' This does not sound like the average man of that day. The man did not speak or act superior to these conquered people. One might wonder what had happened in his rearing to keep the fires of human decency, sympathy, and generosity burning in his heart.

On the other hand, one could wonder if this man, or any man, is indeed worthy of the help and healing of Jesus. Do we ever deserve God's mercy and God's goodness and God's grace? Can we honestly consider ourselves worthy of the healing power which comes from God? To be sure, I think we can never say that in the presence of Jesus. For he is too pure and holy and divine for us to approach him with any thoughts of merit.

The centurion recognized this. For in the very next verse, as Jesus approached him at his house, did he come out to greet Jesus? No! No! No! He sent friends to say to Jesus these profound words, ''Lord, trouble not thyself: for I am not worthy that

Jesus, This Man Deserves Your Help

thou shouldest enter under my roof." The friends, quoting the man, addressed Jesus as "Lord." Does this mean that he had a commitment to Jesus as Lord and Savior, or was this just a statement made because of what he had heard about Jesus? Paul says that no man can call Jesus Lord except the Holy Spirit directs him. And then Jesus had said that not every one who says unto him, "Lord, Lord," shall enter the kingdom, but he who does the will of his Father.

One could also raise the question, "Did this man build the temple out of a great respect for the religion of the Jews and their common faith, or did he build it as a means of social control? A people will give homage to those who build them a place to worship, even though the person who builds the place of worship might be an unbeliever. Nevertheless, he called Jesus Lord. Was even this a momentary commitment or a temporary expediency? Nonetheless, let us give him the benefit of the doubt, for Jesus paid a tremendous compliment to this Roman centurion.

The man made it known to Jesus that he did not feel worthy to have Jesus enter his home. And then he made another statement which wins our respect and admiration. He said to Jesus in verse 7, "Wherefore neither thought I myself worthy to come unto thee." The man made the statement which I have been trying to make—we are not worthy to come into the presence of Jesus. The centurion felt that he was not worthy to come into the presence of Jesus. He did not feel that he deserved any help from Jesus. Nor did he feel that it was an honor for Jesus to come to him. For he felt that Jesus was too holy, righteous, and good for him to stand in the presence of Jesus.

This man was not like the leper Namaan, who felt that the prophet Elisha should come out to greet him and meet him. Elisha just sent him word what to do and where to do it, and all would be well.

This man was on the right road to genuine religion. I just would have loved for him to have made that one final step. He sent Jesus this insightful statement: "But say in a word, and my servant shall be healed." The man was most perceptive when he said, "say in a word." Not just any word, but say the healing word to this my servant, who is so dear to me. Say a word to this condition. A word in due season, how sweet it is! Say a word which has healing and restoration for my servant. Do your healing at a distance. I have confidence that you can do what you will and will what you do, close at hand or miles away.

Then this high official made another statement worthy of our consideration: "For I also am a man set under authority, having under me soldiers, and I say unto one, Go, and he goeth; and to another, Come, and he cometh; and to my servant, Do this, and he doeth it." He recognized the role of authority and its power to keep order and discipline among men, whether in war or at peace.

The man was actually saying to Jesus, "I know from personal experience what a word from one in authority can do. A word from my superiors secures my obedience, and a word from me secures the obedience of my subordinates. Thou, who art under no man and hast authority over unseen powers, hast only to say a word and the sickness is healed.[2]

"If I, who am inferior to you, can get results from my subordinates, without doubt you, are who are superior to me, can get results. I have heard about your words of power and your deeds of power. I have heard about your prayer-power and your praise-power. I have heard about your mighty works of healing. I have faith in you, though I am at a distance from you in race and culture."

This is one of the few times in the life and ministry of Jesus when he was staggered. Not even his disciples had ever expressed so much confidence in him. Christ, who had prayed for Peter to have faith, was stunned to see it shining in this Roman soldier's eyes. Jesus heard his request with astonishment.

Then Jesus said, "I say unto you." I think he was searching

---

2. Rev. Alfred Plummer, *The International Critical Commentary—The Gospel According to St. Luke* (Edinburgh: T & T Clark, Ltd., 1975), p. 196.

Jesus, This Man Deserves Your Help   93

for words worthy enough to decorate the heroism of the man's
devotion. "I have not found so great faith, no, not in Israel." Let
us not make a mistake and marvel at the miracle more than at
the centurion's testimony of confidence and faith in Jesus. He
helped Jesus overcome the humiliation he received in his
hometown where he could do "not many mighty works there
because of their unbelief."

In times like these, we need more faith, and Christ Jesus
needs a few more like the Roman centurion who would show
this kind of faith. If more of us would just be willing to speak and
have the confidence in Jesus that this centurion showed, the
witness of the church would be greater and more effective. "Oh
for a faith that will not shrink!"

Somehow the centurion had learned his lesson well in
another school of discipline. He had developed a mind for judg-
ing men. He knew whom to salute and, from his experience with
men in the military, knew which ones could be trusted with
authority.

What this world needs today is more talent scouts who can
find, in the masquerade, just where the Messiah is. Can you tell?
Can you judge? Can you see? Can you discern? Do you have
faith? Has your faith grown? Is Jesus your Lord and your God?
Do you believe, or are you still sitting on the fence? Will you be
a witness in living and giving until it hurts? Or do you prefer to
play it safe before you make an ultimate commitment?

This centurion spotted the Son of God in remote Galilee,
and everything in his military experience told him instinctively
that here was a man before whom Caesar himself should fall
down. He was able to lay hold of the fact that God himself had
delegated all authority, dominion, and power here Incarnate,
and that one little word from him could dismiss so small a thing
as sickness from any distance.

Even if you do not think highly of Christ Jesus my Lord, you
ought to revere the faith of a Roman centurion who honestly
treated Jesus as if he were the King of Kings. There is no report
that the centurion was ever disillusioned after what Jesus said to

him: "Go thy way; and as thou hast believed, so be it done unto thee."

Luke concludes by saying this: "And they that were sent, returning to the house, found the servant whole that had been sick." Note use of the past perfect tense, he "*had been* sick." But now at the healing word of Jesus Christ, the servant was made whole. He was well and able to function with new power and new strength.

"Oh, for a faith that will not shrink!" That is my prayer; that is my desire. I have faith, but I need more faith. I need more power than I ever dreamed of. Like the father that cried to Jesus, I also say, "Lord, I believe; help thou mine unbelief."

O, for a faith that will not shrink
Though pressed by every foe
That will not tremble on the brink
Of any earthly woe.
   —W. H. Bathurst

O, for a faith that will not shrink though pressed by trouble, pain, prison, ill-health, ill-will, ill-winds, desertion by friends, relatives, loved ones, colleagues, betrayals by brothers and sisters, mother, wife, children, by myself, weak, worn, and weary.

I want a faith that will withstand the storms, knowing that it won't be long.

"Lord, I believe; help thou mine unbelief."

She Needs My Help

Jesus raises the widow's son from death
Luke 7:11-15

Patient/Diagnosis:
A widow's son who had died

Doctor:
Jesus of Nazareth

Cure:
"And he came and touched the bier: and they that bare him stood still. And he said, Young man, I say unto thee, Arise. And he that was dead sat up, and began to speak."

Comments:
In this day and age the definition of death can be complex. However, to make matters simple, we can say that a person who has no heartbeat, no pulse, no breathing, and is cold, is dead. Unless this patient undergoes immediate cardiopulmonary resuscitation, death is irreversible.

Roger G. Smith, M.D.
Internal Medicine
Memphis, Tennessee

Luke presents Jesus as the Great Physician who had the unique capacity to do things which amazed and astounded the multitudes. His ministry of healing and helping people went beyond the common medical procedures of his day and even beyond those of our day and time. For Jesus was able to help and to heal with a skill and rapidity which has never been surpassed. To this day, he has been the incomparable source of inspiration, information, and speculation.

I have tried to get you to understand the fact that Jesus is capable of doing the impossible, that with him nothing is impossible. He has the gift from God to do what God wills in the lives of men and women. God wills wholeness. So in boldness of spirit Jesus came to manifest this awesome fact to us in our own earthly existence.

Let us then march with him through several passages of Scripture which see him at his best as he deals with the problem of death. This is the most dreadful condition confronting men and women. We fear death. It is so final. But in Jesus we have one whom death fears. Death has never been able to compete with Jesus. He confronted death on several occasions and emerged victorious, as we shall see in this sermon where Jesus raised the widow's son from death.

Let us turn our attention to Luke 7, beginning with the eleventh verse. In the passage immediately preceding this one, Jesus had just completed the healing of the centurion's servant. Now we see him in a different light. We see him grappling with the cold hands of death. Nothing tears at the heartstrings of mothers more than the death of a child. We could withstand life with a little more courage if our children were only spared the pains of death, especially when they are just on the verge of living. And this woman had an added burden: the deceased was her only child.

Jesus moved forward with his eye on the cross, but with his heart filled with love for the children of God who walked in darkness. After he had healed the centurion's servant, Luke says, ''And it came to pass the day after. . . .''

She Needs My Help   97

Luke in his own way shows us that Jesus was constantly on the move. He did not spend a great deal of time in any one place. He had a mission and a message designated for more than just one small group or place. He was the universal Savior for the whole world. His work was cosmic in nature and divine in origin.

The day after healing the servant of the centurion, Jesus moved with all deliberate speed to heal and to help others in need. His helpfulness was limitless and flexible. Our Savior cannot be restricted to petty enclaves. He must go beyond our shallow thoughts and narrow minds.

The next day Jesus went to another city, a city called Nain. It is good that Luke gives us this detail. For it helps us to locate Jesus in those obscure areas which we hear so little about in the history of the Jewish people. And yet each city played a special role in the ministry of Jesus and should be given proper recognition.

Nain was a small village on "little Hermon," a hillock 1,690 feet high, overlooking the valley of Jezreel, six miles southeast of Nazareth and two miles northwest of Endor, in the heart of the region of Jesus' Galilean ministry.[1]

This is the only incident that is recorded concerning that city. Nothing else is known of the town from that day forward, so far as Jesus ever visiting or performing some miracle there. But maybe this is enough. No other gospel writer thought enough of this incident to record it. Nevertheless, this one event places Nain at the forefront of those cities and towns in which Jesus did many mighty deeds. It was here that we first got a glimpse of Jesus as not only the Lord of life, but also as the Lord of death.

The writer then goes on to reveal another interesting fact: "and many of his disciples went with him, and much people."

It should be noted that Jesus had more than just twelve disciples. Luke 6:13 states, "And when it was day, he called unto

1. Madeleine S. Miller and J. Lane Miller, Harper's Bible Dictionary (New York: Harper & Row, 1961), p. 477.

him his disciples: and of them he chose twelve, whom also he named apostles." In John's gospel this fact is verified. In John 6:66 we have these words: "From that time many of his disciples went back, and walked no more with him."

Jesus had many disciples as he started his journey, but as they learned more and more about his program, they went back. Some might have become jealous because of those twelve that he selected to walk closely with him. Others, however, might have been unwilling to walk in the pathway of a healer, teacher, and preacher of his nature.

According to John, "Many therefore of his disciples, when they had heard this, said, This is an hard saying; who can hear it?" It was hard for them to understand Jesus when he said:

> Verily, verily, I say unto you, Except ye eat the flesh of the Son of man, and drink his blood, ye have no life in you. Whoso eateth my flesh, and drinketh my blood, hath eternal life; and I will raise him up at the last day. For my flesh is meat indeed, and my blood is drink indeed. He that eateth my flesh, and drinketh my blood, dwelleth in me, and I in him.
>
> As the living Father hath sent me, and I live by the Father: so he that eateth me, even he shall live by me.
>
> This is that bread which came down from heaven: not as your fathers did eat manna, and are dead: he that eateth of this bread shall live forever (John 6:53-58).

Then there were others who just wanted to be in the crowd. They had no desire to be disciples; they only wanted to hear and see the things which Jesus was doing in the name of God. They were spectators—not participators. They were sideline cheerleaders, with no commitment to Jesus as Teacher and Healer and Preacher.

As this group moved to the gate of that city, they were met by another group which was leaving the city. This is life. As

She Needs My Help   99

some enter life, some leave life. As some come to the city, some leave the city. Men and women leave for various reasons: some for new jobs and better opportunities; still others just have the wanderlust and move after the luster of the city wears off.

At any rate, Luke has this to say: "Now when he came nigh to the gate of the city." This is Luke's way of speaking about the main entrance to the city. Or it may be Luke's way of giving us more details about this incident.

"Behold, there was a dead man carried out." Here in stark reality is the story of every city. It does not matter what its location or its size, death reaches into all its nooks and corners. It is there in the most dismal places, and it is there in the most palatial places. Death is real. Death is earnest. It does not select the place nor the person. It will strike the high and mighty and also the low and not-so-mighty.

Death had reached into the home of a widow. The dead man was her only son. Death had stung her twice. She had seen death in the eyes of her husband and now of her son. She had experienced the pain of death at close range. Hers was not a vicarious pain. It was real for her. She had seen death in action and had felt the sweeping numbness which engulfs the body when those die whom we love and love most dearly. Death had been in her home. And you don't really feel death until it strikes you where you live. Then its full impact and import drives you into a sense of hopelessness and helplessness until the grief pangs subside.

There were many people with her. Some say that many of these may have been professional mourners, and musicians with flutes and cymbals.[2]

According to the custom, the mother would walk in front of the bier, and Jesus would naturally see her first. So Luke says, "And when the Lord saw her. . . ." The Lord always sees us before we see him. Death has a way of numbing us so that we

2. Rev. Alfred Plummer, *The International Critical Commentary—The Gospel According to St. Luke* (Edinburgh: T & T Clark, Ltd., 1975), p. 199.

are not able to see straight nor think straight nor act straight. Jesus was always looking for those who needed his help and his healing powers. He came to heal the sick and raise the dead. He was sent by God to us to help us and to heal us. His was a mission of love from the very beginning of his life. This was the cause for which he was sent into our world. He said, "They that are whole need not a physician, but they that are sick." This woman's wholeness had become brokenness. It was up to Jesus to mend the brokenhearted and heal those who had parted. This was Jesus' ministry. This is your ministry and my ministry.

To be seen by Jesus was enough to initiate within him that holy compassion which only Jesus had in an abundant way—"He had compassion on her." She did not ask for his help. He knew that she needed his help. Jesus, I believe, read that woman's heartbeat. Like the psalmist of old, I can hear her saying deep, deep within, "Bow down thine ear, O Lord, hear me: for I am poor and needy" (Ps. 86:1). Or she might have been meditating on the words of David, who said, "Lord, make me to know mine end, and the measure of my days, what it is; that I may know how frail I am" (Ps. 39:4).

Still Jesus might have read from her lips, "My heart is sore pained within me: and the terrors of death are fallen upon me" (Ps. 55:4). Or in her distress, she might have remembered the words of the psalmist who said, "But thou, O Lord, art a God full of compassion, and gracious, longsuffering, and plenteous in mercy and truth" (Ps. 86:15).

Inner compassion leads to outward action. The inner compassion of Jesus reached out to this broken woman. "He had compassion on her, and said unto her, Weep not."

Greek scholars saw that the real translation of that should be, "Do not go on weeping, cease to weep." Jesus was positive that he had the solution to her problem. He wanted her to stop crying immediately. She need not weep any longer about the death of her only son. "I am Lord of life, and I am Lord of death. The grave will not receive this body just now." In fact, I can hear him saying, "I have really come to destroy every grave; every

She Needs My Help   101

tomb will be opened. I am the resurrection and the life. I must
rob the grave and pull the sting out of death. Daughter of
Abraham, I must post on this coffin: Not Ready for Burial. This is
not the time nor the place. Cease repining, my friend."

In this age of women's liberation, I consider it appropriate to
inform you that most of the raising of the dead in the Bible was
done for women. An early incident is recorded in 1 Kings 17:23:
"And Elijah took the child, and brought him down out of the
chamber into the house, and delivered him unto his mother: and
Elijah said, See, thy son liveth."

In 2 Kings 4:36 we read, "And he called Gehazi, and said,
Call this Shunammite. So he called her. And when she was come
in unto him, he said, "Take up thy son."

In John 11:23, Jesus said unto Martha, "Thy brother shall rise
again." Martha, you will recall, said to Jesus, "I know that he
shall rise again in the resurrection at the last day." Then Jesus
said to her, "I am the resurrection, and the life: he that believeth
in me, though he were dead, yet shall he live: And whosoever
liveth and believeth in me shall never die. Believest thou this?"

When Dorcas died in the story in Acts, Peter restored her to
the group by the power of prayer: "But Peter put them all forth,
and kneeled down, and prayed; and turning him to the body
said, Tabitha, arise. And she opened her eyes: and when she
saw Peter, she sat up. And he gave her his hand, and lifted her
up, and when he had called the saints and widows, presented
her alive" (Acts 9:40-41).

Then in the Book of Hebrews there is a general summary of
the great works and mighty deeds of men and women in biblical
history: "Women received their dead raised to life again: and
others were tortured, not accepting deliverance; that they might
obtain a better resurrection" (Heb. 11:35).

Do not go on weeping. Cease to weep. Jesus is standing
close by. And when Jesus stands by, everything which brings
grief will flee if it is his will. He has that divine power to deal with
our pain predicaments. Jesus has in his hand that unique
authority from God to take care of those situations which defy

human comprehension. Man cannot deal with death. Jesus can. Man cannot understand death. Jesus does. Man is frightened by death. Jesus is not. Man has no power to overcome death. Jesus has. Man cringes in the face of death. Jesus does not.

So Jesus took matters into his own hands without asking a single question. His big heart went out to this woman, and he stopped the procession on the way to the graveyard. "And he came and touched the bier." He came to them. He came with a heart full of love to help in this sorrowful setting. He is the Christ who comes. He keeps coming to us and staying with us in spite of us. He comes when we don't want him to come. He comes when we least expect him. He comes when we need him most. Jesus came.

When Jesus comes, he does something. He enters into our pain with some definite plan in mind. "I must work the works of him that sent me." "My Father worketh . . . and I work." "I must work . . . while it is day: the night cometh, when no man can work." His ministry was an action-oriented ministry. He could never be called a do-nothing Savior. "For the Son of man is come to seek and to save that which was lost." This mother had lost her son. Jesus was determined to give him back to her. She was alone and needed the companionship of her son. Jesus was going to act.

So he came close to the procession and touched the bier. His touch was designed to stop the procession. He wanted everything to stand still. He wanted the mourners to stop and the weepers to cease. He wanted the procession to stop and the coffin bearers to lay down their heavy burden. By stopping the procession Jesus also meant to convey the idea that life has a higher claim than death. Jesus was suggesting that death has power, but life has more power.

Jesus came to answer the question the Lord raised with Job when he appeared in the whirlwind: "Have the gates of death been opened unto thee? or hast thou seen the doors of the shadow of death?" (Job 38:17). The psalmist understood that God can open the gates of death. "Have mercy upon me, O

Lord . . . thou that liftest me up from the gates of death" (Ps. 9:13).

"Many of us have been close to the gates of death. Only the mercy and love of God brought us back from the gates of death. Please note that this does not mean actual death, but it does mean that some of us have been close to death. Some of us have been almost dead; close to home, but not quite dead. Job was close to death, but he was not dead.

However, this man was dead. He had been prepared for burial. He was close to the graveyard. His mourners had made all the necessary preparations. In a few moments he would have been six feet under. But for a great and dynamic healer and preacher and teacher, this man would have had the final benediction said at his gravesite by the preacher. But there was another preacher standing there who did not believe in the finality of death over God's children. His faith would not let him believe that this was the end for a son of Abraham.

When Jesus commands, we must act. They who carried the man stopped at the words of Jesus. They stood still. It is good common sense to stand still when Jesus speaks. The blessings he brings are not always delivered when we are on the run. "Be still, and know" is the word of holy Scripture. Stand still and learn. Stand still and listen. Stand still and look. Stand still and feel. Stand still and watch. Stand still and wait. "Stand still, and see the salvation of the Lord." These were the Lord's words for Moses to the children of Israel. They stood with their backs against the wall. There God had a way designed to remove the wall. Walls of water will not stop God. Walls of fire will not stop God. Walls of soldiers will not stop God. Walls, walls, walls, will not keep God from doing what He wills for those who trust and lean on Him.

What walls stand in your way today? What wall do you want removed? What wall is blocking you from the life you could live with God's help? Ask God to remove that wall if it is His will. Walls can be removed. The men and women in Jericho discovered that fact. Walls can be removed. Walls can be destroyed. Jesus is a wall-mover. He stopped the wall of death for this widow. He spoke God's powerful word.

"And he said, young man, I say unto thee, Arise." Take note who said what. It was Jesus, the Son of God who spoke. It was not just anyone, but Jesus, speaking. He did not just say any word but he spoke God's Word. This was the Word that "was the Word, and the Word was with God, and the Word was God." This was the Word that "was made flesh, and dwelt among us, (and we beheld his glory, the glory as of the only begotten of the Father,) full of grace and truth." This was the Word that was said when God said, "Let there be light." This was the Word that was said when God said, "Let there be a firmament in the midst of the waters, and let it divide the waters from the waters." This was the Word that was said when God said, "Let us make man in our image, after our likeness: and let them have dominion over the fish of the sea, and over the fowl of the air . . . and over every creeping thing that creepth upon the earth." This was God's Word. This was God's Son. This was God's Spirit in power coming to this dead man about to be brought back to life. This was the Word.

Jesus spoke the word of power, and this is the word which does not come back to God void. It does what it sets out to do. It revives, restores, restructures, resurrects, reendows with power, reequips for living, restores the brokenhearted, and reconciles those who are parted. So it does. "And he that was dead"—that is the past tense. He *was* dead. At the word of Jesus, the past tense becomes the present tense. He "sat up, and began to speak." He was lying down before Jesus spoke. Before Jesus spoke, he was stiff and dead and lifeless. Before Jesus spoke, he was clothed in his death shroud. He was just about in the grave. He was gone. But Jesus spoke, and he sat up. He sat up and began to speak. This is present tense, living and doing.

"Hello, Mother. Mother, what's happening? Mother, don't be sad. Mother, look, I'm alive! Let us go home, Mother. See what Jesus has done for us. He has put us together again!"

She Needs My Help

Jesus can put dead men and dead women together again. Jesus can mend the brokenhearted and restore those who have parted. Trust him! Test him! Try him!

The next verse says this about Jesus: "And he delivered him to his mother." Jesus gives back to us life. He gives us life. "I am come that they might have life." "I give unto them eternal life." Jesus saves. Jesus saves. This man was almost in the grave, but Jesus saved him. He can do the same for us. Thank God! Amen.

I Must Help This Man
Part I

Jesus casts demons out of the naked man in Gadara
Luke 8:26-39

Patient/Diagnosis:
A certain man who was possessed by demons

Doctor:
Jesus of Nazareth

Cure:
"The man, out of whom the devils were departed, [was] sitting at the feet of Jesus, clothed, and in his right mind."

Comments:
This man exhibited bizarre behavior. A likely diagnosis in this individual is a mental disorder called *psychosis*. Generally, intensive pharmacologic and psychiatric therapy meet with variable degrees of success in achieving a cure. The condition may last for years even with optimal treatment.
Roger G. Smith, M.D.
Internal Medicine
Memphis, Tennessee

I Must Help This Man—Part I

As we walk through the pages of Luke's gospel with Jesus our Lord, we gain new strength for the journey as we look at his mighty deeds of healing and helping those who were victims of physical sickness, mental disorders, moral confusion, spiritual blindness, and even death. Our Lord brought to each of these conditions his own unique divine power, a power which supersedes our capacity to understand. His capacities are not the usual kind. He was endowed with an incomparable ability to bring about changes in people, places, and things. Jesus could perform miracles. Through his earthly miracles, Jesus became for us the "Son of man" and the "Christ of faith."

This double identity of Jesus is for the faithful a bedrock of reality. Jesus for us was not just our Christ after the resurrection; he was our Christ prior to the resurrection and before the hills in order stood. Jesus has and always will be for us the Christ of faith and the Christ of history. His incarnation is just another way God communicates with us as he has done in the past in unique and unusual ways.

Our God is a God who keeps coming to us often and in diverse ways. I would agree with the writer of Hebrews who said:

> God, who at sundry times and in divers manners spake in time past unto the fathers by the prophets,
>
> Hath in these last days spoken unto us by his Son, whom he hath appointed heir of all things, by whom also he made the worlds;
>
> Who being the brightness of his glory, and the express image of his person, and upholding all things by the word of his power, when he had by himself purged our sins, sat down on the right hand of the Majesty on high (Heb. 1:1-3).

So then we see Jesus as the representative of the God who comes to us, is for us, is around us, and flows through us. His coming is for our well-being, our salvation, our redemption, and our release. All of this is embodied in the coming of Jesus. We see this clearly in his healing miracles. In them, we see the depth of God's love and care and concern for the children of this earth who walk in darkness. He comes to bring us light. This light shines in the darkness of our situations and illuminates the darkness so that we might have the right to the light of life. Some have called this the energy of life. At any rate, it sustains us for the long journey back to the Father's house of wholeness and togetherness. We see holistic concern for helpless and hopeless cases as Jesus enters another section of Palestine.

Jesus had just completed a miracle on the Sea of Galilee. He and his disciples were exhausted because they had been caught in a storm on the sea. Jesus was aroused from sleep in the midst of the storm, and he stilled the angry waves. As they landed on the opposite side of the Sea of Galilee, they came to a country called Gadara, believed to have been one of the cities of an area known as the Decapolis. There were ten towns in this location, which was over against the district of Galilee.

According to Luke, as Jesus and his disciples were landing, they met a certain man. Jesus was always meeting men and women in all kinds of conditions. He could hardly move in any direction without confronting those who needed his healing and helping in a most desperate way. In fact, all men needed what Jesus could do for them.

This man was from the city of Gadara. He had what Luke called "devils." Because this word is plural we might say that the man was possessed by demons. Demons are spiritual messengers of the devil. They serve at his call to do his evil will. They afflict men and women in all walks of life. They are real and wreak havoc in the minds of those who become their unfortunate victims.

Paul was confident that evil forces existed in the universe. In his letter to the church at Ephesus, he said:

> Put on the whole armour of God, that ye may be able
> to stand against the wiles of the devil.

I Must Help This Man—Part I   109

> For we wrestle not against flesh and blood, but against principalities, against powers, against the rulers of the darkness of this world, against spiritual wickedness in high places (Eph. 6:11, 12).

Paul was aware of a division in his own personal life—one that was beyond his comprehension. In Romans 7:19, 22-24, he confessed:

> For the good that I would I do not: but the evil which I would not, that I do. . . .
> For I delight in the law of God after the inward man: But I see another law in my members, warring against the law of my mind, and bringing me into captivity to the law of sin which is in my members.
> O wretched man that I am! who shall deliver me from the body of this death?

This man who met Jesus was disturbed by a serious division in his body of "death." In modern terms he would be described as severely neurotic or psychotic.

The man had suffered from this condition for a long time. Mental problems may stay with us for a long time. Many victims are institutionalized indefinitely because modern medicine has not yet found an effective cure for their problems. Our modern procedures are not able at present to erase all of the mental afflictions confronting modern man.

Not only had the man been mentally disturbed for a long time, but, according to Luke, "he wore no clothes." This man was afflicted with physical nakedness as well as mental nakedness. What was happening to him internally was also affecting him externally. There was no "wholeness." He had no sense of where he was or who he was. Just as he was naked inside, he was also naked outside. His nakedness was symbolic of his total wretchedness.

Luke then describes him as not abiding in any house. The

wretchedness of the man had now reached another level of misery. He could not live in a house, nor was he part of any home. He was houseless and homeless. "Houselessness" is being without any shelter for protection from the sun by day and the cold by night. "Homelessness" is isolation from society, away from the warmth and flow of human compassion and relationships. There was no one with whom to communicate or to share the language of the human heart. This alone could drive one mad, for we are not made to live in isolation from one another. We are made to have communication and fellowship one with the other. Without this interaction we become human casualties of neurotic and psychotic behavior.

The final word in this verse says that the man "abode . . . in the tombs." This says more to us about his condition. He lived in and around the tombs in the graveyard. He lived in Tombstone Alley and made his home in Graveyard Valley. Some twisted, distorted, and demented power forced this man to become a living cemetery. Life is drawn to life. The dead draw the dead. This man was dead crazy or crazy dead. He was a walking contradiction to all that stands for what a man should be.

However horrible the man's condition, there was One who could deal with his plight. Jesus came into our world to seek and to save that which was lost. This man was lost in his mental sickness. He was lost to all rational processes that would have allowed him to make a confession of faith in Jesus. Jesus could not allow this potential son of God to remain in his wretchedness. So as the man approached Jesus, Jesus approached the man. The man came toward Jesus, and Jesus came toward the man.

In verse 28 Luke says, "When he saw Jesus, he cried out, and fell down before him." Previously, when this graveyard dweller saw people coming toward him, he had put them to flight with blood-chilling cries. But not this time. Coming toward him now was Jesus, the Son of God. In him was no fear of earthly creatures. He made them and could withstand all the cries and shrills they might make. This was Jesus, who controlled every situation into which he came with the power of God and the might of God.

When Jesus approached, even the devils in the man recognized that here was One who would not flee from them but would challenge and defeat them. So instead of Jesus running from the man, the man came running to finally fall at the feet of Jesus. With a loud, piercing voice he said to Jesus, "What have I to do with thee, Jesus, thou Son of God most high?" This was not the man speaking, but the demons in the man, speaking for him. For the man had been in the graveyard, and no one had taken the time or had the courage to tell him who Jesus was and what Jesus was about. But the demons in the man knew Jesus.

One writer has said, "The victim is the mouthpiece of the demons." This was the case in Luke 4:33-37. The unclean spirits recognized the supernatural powers of Jesus before they were evident to men and took steps to counteract those prayers.

As long as men remain alienated from God they cannot recognize God. Separation from God brings about isolation, estrangement, and frustration. The evil demons are designed to separate us from God and thus draw us to them. Once we are drawn to them, we then become their instruments and do their bidding. We must do either the commands of God or the commands of Satan. There is no neutral ground. We are for God or against God. This is a hard fact, but it is a reality nevertheless.

So the demons in the man made him say to Jesus, "I beseech thee, torment me not." We might well raise the question, "How could Jesus torment a man who was already possessed by devils?" He was already in a miserable and pitiful condition. Was there anything more that Jesus could do to make him worse?

Yes, there was something Jesus could do to torment this man further. For Jesus proposed to cure and save him, and this curing and saving would involve suffering. John Knox has rightly said:

> To be saved we must recognize our need in all of its
> dimensions, and this acknowledgement is difficult

and costly; it is easier to keep our illusions about ourselves. The first step toward wholeness and inner
security is to face the facts; and the facts are
disagreeable. It is pleasanter to "escape" from our
wretchedness than fully and honestly to recognize
and seek to understand it.[1]

Henry Nelson Wieman has written illuminatingly about a
statement from Arthur N. Whitehead: "Religion . . . is the transi-
tion from God the void to God the enemy, and from God the
enemy to God the companion." He says:

When we find ourselves confused and distraught,
torn apart by many conflicting reactions to many
diverse situations, lacking that knowledge of God
which would unify our experience and give peace
and wholeness to the soul, God is "the void." But
when God first confronts us, he does so as "the
enemy." He demands something of us which we find
painful to give—a radical readjustment and reorienta-
tion, a new discipline. At this stage God is the
"tormentor," more tormenting than the many
demons which possess us. But as we make the required acknowledgment and inner adjustment (this is
repentance), God becomes "the companion," sustaining and strengthening, the source of life and
peace.

Facts, especially permanent and important facts,
often have this double character—hostile if we
challenge and thwart them; friendly and supporting if
we accept and respond appropriately to them. God is
ultimate fact, the really permanent and important
fact; and we must often know the pain of his judg-

1. The Interpreter's Bible, Vol. VIII, Luke-John (Nashville: Abingdon Press, 1952),
p. 157.

ment before we can know the joy of his salvation.[2]

Jesus brought his tormenting power and divinity into this situation. He brings it into our situations too. When he comes, the evil in us cannot stand the confrontation. He is too good, clean, pure, and God-filled for that which is evil to remain in us. This is especially true when God in Jesus decides to act. The self-initiating action of God demands radical departure from all that is vile and base.

This was true with Moses on the slopes of Sinai when he heard God's words, "Moses, pull off your shoes, for the ground you are standing on is holy ground." God was saying, "I am here, and in my being I sanctify everything and everybody when I come." God can clean up the most vile and degenerate condition.

This is what Isaiah felt when he saw the coming glory of the Lord. He said:

> I saw also the Lord sitting upon a throne, high and lifted up, and his train filled the temple (Isa. 6:1).

The the seraphims began singing the anthems of heaven:

> Holy, holy, holy, is the Lord of hosts: the whole earth is full of his glory.
>   And the posts of the door moved at the voice of him that cried, and the house was filled with smoke (Isa. 6:3, 4).

Isaiah was filled with dread, awe, and holy reverence and cried,

> Woe is me! for I am undone; because I am a man of

---

2. *Ibid.*, pp. 157-58.

unclean lips . . . for mine eyes have seen the King, the
Lord of hosts (Isa. 6:5).

This was the torment of Isaiah. He saw his wretchedness.
This is the torment of every child of God who sees and knows
God. We cry, "Woe is me!" God is too pure and too holy for us
to behold unless God acts to clean us up. This he did for Isaiah
as he had done for Moses. He made it possible for them to worship, hear, and obey.

God sent the seraphims unto Isaiah, having a live coal in his
hand, which he had taken with the tongs from the altar:

And he laid it upon my mouth, and said, Lo, this hath
touched thy lips; and thine iniquity is taken away, and
thy sin purged (Isa. 6:7).

God the tormentor gets him ready for the holy purpose of
using him. God the tormentor cleans him up for the task of
preaching. God the tormentor purges him for the journey
ahead. God the tormentor endows him with Holy Ghost power
to become a power. God the tormentor shakes his foundation
so that he can help build a new foundation. God the tormentor
inculcates in him the "is-ness" of goodness, graciousness, genu-
ineness, and greatness.

God the powerful endows the powerless to speak to the
hopeless. God the tormentor drives out the dross so that Isaiah
might pick up a cross. God the tormentor surrounds him,
engulfs him, envelops him for the task of ministry. God the
tormentor fortifies him with strength, courage, and fortitude.
God the tormentor redirects his life for the coming kingdom of
God. God the tormentor flows through him and claims him for
heavenly habitation. God the tormentor comes to save and to
cure His chosen vessel.

God comes! God does when He comes! God sends! God
sends in power and might. His will will be done. His cause is victorious. His kingdom is forever and ever. Amen and amen.

I Must Help This Man—Part I   115

Jesus, as the Son of God, the unique Son of God, had already commanded that this unclean spirit come out of this dreadful creature which had roamed naked and screaming from the graveyard. As the Son of God, which God had attested to on several occasions, Jesus was able to command that these demons leave this man and his being. God had said that Jesus was His Son at Mary's conception. The angel at his birth sang praises to him as the Savior of the world. Jesus at the age of twelve spoke of his Father's business. He was conscious then of his unique relationship to God. He was claimed by God as His Son when he was baptized. God also claimed Jesus on the Mount of Transfiguration. The centurion bore witness to Jesus as the Son of God when he was crucified.

William Barclay has said that there was a unique and intimate relationship between Jesus and God; there was a unique obedience and unique knowledge which issued in a unique power.[3]

This unique power had spoken to this man and his demons. It was at work, driving the demons from the body and mind of this man. This was the power which was let loose in the world to redeem and to save the world. It would heal those who believe and break those who did not believe. To them who believe, he gave the power to become the sons of God.

I believe! Do you believe? Then go! Do and be! Make and become!

3. William Barclay, *Jesus As They Saw Him* (New York: Harper & Row, 1962), p. 65.

I Must Help This Man
Part II

Let us now renew our journey with Jesus as he was confronted by the demoniac who lived in the graveyard at Gadara. This man had been so demoralized by the demons that they had become his spokesmen. He could not speak for himself. His voice became the unconscious and the conscious voice of the devils. Just as we are to have the mind of Jesus, we can also have the mind of the demons. Man is never neutral. He either stands for good and does good, or he stands for evil and does evil. We will either be occupied by the high and the mighty or by the low and the blighted.

Speaking for the man, the demons said to Jesus, "What have I to do with thee, Jesus, thou Son of God most high?" The man could not have known who Jesus was. His mind had been irrational for a long time. And there was no way possible for him to have heard about Jesus and retain a degree of remembrance. For when the mind goes, unless there is help from above or from some other source, there is very little chance for it to retain a high degree of functionality. It would seem to me then that the demons were in complete control of this man's body and mind. They knew Jesus and had the man say to him, "What have I to

I Must Help This Man—Part II

do with thee, Jesus, thou Son of God most high?"

We will not deal with this again in this sermon, but I want us to remember that it is a very important concept in the thought world of the Bible. Jesus is God's Son by right and origin. He was begotten of the Father and was full of grace and truth. He was and is of the very essence of the Father. *He is the Son of God.* Jesus said, "I and my Father are one." On another occasion he said, "He that hath seen me hath seen the Father." When Jesus prayed, he could say with unique authenticity, "My Father."

On the other hand, we are God's sons by adoption. We are sons but not in the same way that Jesus is and was. We should spell "sonship" with a small "s." When we pray, we should say, "Our Father." And there is a difference. We are sons and daughters of God. Jesus is *the* Son of God. Jesus' sonship comes from a high quality of direct intimacy. "I know the Father. No one knows the Father but me. And no one knows the Son but the Father."

We become a son by hearing the Word. Jesus brought the Word, and it was God's Word. In a real sense, Jesus is more than our elder brother, as Paul taught. He is our elder Brother and our elder Father. He holds an unparalleled double relationship with us.

Let us turn our attention to the next thing this man and those demons said to Jesus: "I beseech thee, torment me not."

"To beseech" is "to beg, to plead, to ask." It is a plea to someone who can—or cannot—help. It may be positive, or it may be negative. In this instance, it was a negative plea to be left alone. The demons wanted to have nothing to do with Jesus. They knew that they could not occupy the same place at the same time with Jesus. They could not stand in his presence. He would not stand in their presence. There is a physical principle which comes to mind here: Two objects cannot occupy the same space at the same time.

There are two kingdoms in this world: the kingdom of God and the kingdom of Satan. They are not compatible. They do not get along well. They are out to destroy each other. They will not exist side by side. There can be no peaceful co-existence. This is implied in Jesus' declaration: "My kingdom is not of this world." Jesus also said: "Every kingdom divided against itself is brought to desolation; and every city or house divided against itself shall not stand" (Matt. 12:25).

Satan's kingdom is fighting to destroy God's kingdom, and God's kingdom is fighting to destroy Satan's kingdom. God's kingdom will be victorious.

This is what we see in this passage of Scripture. The demons did not want Jesus to come near them or the man. They recognized that they were in a no-win situation. With Jesus on the scene, they could not retain their hold on this man. The man might have disobeyed the demons and run to Jesus against their wills. They had so tormented the man that they could no longer control him.

So they had the man hurl this charge at Jesus: "Torment me not." As they tormented the man, they made him say this to Jesus. It was all right for them to harm him, but they did not want Jesus in this man's life. They felt that if Jesus did torment the man, it would only be for a moment. Their tormenting would last forever and ever. The tormenting that Jesus would bring into the man's life would be temporary, tentative, and tactful.

This might not appeal to your thinking. Can and does Jesus torment us? Did Jesus come to torment us? Is he in the tormenting business? Yes; I will say "yes" a thousand times!

Jesus does come to torment us. Jesus proposed to cure and save this man; and this curing and saving will involve suffering. As John Knox has said, "To be saved we must recognize our need in all of its dimensions, and this acknowledgement is difficult and costly."[1] It is costly because it means that we will have to give up that which has become dear to us. We do not like to depart from the habits and customs which have become an essential part of us. This is true even when that and those we love hurt us.

1. The Interpreter's Bible, Vol. VIII, Luke-John (Nashville: Abingdon Press, 1952), p. 157.

I Must Help This Man—Part II

Jesus demands a radical departure from that which holds us and binds us. When this happens, God and Jesus become the "tormentors," more tormenting than the many demons which possess us. We hate to depart from that which is usable in any form. This is true of those who are rational, and it is also true of those we would call irrational. Habits are habits, in season and out of season.

Every would-be disciple must learn to put Jesus first. He will not accept a secondary role in our lives. He wants to be first. He must be first. "If any man will come after me, let him deny himself, and take up his cross, and follow me." To come to Jesus is a costly experience. Only the pure in heart can respond. Jesus makes this possible for us. He creates the climate to which our souls can respond.

When Jesus gave the terms of discipleship in the gospels, he made it plain and emphatic that there was no middle ground. Either a person is for him, or he is against him. Either we obey, or we disobey. It is plain and simple. If we want his life and life-giving powers, we must submit to his terms. "For whosoever will save his life shall lose it: but whosoever will lose his life for my sake shall find it."

Jesus brought to this situation his life-giving power. He brought to this condition the power of God and the glory of God. And he still brings all that heaven has to the healing situation. Satan was there with all he had. Jesus would not bring half his resources, for they would not do. He had to have all power and might, for the man was in a desperate condition.

The Scripture says, "For oftentimes it had caught him: and he was kept bound with chains and in fetters; and he brake the bands, and was driven of the devil into the wilderness" (Luke 8:29). Here is the stark reality of a man made mad and crazy by the devils which controlled him. He was not in control of himself, but the devils controlled him.

This negative and destructive influence of the devil and his demons can only be counteracted by a positive and creative power for good, for it seems as though all of us are influenced by one or the other. Our Lord was directed by the positive power and was thus not willing to submit to the negative power of the devil.

In Luke 4:1 this profound passage is recorded by the physician: "And Jesus being full of the Holy Ghost returned from Jordan, and was led by the Spirit into the wilderness." Jesus was full of the Holy Ghost. He was full of that creative power which kept him on course all his life. It did not allow him the opportunity to yield to Satan's power and might. The will, purpose, and plan of God were always on his mind. He was full of that presence which kept him steady in the storms and stresses of the pilgrim's journey.

Note that Jesus "was led by the Spirit into the wilderness." We can go anywhere if God's Spirit and power go with us. Our wilderness experiences will not be unbearable if God's Spirit is with us. Jesus was led to the wilderness by the Spirit. In that wilderness Jesus was tempted by the devil for forty days. God had filled him with His power and presence, and Satan was trying to fill him with his power and presence. Jesus would not yield to the temptations of Satan.

Though physically weak and thirsty, Jesus was able to fight the wiles of the devil. The devil made some mighty big promises to Jesus. He struck at the very nerve center of every hungry man. "Make bread when you are hungry, if you have the means to do so." Jesus refused. Satan offered him the kingdoms of this world. Jesus refused. Finally, Satan tried to get Jesus to tempt God by jumping down from the pinnacle of the temple, hoping that God would come to his rescue. Jesus refused. He was too full of the Holy Spirit. The Holy Ghost called the tunes in the life of Jesus. He heard the sweet music from God's throne in glory. "I am the Lord thy God. . . . Thou shalt have no other gods before me."

Even though the man had been driven into the wilderness by the demons, when Jesus saw him and observed his chaotic condition, Jesus immediately went into action to relieve this man of his demonical condition. Luke says, "For he had commanded the unclean spirit to come out of the man" (8:29). Jesus was will-

I Must Help This Man—Part II

ing to act because of the man's condition. He was the self-giving Savior. He was the giver of life before this man could ask for help. He was willing to help and to heal. The urgency of the task was all that Jesus needed. He was willing to do when he saw the need. He was also very capable of doing the deed.

The self-activating love of God pressed the man for a name. "What is thy name?" he asked. This man's name identified him. He was given a name at birth or before birth. This set him apart from others in his city or village. It was his badge of identity. It gave him a reference point for which he would always be identifiable. At the sound of his name, he would gradually come to a consciousness which told him who he was. In time he would automatically respond to the name given at birth as the human body does to water when thirsty.

Jesus also wanted to make the man feel a deep sense of personal worth. Jesus was the only one in a long time who dared to approach him with the question, "What is your name?" Others had run from him and left him in the wilderness alone. Jesus did not run from him. Jesus did not fear him. Jesus could face him and his rantings and ravings. His madness and badness did not disturb the goodness and Godness in Jesus.

I am glad that Jesus did not run. It helps me to know that when the demons get loose in me and you, there is one who will understand and help us to face them. Others will run from us and isolate us from polite society. Jesus, however, knows us. He knows that there are times when we are weak, weary, and worn—times when the demons will pounce on us and leave us beaten, tattered, and torn. We do not have the resources to deal with them and the moments of depression and sadness and loneliness that they inflict upon us.

Jesus knows that there are also ancestral ghosts which roam around inside our ancestral heritage. They live in the basement of our beings and try from time to time to mount the steps to the second level or even to the third level. We cry like Paul, "O wretched man that I am! who shall deliver me from the body of this death?" Then, in those lonely hours, I can hear Jesus saying,

"Peace, be still." I can hear him saying, "There are ancestral ghosts, but never forget the power of the Holy Ghost." Then we can sing with new meaning, "Blessed assurance, Jesus is mine" or sing with boldness:

> Return, O Holy Dove, return
> Sweet messenger of rest;
> I hate the sins that made Thee mourn,
> And drove Thee from my breast.
> —William Cowper

"What is thy name?" Jesus raised the question with this man and received an irrational answer. This was not the man's real name. No Jewish mother in her right mind would name her child "Legion." "Legion" was Latin for an army of about 6,000, but the word had also been naturalized in Aramaic. According to popular diagnosis, the severity of an affliction was proportionate to the number of demons who had caused it. Mary Magdalene was one from whom seven demons had gone out. But this man housed an army of them.

Leslie Weatherhead, in his book *Psychology, Religion and Healing*, has suggested, "that the word *legion* was a key to the origin of the shock which had brought on the illness." He goes on to say:

Here, in St. Luke's story, we have a man muttering the word "Legion," and it is not fanciful to suppose that he had suffered some shock at the hands of the Roman legion. We know from the story of the massacre of the innocents the kind of thing the Roman legion could do, and, indeed, it is possible that this patient had witnessed this dreadful affair. If he had seen tiny children slaughtered, and had rushed in from the sunny street terrified of the approaching soldiers whose swords were dripping red with blood, and had cried, "Mummy, Mummy, legion!" (if we may modernize his language), then it

I Must Help This Man—Part II

would be no flight of imagination to suppose that the childhood's shock, especially if the patient had a hereditary emotional unbalance, would be quite sufficient to drive him into psychosis. And now the community had exiled him right out of the security of their own fellowship into a wild graveyard in a foreign land, where he is left to live amongst the pigs, terrified by spasms of fear which leap up from his repressed memories into the consciousness, and express themselves in maniacal frenzies and in loud cries.[2]

It does not matter whether we accept this scholar's point of view or not. The fact is that the man was in a pathetic state. Luke says, "many devils were entered into him" (8:30).

Something alien to his real personhood had disoriented his perception of who he was. "My name is Legion. My name is Mob! My name is Many! There are many of us!"

Whenever there are too many of us in one human body, we cannot function effectively and efficiently. We need to have ourselves well integrated and organized. We don't function at optimum levels when we cannot make the "us-ness" of our existence function harmoniously. There were agents in the man which made this impossible. The man might not have known this, but Jesus knew that there was an element in this man which did not belong. So Jesus sought to drive this negative force out before the man spoke to him. In fact, the demons themselves knew that they did not belong and said to Jesus, who was invading their temporary abode: "What have I to do with thee, Jesus, thou Son of God most high?"

When they realized that they could not stay in the man, they said to Jesus, according to Luke, "And they besought him that he would not command them to go out into the deep." Legend

---

2. Leslie D. Weatherhead, *Psychology, Religion and Healing* (New York: Abingdon-Cokesbury Press, 1951), p. 56.

has it that the devil and his demons dread the depths of the water. So the demons said to Jesus, "If you must drive us out of this man, don't drive us in yonder's depths." This idea is similar to what John records in Revelation 20:1-3:

> And I saw an angel come down from heaven, having the key of the bottomless pit and a great chain in his hand.
> And he laid hold on the dragon, that old serpent, which is the Devil, and Satan, and bound him a thousand years,
> And cast him into the bottomless pit, and shut him up, and set a seal upon him, that he should deceive the nations no more, till the thousand years should be fulfilled: and after that he must be loosed a little season.

The demons did not want to leave the man, but if they had to leave, they preferred another abode. So we see them asking for permission to enter a herd of pigs in verse 32. Evil wants to remain around and alive. It needs some form to inhabit. It needs earthly shelter.

Jesus in his permissive will allowed evil to select another abode. Someone has raised the question, "Why did not Jesus kill these devils?" We may only conjecture that the time had not come. There will come a day when evil, Satan, demons, dragons, and that old serpent will cease to trouble those who love the Lord. Until that day, we are to stay close to Jesus. He will protect us from all hurt, harm, and danger.

Our Lord granted them their wish. "Then," the writer says, "went the devils out of the man, and entered into the swine: and the herd ran violently down a steep place into the lake, and were choked." It is interesting that all of the demons went together. They had been torturing the man together, and now they entered the pigs together. In each situation their presence led to self-destruction on the part of the man and now on the part of the pigs.

I Must Help This Man—Part II

Satan is destruction-oriented. He is the author of destruction. Nothing stands when Satan comes. He is more destructive than Mount St. Helens. This is the record according to Job when Satan had finished with him:

> Naked came I out of my mother's womb, and naked shall I return thither: the Lord gave, and the Lord hath taken away; blessed be the name of the Lord (Job 1:21).

You may wonder why Jesus would permit the destruction of some innocent farmer's property in this manner. But it was better to have a hog shortage than to have a man shortage. The owner could replace the hogs, but who else could restore a madman to health and happiness again?

To Jesus, the man was more important than the hogs. Hogs will always be around, but this man needed Jesus' help then and there.

This Man Has My Help
Part III

Our Lord was confident that his mission was to destroy the works of the devil. The devil's work was not greater than the work of God. God's power and God's might had to be displayed by God's Son in order that the world would come to accept the central fact that the kingdoms of this world must become the kingdoms of our Lord and of his Christ.

The consciousness and awareness of his Father's supreme power gave to Jesus the confidence he needed to defeat the works of Satan and all his demons. Therefore, he could say with bold assurance, "If I cast out devils by the Spirit of God, then the kingdom of God is come unto you" (Matt. 12:28). When he sent the disciples out on their first mission, he empowered them with this same authority:

> . . . Go not into the way of the Gentiles, and into any city of the Samaritans enter ye not:
>
> But rather go to the lost sheep of the house of Israel.
>
> And as ye go, preach, saying, The kingdom of heaven is at hand.

This Man Has My Help—Part III

Heal the sick, cleanse the lepers, raise the dead, cast out devils: freely ye have received, freely give (Matt. 10:5-8).

The church of Jesus has this same power today. Jesus did not leave us without power. Our power is limited only because we lack faith and commitment. If we have faith, God will remove the demons and satanic forces which keep us from being and doing what God wants us to be and to do.

This community came out to see what had taken place. They wanted to know just what had happened. The news had upset them—two thousand pigs dead, and one sane and whole man alive. This was too much of an economic loss if one regards it in a business sense. Pigs are worth more than one insane and worthless man. The whole village had renounced this man, but God had not given up on him. This is the beauty of our religion. Men may give up on us, but God the Father never gives up on us. He knows that we are valuable, and that He and He alone can bring out the beauty and the grandeur hidden in every breast.

This is why Jesus kept working with Peter. One observer spoke of a "hidden splendor" lurking beneath the surface of Peter's outer shell. What gem, what precious jewel, what golden thread runs through the spirit of man and the spirit of woman? Only God knows.

The people in this city unwittingly asked Jesus to leave their region. They did not want that kind of man in their midst. They preferred the dirty hogs to a clean man. They preferred filth to cleanliness. They preferred hog grunts to a man's praise and adoration to God. They preferred the hooves of swine to the footprints of a man proclaiming the glory and wonder of God. They preferred hairy hogs to a revitalized man, filled with God's power and God's might. This was that town—but it could be our town. We still prefer business as usual over the call to high Christian discipleship.

It is strange that this cure caused a community catastrophe.

Instead of rejoicing, there was anger. Instead of relief, there was open rebellion. Instead of praise and celebration, there was consternation and alienation.

This could well be a parody on the people in our village. We do not want to pay for costly cures for those who sorely need the cure. We don't mind if some big shot needs help, but something in us withdraws in anger and protest when some little shot needs healing and help. This is the reason for the anger over the federal budget and local and state budgets. It costs too much to heal those who are down and out. We don't have the resources for so many. Yet we can waste billions on defense and more on inept politicians and business barons who mismanage corporation monies. We can find the money to build super-skyscrapers, supertankers, superplanes, supertrains, superhighways, supermissiles, superstadiums and coliseums. Yes, for all that gives a few folks satisfaction we can find the money. For that which benefits the masses we are sadly lacking. This is your country. This is my country.

Jesus is not willing to stay where he is not wanted. If we ask him to leave, Jesus will leave. It is a sad day in the life of any community when that community asks the Son of God to leave. The great tragedy in this passage is that they asked Jesus to leave them. They could have asked him to remain and cure all the other sick people in that region. They could have made him the resident psychiatrist and opened a mental clinic there for men and women from miles around to come to and have their neuroses and psychoses dealt with tenderly and gently.

I wonder why this community did not see the possibility of that. Other communities did try to get Jesus to do just that, but not this community. "Leave our town! Leave our region!" That town and that region could have gone down in history as one of the great medical and mental centers of the world. Had they allowed Jesus to remain in their town, they could have been blessed with all the benedictions of God Almighty.

Jesus will leave when we ask him to leave. He will not stay where he is not wanted. He will not give what is not wanted. He

This Man Has My Help—Part III

will not serve those who refuse his service. He will not cure unless we are willing to be cured. The Jesus of history and the Christ of faith now acts in accordance with their wishes. Luke says of that pathetic departure, "and he went up into the ship, and returned back again" (8:37).

Some mother in that crowd with a sick child should have cried, "Don't leave, Jesus!" Some sick person in the crowd should have begged, "Don't leave, Jesus!" Someone in that crowd should have requested that Jesus remain. Jesus might have remained a few more days as he did on several other occasions. We ought not to ask him to leave. We ought to beg him to stay. Jesus has too much to offer us. He has too much to do for us. He had the power of God and might of God in his hands. Why would we want the Son of God to leave?

I am glad that there are still some brave voices in our cities, states, and country who cry to Jesus, "Stay with us! Do not leave us!" In schools the cry is heard, "Stay with us, Lord Jesus." In courtrooms the cry is heard, "Stay with us, Lord Jesus!" In the halls of congress the cry is heard, "Stay with us, Jesus!" In churches the cry is heard, "Stay with us, Lord Jesus!" "Stay with us and heal us and make us whole!"

Jesus left that village, but let us not ask him to leave us. In fact, he has promised never to leave us alone. "Lo, I am with you alway, even unto the end of the world." I am most thankful that Jesus has promised to be with us in our most trying, testing, terrible times.

Now the man does something which is very interesting. Luke states the case this way:

> Now the man out of whom the devils were departed besought him that he might be with him: but Jesus sent him away, saying,
> Return to thine own house, and shew how great things God hath done unto thee. And he went his way and published throughout the whole city how great things Jesus had done unto him.

The man besought Jesus (v. 28) not to have anything to do with him. He did not want the devils within him to stand in open confrontation with Jesus, the Son of God. He knew that they could not survive in the presence of Almighty God. That is why we sing, "O Satan, Jesus is going to tear your kingdom down!" Satan flees from Jesus with a quick pace, as the night flees with the breaking of the dawn.

Then the Gadarenes besought Jesus to depart from their city. They did not want him around them any longer. They sought to get him to leave. Theirs was a negative reaction, just as the devils' request was a negative reaction. To be sure, all of Satan's actions are negative. He seeks to negate the good that God wills for our lives. Jesus had done good. The good is positive, wholesome, and healthy. Jesus wills the good for each child of God. "I am come that they might have life, and that they might have it more abundantly."

He seeks to bring into our lives the best that God has. The kingdom of God means healing, help, and hope. This is what John means when he says in the Book of Revelation, ". . . and the leaves of the tree were for the healing of the nations." God desires that we be healed. The healing begins here and now. The final healing will be in the new heaven and the new earth which John saw with unusual clarity and beauty. "And I saw a new heaven and a new earth: for the first heaven and the first earth were passed away; and there was no more sea."

In that glorious vision John saw something which will help those of us who press on the upward way. "Behold," he says, "the tabernacle of God is with men, and he will dwell with them, and they shall be his people, and God himself shall be with them, and be their God." God is getting us ready to be His. Once we are His, God will do wonderful things for us. Once we belong to Him completely—and that will be on the other side of this vale of sorrows—John says, "And God shall wipe away all tears from their eyes; and there shall be no more death, neither sorrow, nor crying, neither shall there be any more pain: for the former things are passed away."

This Man Has My Help—Part III

This is why I urge you to study your Bibles. You must worship frequently! Pray constantly! Serve with all your might and power! These are the keys to peace of mind. Also you must ask God to fill you with the gift of the Holy Spirit.

Jesus kept the disciples filled with his words, his power, and his presence as long as he was with them on earth. But when he went back to glory and sat down at the right hand of the Father, they needed a new presence and a new power in their lives. So he told them that he would not leave them without power and a presence. He and the Father would send them something which would fill their lives for the journey ahead. Jesus knew that they could not do kingdom work without kingdom power. He knew that they needed a guide from the kingdom.

After Jesus rose from the grave and demonstrated to them and more than 500 others that he was alive and alive forevermore, he told them to go to Jerusalem and wait for the power—wait for the power of the Holy Ghost. They waited for ten long days in prayer and fellowship. They were obedient to Jesus and to the words he taught. They waited and waited. Then it happened.

Luke, in Acts 2:1-4, states the case with beauty and profundity:

> And when the day of Pentecost was fully come, they were all with one accord in one place.
>
> And suddenly there came a sound from heaven as of a rushing mighty wind, and it filled all the house where they were sitting.
>
> And there appeared unto them cloven tongues like as of fire, and it sat upon each of them.
>
> And they were all filled with the Holy Ghost, and began to speak with other tongues, as the Spirit gave them utterance.

We must take note that all of them received the new power from on high. Every disciple in that room received the gift of

God's Holy Spirit. There was no discrimination. All enjoyed the benefits of that miraculous power. They were equipped, empowered, enlightened, engulfed, and enlarged for bold mission for Christ Jesus, our Lord and Savior. Satan could do them no harm. They were sealed until that day when all the saints of God are gathered home.

In a real sense Jesus had given them power over the demons when he first sent them out. "Then he called his twelve disciples together, and gave them power and authority over all devils, and to cure diseases" (Luke 9:1). Jesus also sent seventy other disciples out on a mission for him. He gave them power and authority; and when they returned, they reported to Jesus, "Lord, even the devils are subject unto us through thy name."

It is in the name of Jesus that we must work. We must pray in his name. We must teach in his name. We must sing in his name. We must serve in his name. We must live in his name. We must give in his name. We must baptize in his name. We must preach in his name. In the name of Jesus we live, we move, we have our being, and we die. I glory in the name of Jesus.

The name of Jesus is so sweet,
    I love its music to repeat;
It makes my joys full and complete—
    The precious name of Jesus.
Jesus, O how sweet the name!
    Jesus, every day the same;
Jesus, let all saints proclaim
    His worthy name forever.
        —Rev. W. C. Martin

When Jesus sent the man away, he did not just send him away. The healing involved responsibility. Jesus gave this man an assignment. You and I must never come to Jesus and receive his blessings and benedictions without receiving an assignment. The power is given for service. The power is given for work. The power is given to be used for the kingdom which is on earth,

This Man Has My Help—Part III

though in small beginnings. You and I have the sacred privilege to participate in the kingdom of God on earth. Hence, we are to be instant in season and out of season. We are to spend our time working for the master. If we work for him, God will supply the power. We need more power. God gives more power. It is given in accordance to our faith. Little faith, little power. Much faith, much power. Little work, little power. Much work, much power.

You don't need as much power to plow ten acres as you do to plow fifty acres. You don't need as much power to build a doghouse as you do to build a hen house. You don't need as much power to pastor ten persons as you do to pastor one thousand persons. Power is given in proportion to your task. It may not be given at all if you are not going to use it.

Jesus gave this wild man, who had become mild, meek, and sane, an assignment: "Return to thine own house, and show how great things God hath done unto thee."

Jesus sent him back into the community from whence he came with a new life and a new mission. "Return to your home, wife, children, relatives, and friends. When you get there, tell them what great things God has done for you. Tell them how God has made you whole. Tell them how God has healed you. Tell them how God has brought a change into your life. Tell them how God has acted in you and around you to change your midnight into day. Tell them what has happened out there in the graveyard. You tell them the story. It will be more convincing than if I were to try to tell it. You have a story to tell. If you tell the story, and they see you acting like a new man, they will have tangible evidence by which they can lay hold onto faith for themselves."

In that last verse, the man sought to do more than Jesus commanded him to do. "And he went his way and published throughout the whole city how great things Jesus had done unto him."

Luke says that Jesus told the man to go and show himself. Mark says that Jesus told the man to go and tell. Luke says that

Jesus told the man to go home and show. Mark says that Jesus told the man to go home "to thy friends, and tell them how great things the Lord hath done for thee, and hath had compassion on thee." Mark would have him share with his friends. Luke has him staying at home. Both, however, agree that the man did what Jesus said and then did some more. Extra effort wins! He went and told what Jesus had done for him in the surrounding areas. The man could not keep it to himself. He had to tell the story! He had to proclaim the news! It was more than he could keep to himself and his family only. He went and told the story "throughout the whole city."

If God has brought joy and happiness into your life, you ought to tell the story. If God has lifted your head when it was bowed down, you ought to tell the story. If God has put bread on your table when there was no bread, you ought to tell the story. If God has opened doors for you, you ought to tell the story. If God has put shoes on your feet, you ought to tell the story. There should be some storytelling here this morning. If God has given you a place to stay, you ought to tell the story. If God has healed your body, you ought to tell the story. If God has been your bread when you were hungry, water when you were thirsty, has given you a home when you were homeless, you ought to tell the story. You ought to tell the story if your name's been changed, been written on high, recorded in the Lamb's Book of Life.

You ought to tell the story!

This Man Has My Help
Part IV

Our blessed journey with Jesus through the Gospel of Luke should make us more conscious of the role the good doctor played in recording the healing ministries of Jesus. His reports made them authentic, for he was trained as a physician and therefore obliged to present the facts as they were given to him. This is why I love to think about what Luke recorded.

The demons did not want to leave this man from Gadara. They wanted to remain within him. They needed human shelter to perform their deeds of destruction. So they petitioned Jesus to let them remain in the man. It was not enough for them to see that the man was horribly afflicted. They wanted to add to his misery continuously. Evil is like that. It is never satisfied until we submit to its power. It seeks to completely destroy us. This is why evil is so diabolical. It demands complete control.

Jesus granted them their wish. He could have done away with them, but he permitted them to remain for reasons unknown to us. Maybe it was not time for the demons to be destroyed. There is a time for all things. Perhaps this is what the preacher had in mind when he wrote:

> To every thing there is a season, and a time to every
> purpose under the heaven:
> A time to be born, and a time to die; a time to
> plant, and a time to pluck up that which is planted;
> A time to kill, and a time to heal; a time to break
> down, and a time to build up;
> . . . A time to keep, and a time to cast away (Eccles.
> 3:1-3, 6b).

Jesus knew that this was not the time to destroy the demons. Their day would come. He was in the healing business, the saving business. I have come "to seek and to save that which was lost" are his words to those who are sick, lost, and disturbed.

The demons had to have shelter. Evil wants a place to abide. We must be careful that we do not become that place where evil abides. The evils of body, mind, and spirit have to have places to abide.

Satan, as was pointed out previously, went searching for someone within whom he could lodge himself. Job became this object through the permission of God. While Satan stood on the outside of Job's body and tormented him, he was never able to get inside Job, for in Job's heart there was no altar erected to Satan. "Though he slay me, yet will I trust in him." That was genuine confidence at the very core of Job's being. In that kind of religious stance, there is no entranceway for Satan. Each time Satan sought to ascend the stairs of Job's consciousness, Job would cry out, "I know that my redeemer liveth;" or Job would say, "Though he slay me, yet will I trust in him." Or with steadfast optimism, he would say, "When he hath tried me, I shall come forth as gold."

It is still true; He will keep us in perfect peace, if we keep our minds stayed on Him. This is Isaiah's assurance: "Thou wilt keep him in perfect peace, whose mind is stayed on thee: because he trusteth in thee" (26:3).

The pigs were choked. The text does not say that the devils were choked, but that the pigs were choked. The demonic

This Man Has My Help—Part IV

nature of the devils had destroyed them. They had been driven to self-destruction by the devils. They had not known possession before. This was the first experience for them. A berserk man or animal may self-destruct.

Rampaging hogs will cause trouble in any community. They are like wild men. Wild, crazy men and women will cause trouble. We see this in our world today. Men go wild. Women go wild. Juries go wild. Judges go wild. Police go wild. Politicians go wild. Arsonists go wild. This is a wild and woolly world. Pigs gone mad are like men gone mad. Madness is madness. Hog madness is no different from man madness. *Madness is madness!*

If Jesus had not come along, the wild man Legion in time would have destroyed himself. He could not have lasted long, cutting himself and running naked and living among the tombs of the dead without shelter or homelife. His madness was a sickness unto death. Thank God, Jesus came along and helped this man in his most wretched condition. Jesus came to seek and to save that which was lost. This man's lostness was complete.

The violent action of the hogs caused an immediate action on the part of the men who kept the hogs. Verse 34 says, "When they that fed them saw what was done, they fled, and went and told it in the city and in the country." They saw what had happened. They fled from what had happened and ran and told what they saw. Their flight was one of dread and fear and consternation. They did not understand what had happened. Nor did they wait to ask Jesus for an explanation. They felt that this was something which the whole town needed to know about. So they went in the fullness of their strength and told the whole town and city.

Our reaction to Jesus is either one of acceptance and joy or of fear and dread. We are either for Jesus or against Jesus. We either appreciate Him or we disrespect him.

The multitude that heard the startling news thronged to the place to see what had happened. In verse 35 we find:

Then they went out to see what was done; and came

to Jesus, and found the man, out of whom the devils were departed, sitting at the feet of Jesus, clothed, and in his right mind: and they were afraid.

They came to Jesus. Jesus confronts every city with his being and personality. He has to be dealt with. We can deal with him individually or collectively. He has to be faced and seriously considered. And until he confronts us, we have not really been confronted. For Jesus confronts us in mercy and truth and grace, or he confronts us with judgment and wrath.

When they came to Jesus, they not only found Jesus, but they found the man. *Our brother is always found in the presence of Jesus.* In fact, we cannot find Jesus until we find our brother. This is what Jesus meant when he said, "Therefore if thou bring thy gift to the altar, and there rememberest that thy brother hath ought against thee; Leave there thy gift before the altar, and go thy way; first be reconciled to thy brother, and then come and offer thy gift" (Matt. 5:23, 24). Jesus is found in the bosom of our brother, and our brother is found in the bosom of Jesus.

They not only found the man, but they found him sitting at the feet of Jesus. This was startling to them. For they had never seen this man sitting at the feet of anyone before. Now here he was, sitting as a gentle child at the feet of the Master. The last time they had heard from this man he was running wild and naked in the graveyard. His maniacal shrieks and cries could be heard in the surrounding countryside. Now there was a dramatic change. There were no cries. There was no raving. There seemed to be no madness. The man not only sat there, behaving himself, but according to the writer, he was "clothed, and in his right mind."

We don't know where he got the clothes from, and that is not important. It could be that Jesus and the disciples had some spare garments in the boat or that the man had just a blanket around him. The good news is that he was not meant to be naked but to be clothed. Like Adam, he recognized the need for clothes in the presence of God's holy Son. The agony of his past

This Man Has My Help—Part IV

nakedness was now more than he could stand.

Not only was he clothed, but the Word says that he was now in his right mind. They had seen him in his wrong mind, but now they see him in his right mind. They had seen him mad; now they see him glad. They had seen him hysterical; now they see him rational. They had seen him shackled; now they see him free. They had seen him wild; now they see him mild. They had seen him illogical; now they see him logical. The had seen him broken; now they see him whole. They had seen him godless; now they see him fearing. This was the mind of the man *now*. That was the mind of the man *before he met Jesus*. Then and only then does he regain *sanity* and *stability* and *wholeness*.

Luke went on to say this about those who came out to see what had happened: "And they were afraid." They were afraid of the man in his insane condition; and now that his sanity had been restored, they were afraid of him. Before and after, they were afraid. We too are afraid of the unknown. We are also afraid of the known. It works both ways. We fear that which we know and that which we don't know. This paradoxical nature of our being keeps us hovering between the devil and the deep blue sea. We want to know, and at the same time we don't want to know.

We cry like Job when God confronts us with too much of Himself: "Behold, I am vile; what shall I answer thee? I will lay mine hand upon my mouth. Once have I spoken; but I will not answer: yea, twice; but I will proceed no further" (Job 40:4, 5). We are all like Christopher Morley in *Inward Ho!*: "I had a thousand questions to ask God; but when I met him, they all fled and didn't seem to matter."

In the next verse, 36, we find that the men who fled to town gave a full report to those who came to see what had happened to their hogs: "They also which saw it told them by what means he that was possessed of the devils was healed." They gave an eyewitness report. They saw what Jesus did, and they reported what Jesus did. They did not try to keep hidden the fact that Jesus was responsible for the pigs' destruction and the man's reconstruction. They told both sides of the story. At least this makes them objective witnesses. Dependable witnesses are hard to find, but not in this case. They were reliable witnesses. They reported the facts as they saw them.

The man had been possessed, but now he was dispossessed. The man had been insane, but now he was sane. The man had been destructive, but now he was constructive. The man had been full of demons, now he was free from demons. This was the story. Jesus had done this. He was responsible for both the man's restoration and the pigs' destruction.

As I have said previously, Jesus confronts us with live options. After an encounter with him, we are either for him, or we are against him. There is no neutral ground where Jesus is concerned. He must reign in our hearts, in our cities, in our nations, and in our world. Jesus will not take a back seat. I am here reminded of what Paul said of him in Philippians 2:9-12:

> Wherefore God also hath highly exalted him, and given him a name which is above every name:
> That at the name of Jesus every knee should bow, of things in heaven, and things in earth, and things under the earth;
> And that every tongue should confess that Jesus Christ is Lord, to the glory of God the Father.

So these people in this city and the surrounding country came out to see Jesus. When they discovered what had happened, they made an unwise choice. They did what most folks do: they took the wrong turn in the road. They were more concerned about pig profits than man profits. They were more concerned about economics than they were about salvation. They were preoccupied with business rather than religion. Thus they "besought him to depart from them." They requested Jesus to leave their community. They wanted him out of their town. They did not want the Son of God and the healer from Nazareth in their midst. They did not want the chief psychiatrist there.

This Man Has My Help—Part IV 141

"Leave our town, Jesus! Leave us alone with our hogs and our madmen. Let us have our city with all that leads to sickness and desolation and decay. Leave us alone so that we might try to build our lasting monuments to our own glory and technology. Leave us alone! Go thy way! Never return to this city. We have our way, and that way is right. You are an imposter! We want nothing to do with you. Begone from us, and let us be!"

They did not know the way without Jesus. They did not have the key to life without Jesus. They did not know the way to life and light and liberty without Jesus.

Let us go easy with them. We in our day and time are trying to build without the Jesus of history and the Christ of faith too. We know how to come to Jesus and be saved, but we walk away. We know what we ought to do, but we will not do it. We know how to give, but we will not give. We know how to serve, but we will not serve. We know the way, but we will not walk therein. Jesus, leave us alone! Even in his church, this demand is made. Jesus, leave us alone! Jesus, leave us alone! We try in many ways to escape the demands of Jesus. But Jesus cannot be turned off with a flip of the wrist. He keeps knocking on the door. We may not open that door, but Jesus is there knocking. "Behold, I stand at the door, and knock. . . ." He stands at the door of every heart. He stands at the door of every house. He stands at the door of every city. He stands at the door of every region. He stands at the door of every nation. He stands at the door of our cosmos. "Behold, I stand."

Jesus stands there with life, light, and liberty in his precious hands. Only those who want to see the kingdom of his Father will accept the lifeline. Once you accept the lifeline, you are supposed to throw it out to others. This is the mission of his church. We are here by Christ's grace to throw out the lifeline. Let us not act like those in Gadara and ask our Lord to leave. "Behold, I stand at the door, and knock." Who will let him in? Who will open the door?

Help, My Daughter Is Dying!

Jesus raises Jairus' daughter from the dead
Luke 8:41-53

Patient/Diagnosis:
Jairus' twelve-year-old daughter who was dying

Doctor:
Jesus of Nazareth

Cure:
"He put them all out, and took her by the hand, and called, saying, Maid, arise. And her spirit came again, and she arose straightway: and he commanded to give her meat."

Comments:
Here we have another example of a moribund individual. Without immediate, intense resuscitative maneuvers, death is imminent.

Roger G. Smith, M.D.
Internal Medicine
Memphis, Tennessee

Help, My Daughter Is Dying!

143

We continue the healing and helping ministry of the Lord Jesus Christ as recorded by Luke. This continuing saga of the Savior's power and authority grows more profound as we march with Luke while he records in detail the healing miracles of Jesus. This trained doctor leaves no stone unturned to give us a record of what Jesus did in some difficult and testing situations. It is to his credit that he was willing to take the time and energy to give us the details of our Lord's mastery of sickness, blindness, lameness, dumbness, and deathness. Truly, Luke pictures Jesus as the divine physician. Jesus had said himself, "They that are whole have no need of the physician, but they that are sick. . . ."

Jesus, therefore, at the very beginning of his ministry sets the record straight concerning his divine intent and mission of healing and helping men and women in all walks of life caught in the horribleness of human existence. From the very depths of human misery Jesus sought to lift men and women to higher levels of human existence.

According to Dr. Luke, Jesus regarded healing as an essential part of his work. Jesus regularly connected the kingdom of God with the healing of the bodies of men. "[He] went about all Galilee, teaching in their synagogues, and preaching the gospel of the kingdom, and healing all manner of sickness and all manner of disease among the people" (Matt. 4:23). As we have pointed out before, when Jesus sent out the apostles on their mission, his instructions to them were that they were to preach that the kingdom of heaven was at hand, and as they preached, they were to "heal the sick . . . raise the dead, [and] cast out devils" (Matt. 10:7, 8).

William Barclay has stated the case beautifully:

> In Jesus' mind there was clearly the closest connection between the coming of the kingdom and the conquest of suffering and the defeat of disease and pain

144   HELP ME, SOMEBODY!

and death. If Jesus was the bringer of the kingdom,
then he was necessarily the healer of men, both in
body and soul.[1]

Jesus brought healing and help to men in all walks of life.
Those who came were helped, provided they were receptive to
the healing powers at work in him.

Hence, Luke gives to us a unique and beautiful incident in
our Scripture for this sermon. In fact, two healing miracles are in-
terwoven here. At this time we want to look at the healing of
Jairus' daughter. Later we will consider the miracle of the
bleeding woman.

According to Luke, Jesus had just completed the healing of
Legion, the wild man of Gadara. When the people asked Jesus
to leave their vicinity, he did as they requested, and as soon as
he returned to the other side of the lake, a man met him.

And, behold, there came a man named Jairus, and he
was a ruler of the synagogue: and he fell down at
Jesus' feet, and besought him that he would come
into his house.

Jairus was no ordinary man. He was a ruler of the
synagogue. He was responsible for the administration of the
synagogue and the ordering of public worship. Some say he had
reached the highest post life could give him in the respect of his
fellow men. He was well-to-do and had climbed the ladder of
earthly ambition and prestige. He was at the pinnacle of social
power and prestige and religious power and prestige.

Regardless of this man's position, he had a desperate need
to come to Jesus. In spite of his wealth, his money could not buy
health for his only child. On the other hand, Jesus had no earthly
wealth, but he had healing power and authority. Jesus pos-

---

1. William Barclay, *Jesus As They Saw Him* (New York: Harper & Row, 1962),
   p. 205.

Help, My Daughter Is Dying!   145

sessed the one thing that money cannot buy. It cannot buy healing power from God.

The ruler "fell down at Jesus' feet, and besought him that he
would come into his house." We should pay careful attention to
the fact that Jesus does not refuse the homage. Others refused
to accept this kind of divine homage. Peter, in Acts 10:25, 26,
refused the homage of Cornelius:

> And as Peter was coming in, Cornelius met him, and
> fell down at his feet, and worshipped him.
> But Peter took him up, saying, Stand up; I myself
> also am a man.

When the men at Lystra tried to make Paul and Barnabas
gods they refused, saying,

> We also are men of like passions with you, and
> preach unto you that ye should turn from these
> vanities unto the living God, which made heaven, and
> earth, and the sea, and all things that are therein (Acts
> 14:15).

Even the angels refused homage from John on the Isle of
Patmos:

> And I fell at his feet to worship him. And he said unto
> me, See thou do it not: I am thy fellowservant, and of
> thy brethren that have the testimony of Jesus: wor-
> ship God: for the testimony of Jesus is the spirit of
> prophecy (Rev. 19:10).

Jairus forgot his position in society and came to Jesus. In this
act of humility, he showed how desperate he was. And not only
did this religious leader come and fall at the feet of Jesus, but he
invited Jesus to his home. It is apparent that the clash between
Jesus and the religious establishment had not reached the

hostile stage. The storm clouds were gathering, but they had not reached the level of a major storm which developed later in the ministry of Jesus. Then, too, these events took place in northern Galilee. This was a place of toleration as compared to southern Judea, at the temple in Jerusalem.

The reason Jairus came to Jesus is found in verse 42: "For he had one only daughter, about twelve years of age, and she lay a dying." One daughter was all Jairus had. It is apparent from the story that he loved this child. Only Luke gives us this information. Luke was more concerned with details than some of the other writers and was most interested in the human stories which traversed the landscape of Palestine as Jesus made his journey from Galilee to Judea.

Being an only child, this daughter must have been the light of Jairus' life. This light was going out when Jairus left home. There was darkness in that house when he went to find this healer and physician. The child was about twelve years old; she was at the dawn of womanhood. Children in the East develop faster than do children in the West. Some say she might have been contemplating marriage at that age. What might have been the dawn of her life was about to be the darkness of life for her. For Luke says, "she lay a dying."

Jesus responded to the request of Jairus. He started to go with him without asking any questions. "But as he went the people thronged him." That is to say, the people gathered around Jesus from all sides. They wanted to see him, touch him, hear him, and be with him, albeit there were those who had no real purpose other than just being in the crowd. Others were there because it perhaps gave them something to do, to watch this miracle worker at work. Still there might have been those who felt that God in some strange and unique way was breaking through the code of custom once more.

Jesus was to be surrounded by the crowd until he revealed the commands and demands of the kingdom. The kingdom for him was more than bread and wine, fish and loaves, new limbs and new bodies. It was, in the final analysis, doing the will of

Help, My Daughter Is Dying! 147

God, and this involved suffering, sacrifice, and service.

Before Jesus could go to Jairus' house, a bleeding woman delayed him. She too was in need of help. Jesus performed a miracle on her behalf just as he was to do for Jairus. He was no respecter of persons. Whoever came to Jesus received his help if they came in faith, hope, and love. Jesus still stands at the door of our hearts trying to get in and save us from the ravages of disease and sickness. He is still in the healing and helping vocation. He is still the divine physician.

Just as Jesus completed the miracle for the bleeding woman, a messenger came from Jairus' house with this fateful message: "Thy daughter is dead; trouble not the Master."

The word *dead* here leaves us cold and angry. This was Jairus' only child, and now she lay dead. Life seems to deal hard blows to those who love with an eternal love. This was Jairus' pride and joy, but now the cold and strong hand of death had stilled her voice forever. This is what death would have us believe. Our Lord came into this world to stop the march of death. He was to rob it of its sting and pull the victims from the graveyards of this earth. He had to start in life, because life comes from life; nothing comes from death but death.

The messenger who brought the sad news went on to say, "Trouble not the Master." He was convinced that there was nothing that Jesus could do for the child. He felt that it was useless to plead with Jesus for assistance now that the child was dead. At least he had faith until death came. He did not lose faith before death came. He believed in the possibility of recovery. He did not give up and give out as some would have us to do today. They take the position that when life becomes mere existence, cut off the support systems. They call it "dying with dignity." I prefer to call it "dying in ignorance." God, I believe, is able to bring back to life the most hopeless cases. Life is not in our hands. It comes from God and is sustained by God. It will be reclaimed by God when God is ready.

"Trouble not the Master." Yet Jesus says to us,

Ask, and it shall be given you; seek, and ye shall find; knock, and it shall be opened unto you:

For every one that asketh receiveth; and he that seeketh findeth; and to him that knocketh it shall be opened (Matt. 7:7, 8).

Jesus has also said,

And whatsoever ye shall ask in my name, that will I do, that the Father may be glorified in the Son.

If ye shall ask any thing in my name, I will do it (John 14:13, 14).

Jesus gave to his disciples this open invitation. In John's gospel Jesus stated this divine prerogative:

Ye have not chosen me, but I have chosen you, and ordained you, that ye should go and bring forth fruit, and that your fruit should remain: that whatsoever ye shall ask of the Father in my name, he may give it you (John 15:16).

Jesus concludes the offer of this gracious blessing by saying in John 16:23:

And in that day ye shall ask me nothing.

Verily, verily, I say unto you, Whatsoever ye shall ask the Father in my name, he will give it you.

Can you understand why I say we must never stop knocking on the door of heaven in the name of Jesus? God might open the door to his wonderful blessings. If not, then we gather valuable knowledge by advancing in spiritual depth beyond the shores of weak, pathetic faith. We advance in spiritual depth in victory and in defeat. We are in good hands with God in control. God is able to turn our earthly defeats into heavenly victories.

Help, My Daughter Is Dying! 149

Jesus knew this and went to Calvary with a song of victory on his holy, blessed lips.

The man told the ruler not to trouble Jesus. He felt that all hope was gone. "Trouble not the Master." Jesus heard what the man said. He said to the ruler of the synagogue, "Fear not: believe only, and she shall be made whole."

Jesus spoke before Jairus became burdened in disillusionment and faithlessness. He came to Jesus in faith, and Jesus wanted him to remain in faith. To continue in faith is the hallmark of a true child of God. We must remain in the household of faith in the dark and dismal days of our existence.

Faithfulness is what Paul discovered in the dark and dismal days of his life. He carried to Jesus many trials and tribulations. The most important was a bodily ailment which Paul wanted removed. Jesus said to him,

> . . . My grace is sufficient for thee: for my strength is made perfect in weakness. Most gladly therefore will I rather glory in my infirmities, that the power of Christ may rest upon me (2 Cor. 12:9).

As a kind of holy benediction to faithfulness, Paul continues,

> Therefore I take pleasure in infirmities, in reproaches, in necessities, in persecutions, in distresses for Christ's sake: for when I am weak, then am I strong (2 Cor. 12:10).

"Fear not," says Jesus. Fear is the great obstacle to faith. If we could live without fear, our lives would be more productive. Most of us are tied down by fears of all kinds—moral, spiritual, mental, and even physical fears. All fear is anti-productive. Perfect love will cast out all fear. If we would just perfect our love, we would fear less. Jesus has shown us the way to perfect love. If we lose our lives for his sake, we will find our lives. It is the life of perfect love.

Jesus also said to the dying child's father, "Believe only." Jesus would have the man to hold on to the belief which brought him to Jesus in the first place. His initial belief was the first step in the healing process. Those who come to God must believe that God *is*, and that He is a rewarder of them that seek him.

> Only believe; Only believe,
> All things are possible
> Only believe.
> —Paul Rader

Jesus gives the blessed assurance that the child will be made whole. This is Jesus' way of saying that nothing on earth can stand in the way of divine healing and help. His power is able to bring back to life even those who have fallen asleep. We can call it sleep because that is what it is in the eyes of Jesus. It is merely death from our vantage point. That is because we don't know any better. We are not advanced enough in kingdom knowledge to call death anything but death.

Jesus entered the house where death lurked in and around the bedside of Jairus' only daughter. He would not allow all who had followed him to enter the house. He excluded the many but included a few witnesses: Peter, James, and John and the father and mother of the maiden. These blessed few were to see the mighty power of God working in Jesus, the Savior.

The crowd was not permitted to enter the room where the sick child was. Jesus and the others were about to enter the room, and the weeping and mourning became too loud for Jesus, the blessed one of God.

Luke gives us a vivid picture of the situation:

> And all wept, and bewailed her: but he said, Weep not; she is not dead, but sleepeth.

Jesus used the same words when they brought him the message that Lazarus was sick. He said to his disciples: "Our

Help, My Daughter Is Dying!

friend Lazarus sleepeth; but I go, that I may awake him out of sleep" (John 11:11b). The disciples did not understand that Lazarus was dead and said to Jesus, "Lord, if he sleep, he shall do well."

Then Jesus said to them forthrightly, "Lazarus is dead. And I am glad for your sakes that I was not there, to the intent ye may believe; nevertheless let us go unto him."

In verse 53, the people laughed at Jesus. They knew that the child was dead. They knew the language of earth, but not the language of heaven. We tend to ridicule that which we do not understand, and sometimes we belittle those who try to help us understand. We should be careful how we laugh at Jesus. All of the returns are not in yet. The polls have not closed. They are still voting on the idea that Jesus can do the impossible.

One of Eugene O'Neill's plays is called *Lazarus Laughed*. One of its characters was a man who had been resurrected. It is interesting to note that no emperor or society could scare him into doing anything anymore, because the threat of death still hung over his head.

Be careful how you laugh at Jesus, lest the daughter of Jairus, the widow's son, or Lazarus have the last laugh on you!

Jesus then dismissed them all, except that blessed few, who went with him into the room where the child was. Someone has rightly said, "The birthplace of a miracle has no room for scorn; first Jesus cleared out doubt."

I wonder what miracles would take place in the house of God if all of those who no longer took Christ seriously were evacuated. Only a handful might be left, but that is all a miracle from God needs. In a sense, no great things will come from the house of God today until all prerequisites are met. "It is hard for faith to fight in the smug and stifling atmosphere of its enemy, arrogant disbelief, or, worst of all, that treasonous saboteur, pretending faith."[2]

---

2. David A. Redding, *The Miracles of Christ* (Westwood, NJ: Fleming H. Revell Company, 1964), p. 157.

Judas was a pretender of the faith. That is why he never felt close to the others and Christ. He did not belong there and was not willing to undergo the prerequisites to becoming what the others went through.

If we could get rid of the doubters and disbelievers in the fellowship, there is no secret what God could and would do. Let us resolve that we will not doubt. Let us move forward in faith and come to Jesus in bold confidence that our Christ is able. He is able! He is able to do far more than we are willing to let him do. "Lord," we ought to cry, "I believe; help thou mine unbelief." Jesus would hear this prayer, and the prayer he hears with faith is the prayer he answers in faith.

Jesus then "took her by the hand, and called, saying, Maid, arise." The Aramaic words which Jesus spoke are, "Talitha cumi," which means, "Get up, my child." This is practically the same statement Jesus spoke to the widow's son in Luke 7:14: "Young man, I say unto thee, Arise." In a similar vein Jesus spoke of Lazarus, saying, "Lazarus, come forth."

When Jesus spoke, something happened. Something marvelous happened. The boy in Luke's gospel sat up and began to speak. In John's gospel there was movement in the tomb: "And he that was dead came forth, bound hand and foot with graveclothes: and his face was bound about with a napkin." Our Lord saw Lazarus and said to those standing there, "Loose him, and let him go." When our Lord, our Master, our Guide, our King, our Savior and Deliverer and Liberator spoke to this girl, something happened. "And her spirit came again, and she arose straightway," that is to say, immediately. Jesus was an instant healer. It did not take all day for him to get the divine healing done. He is like his Father. The Father spoke and there was light. He spoke and there was water. He spoke and there was vegetation. He spoke and there were wild beasts. He spoke and the hills in order stood. He spoke and man was.

God is like Jesus, and Jesus is like his Father. They were and are unlimited in power and authority over this mundane life we live. We must never forget that this is our Father's world. God

Help, My Daughter Is Dying!   153

sustains it. God controls it. God directs it. God supplies it. God revives it. God denies it, and God will judge it. This is our Father's world.

Nothing happened until Jesus came and the others left. When Jesus comes, everything else has to leave. Darkness must give way to light. When Jesus comes, sickness gives way, brokenness gives way, mourning gives way, lostness gives way, grief gives way, burdens give way, pain gives way, faithlessness gives way, and even death gives way. Jesus is the Light of the world.

Trench describes this moving moment in the house of Jairus:

> The house was now solitary and still. Two souls believing and hoping, stand like funeral tapers beside the couch of the dead maiden—the mother and the father. The church is represented in the three chiefs of its apostles.[3]

Jesus raised this little girl effortlessly, in secrecy and with profound results. Immediately the girl got up and walked about; she was twelve years old.

Jesus then commanded that they give her something to eat. He knew the nature of children. They are ever ready to eat. "Give her something to eat. Let her have some food. She needs some nourishment. She is alive again and will be with you for a long time. Take care of her. The blood flows warm in her body. Here is your child, Jairus. She is whole! She is well! She is alive! Death hath no dominion over her. I have dominion over life and death. I am the resurrection and the life!"

Luke then says that the parents were astonished. They were amazed at what Jesus did. They could not understand. They were bewildered. They were shocked. They got what they wanted, but they could hardly believe that it had happened. Life is like that sometimes. The things that we ask God for are given

3. Ibid., p. 158.

to us, and then we are amazed when God grants the wish. Nevertheless, there was joy in that house. Their child was alive and alive forevermore.

There is some doubt that Jesus spoke this last statement to the parents: "But he charged them that they should tell no man what was done." And yet there were times when Jesus did just that. He demanded that certain things be kept from the multitude. This is true in the Gospel of Mark also. Over and over again Jesus tried to get those who were helped by his love and care to keep what he had done for them a secret.

The International Critical Commentary has some interesting remarks in this regard:

> . . . The object of it cannot have been to keep the miracle a secret. Many were outside expecting the funeral, and they would have to be told why no funeral was to take place. It can hardly have been Christ's intention in this way to prevent the multitude from making bad use of the miracle. This command to the parents would not have attained such an object. It was given more probably for the parents' sake, to keep them from letting the effect of this great blessing evaporate in vainglorious gossip. To thank God for it at home would be far more profitable than talking about it abroad.[4]

However, I believe that Jesus did not want the witnesses to tell what method he used to raise the girl. His words and actions would have been the kind of fuel that fake healers could use to exploit people. In order that this might not be done, Jesus told them not to tell what was done. All that the multitude needed was to see the girl alive. They did not need to know how it was done. How it was done was the divine physician's method. His

---

4. Rev. Alfred Plummer, The International Critical Commentary—The Gospel According to St. Luke (Edinburgh: T & T Clark, Ltd., 1975), p. 238.

Help, My Daughter Is Dying!

procedure was a divine secret. Men could lay hold of the fact of the cure, and that would suffice. Faith in him was more important than a particular methodology. Jesus wanted them to see and know that he saw beyond life and death, crown and cross, glory and shame, tragedy and triumph, rejection and enthronement.

Jesus saw beyond. He wants us to see beyond. There is more to come, and that that is to come is more lasting than that that is. Thank God! Glory to His name!

Help Me, Somebody!

Jesus heals the woman with the issue of blood
Luke 8:40-48

Patient/Diagnosis:
   A woman having an issue of blood twelve years

Doctor:
   Jesus of Nazareth

Cure:
   "[She] came behind him, and touched the border of his garment: and immediately her issue of blood stanched."

Comments:
   This case of a woman who had been bleeding for twelve years could describe an individual with a clotting factor defect or a condition called *thrombocytopenia*. In either case, without the work of a blood specialist the condition would most likely continue for years.
                    Roger G. Smith, M.D.
                    Internal Medicine
                    Memphis, Tennessee

Help Me, Somebody! 157

There is no greater need in this world than the need for help. People in all walks of life experience this need from time to time. There are all kinds of needs in this world. There are, among others, economic needs, political needs, educational needs, social needs, and religious needs. Each need in its own way might impinge upon the other and thereby force the whole problem of life to be seen as hopeless.

Needs are not only private but public. That is, certain private needs might remain private, but then those who need stay in need for so long that that which was private becomes public. The public soon discovers what was private, and it becomes public. This is true because our private lives are never lived in isolation from those who live around us. They come to know and understand when things are not going right with us; and so in many ways they try to help and provide the kinds of moral, physical, and personal supports which will see us through the bad times.

In our Scripture for this sermon, Luke 8:40-48, we see a child of God in desperate need for help and healing. This is the most difficult problem facing us as humans. We want to be healed of our afflictions and infirmities. We don't like to be sick without hope for recovery. Help is needed by most of us when we have done all we can do, and there is nothing more to do but wait on God. We have to stretch our hands to God.

The woman in our story faced a bleak and dark future. As the victim of a rare blood disease, her illness could not be diagnosed by the medical doctors of her day and time. They were baffled by her condition. This was her dilemma. How does one get well when the doctors cannot help?

This woman had suffered for twelve years. Luke puts it like this, "And a woman having an issue of blood twelve years. . . ." There is no name given for this woman. Legend has it that her name was Veronica. Regardless of her name, she had been sick for twelve long years. That is a long time to be sick. However, that might not seem like such a long time for us today, for our lifespan now is statistically much greater. In those days, twelve years might be equivalent to half of one's life. It was a very serious problem for this woman. Half of her life had been spent in and out of the doctor's office.

There was a bigger problem here than the fact that she was sick. The next idea in this passage states the problem: ". . . which had spent all her living upon physicians, neither could be healed of any." We do not mind spending our money for our health's sake. But if, after we spend our money, there is no improvement, we lose faith, hope, and love. There is the tendency to forget that God is still for us and concerned about our problems and difficulties.

This woman had spent all her living. She had given one paycheck after another to physicians, who, in turn, had given her all kinds of prescriptions and had made all kinds of diagnoses. Each diagnosis led to a poor prognosis. There was no improvement in her health but a constant weakening of her vital signs and organs. There was a constant flow of blood from that poor victim's body. So Luke goes on to say of her, ". . . neither could be healed of any."

This word *any* connotes the fact that several physicians may have been consulted. None had been able to do her much good. Not one had been able to stop the flow of blood from her emaciated body. Each had tried in his own way, but to no avail. One could use the phrase for these doctors, "worthless physicians." Mark's account says she was no better but "grew worse." This was her state—gradually dying while futilely changing from doctor to doctor.

And yet, we must not justly condemn them, for they had used their medical skills on others and had helped them. Perhaps it was just this case which baffled them. There might have been others, but this case was unusual because it is included in the healing miracles of our Lord and Savior. The doctors had to refer this case to the Doctor of Doctors. They could not deal with it, but there was One on the road who could.

Mark says that this woman had heard the reports about Jesus, a statement which Luke does not record. I would like to

Help Me, Somebody!   159

believe that she had heard about this young healer. I would also like to believe that a friend had told her about Jesus. I don't care how sick you get, there will be some friends who will bring you good news. There are friends who stick closer than a brother or sister. They will be there when the storms of life are raging. They will be there when money is gone. They will be there when life loses its beauty. They will be there when the dark and dismal days stretch into long months and hard years. They are your true friends. It may be that this woman had one such friend. We all need a friend! We need friends until the real Friend comes along—Jesus of Nazareth. That is why we ought to sing with renewed fervor and fire:

> What a Friend we have in Jesus,
> All our sins and griefs to bear.
> What a privilege to carry
> Everything to God in prayer!
> —Joseph Scriven

This woman in her condition was determined to find a source for her healing. She had not given up her quest for healing and help. She remained constant and steadfast in the firm belief that someday she would be made well. This kind of determination will be rewarded. Now she was about to be rewarded for twelve long years of patience and persistence.

Verse 44 states several things which we will consider at this time. First, she "came behind him. . . ." Either she was too weak to come in front of Jesus, or Jesus had just about passed her house when the word was brought to her that Jesus of Nazareth was passing by. At any rate, she came behind Jesus. She might have been embarrassed to come in front of Jesus, for she had been sick for a long, long time. During that time, her physical features had probably deteriorated, and her body might have been deformed from the constant loss of blood. Also, there was a crowd around Jesus, and this might be as close as she could have gotten to him. She might not have had time to get in front of him. Deep down within, this desperate woman might have been singing,

> Pass me not, O gentle Saviour.
> Hear my humble cry;
> While on others Thou art calling,
> Do not pass me by.
> —Fanny J. Crosby

And deep down within her sick, weak, weary, and worn body she cried,

> Saviour, Saviour, do not pass me by
> While on others Thou art calling
> Do not pass me by.

She wanted help! She needed help! She sought help! Twelve years of pain, tears, groans, agony, frustration, rejection, isolation, loneliness, misery, hopelessness, helplessness, confusion, moments of doubt, hours of darkness, days of weariness, months of tiredness, years of weakness combined to provoke this dramatic, desperate action. At this point she was going to try Jesus. The healer from Nazareth was passing by.

Jesus was on his way to heal and help Jairus. This woman was not the primary subject of his healing mission on this occasion. However, she could have been had she requested the help of Jesus. Jesus never fails a child of God who reaches out in faith for his gracious healing gift. Jesus will not fail us. He still finds the time to hear a child's prayer. Certainly he would hear this woman's prayer, for she had been in prayer for more than twelve years. That is a long time to pray.

But we all must remember that we cannot hurry God. God takes His time. He comes when He is ready to fulfill a moment of divine healing and helping. Let us never forget this. It does not matter how unbearable the pain and agony of our days. God will place on us no more than we are able to bear. He knows just

Help Me, Somebody!

how much each of us can bear. Yes! He knows just how much we can bear. Though the load gets heavy, you're never left alone to bear it all. Just ask for strength and keep on toiling even though the teardrops fall. You have the joy of this assurance—the heavenly Father will always answer prayer, and He knows, yes He knows, just how much *you* can bear.

God the Father knew that this woman carried a heavy load. Her faith in Jesus was motivated by her trust in God, who gives faith to the faithless and hope to the hopeless. In that attitude of faith she did what every child of God must do—she "touched the border of his garment." Touching Jesus by faith is all that is needed by those who seek him. For when you seek him in faith, he is there in grace to provide whatever is needed to help you lay hold of wholeness, health, and strength.

We are told that she touched Jesus, not that Jesus touched her. This was a conscious and deliberate act on her part. Jesus was not aware that she was in the process of touching him until the act was done.

There were others in the crowd that day. But we are not told that any of them were healed. This woman, however, was in a different category. Her touch was a touch of faith and hope and confidence. Her touch was filled with the pain of twelve long years. In her touch were tears mingled with prayers which had gone up to heaven and had alerted Jesus to be on the lookout for such a peculiar touch and desperate need. This touch was like that of the man at the pool of Bethesda who had been coming for thirty-eight years. His suffering, sacrifice, and sickness so sensitized Jesus that his case became priority one in that pool of misery.

Matthew and Luke are most explicit. It was the fringe that she touched. A sacred tassel was tied by a blue thread to each of the four corners of the outer garment—a cloak that served as clothing by day and a blanket by night (Num. 15:38-39; Deut. 22:12). It was believed that such tassels were intended to remind Israelites of their obligations to the law, and are still fixed to the prayer shawl worn by orthodox Jews today. The loose

162 HELP ME, SOMEBODY!

end of the cloak would have hung over Jesus' left shoulder, and
the sacred tassel attached to it could have been touched by one
who came up behind him—perhaps because that one was cere-
monially unclean.[1]

When this woman touched the garment of Jesus, something
glorious happened to her. It is beautifully stated by Luke: ". . .
and immediately her issue of blood stanched." She stopped
bleeding as soon as she put her hands on the hem of the
Master's garment. There was no delay. Her healing was instant.
He is an instant healer and Savior. It does not take Jesus long to
take care of our needs. He took care of all our needs in just
three years of healing, teaching, preaching, serving, dying, and
rising again from the dead. It does not take Jesus long to deal
with our needs. That is why we should always remember to take
our burdens to the Lord. He can deal with them. When no one
else can handle the heavy load, go to Jesus. We should take our
burdens to our instant healer and helper. Jesus can help us.

Do you, my brothers and sisters, understand what I am suggesting to you? Let go and let God. Let go and let Jesus. He will
take care of you. He will heal you! He will help you! He wills that
you be whole. He wills that you be healthy. He wills that you
walk. He wills that you see. He wills that you hear. He wills that
you talk. He wills that you move your limbs. He wills that you get
up and live. He wills that you overcome the physical, mental,
and moral dilemma that you face. He wills, I tell you! Yes, I know
he wills.

The blood stopped flowing in this woman's body. In spite of
the multitude pressing around him, Jesus asked, "Who touched
me?" Jesus was sensitive enough to know that someone had
touched him with a touch of faith and hope. He knew that a child
of God had reached out in quiet desperation.

Jesus was not really seeking information. He knew that
someone had touched him with purpose and need. Jesus

---

1. *The Interpreter's Bible*, Vol. VIII, Luke-John (Nashville: Abingdon Press, 1952),
p. 161.

Help Me, Somebody! 163

wanted this woman to admit that she had touched the Master. He wanted her to publicly confess that she had touched his garments with a degree of faith and hope. For this is what he needed to include her in the work of the kingdom. He needed her private and public testimony.

Jesus needs from us, too, our public and private testimonies. He knows that many of us are reaching for him in faith. He knows that there are times when he answers a prayer of desperation. And Jesus wants us to tell what great things God has done for us. Let the world know if God has helped you.

All the people there denied that they had touched Jesus. No one was willing to say that they had touched the healer and helper. This was strange. For all of them ought to have been there for healing and help themselves. Obviously this was not the case. At any rate, Peter spoke up and said, ''Master, the multitude throng thee and press thee, and sayest thou, Who touched me?''

Peter was always the first one to speak up. He was the big fisherman. He had a lot to say. Some of it was wrong, and some of it was right. Nevertheless, he never missed an opportunity to say what was on his mind. There was no holding back for Peter. Jesus, however, knew more than Peter, and countered his statement by saying, ''Somebody hath touched me: for I perceive that virtue is gone out of me.''

Jesus could have been saying,

Somebody who needed help has touched me!
Somebody who has been bleeding for twelve years has touched me.
Somebody who has spent all their living on doctors has touched me.
Somebody who has been living on Misery Street has touched me.
Somebody who has gone the last mile of the way has touched me.
Somebody who is desperate has touched me.

Somebody who is penniless has touched me.
Somebody who is friendless has touched me.
Somebody who is tired has touched me.
Somebody who has been praying for a long time has touched me.
Somebody who has been crying for a long time has touched me.
Somebody who has known dark days and sick nights has touched me.
Somebody who is frightened by death has touched me.
Somebody who knows what pain is has touched me.
Somebody who is unclean has touched me.
Somebody who has spent all has touched me.
Somebody who needs somebody who knows something and can do something for somebody who thinks that they are nobody has touched me.

"Peter, I tell you, somebody has touched me in this crowd with a touch of faith, hope, and love. When they touched me I felt the healing power from glory go out of me and fill their body with life, new life and energy. Somebody is new, Peter. Somebody is whole who was broken just a few moments ago. Somebody is well who was sick. Somebody is clean who was dirty."

Who was it who cried, "Help me, somebody?" The woman knew that Jesus was right. Jesus is always right. I am so glad he knows when we reach out in faith, hope, and love. "The woman saw that she was not hid. . . ." She had gone back into the crowd and sought to hide. She did not want to be exposed. She was frightened and thought that this blessed cure might be taken from her as suddenly as it had been given. Or she might have been reluctant to let it be known that she who once was unclean had touched the teacher and healer.

Just as she came to Jesus to touch him, she came to him

Help Me, Somebody!

again. She came trembling and falling down before him. She came to Jesus trembling. This is the appropriate way for all of us to come. We ought to come into his blessed presence with fear and trembling, never bold and brash, but with fear and trembling. The lower we are when we come, the higher Jesus can lift us. This woman not only came with a degree of awe and humility, but when she came she fell in front of Jesus. The first time she came behind Jesus. This time she came in front of Jesus. This was because she was now whole and healthy. She came in front now because her condition had been changed.

Jesus does alter our positions. He changes us from back-door people to front-door people. Because of Jesus, all of us can come boldly to the throne of grace that we might find relief and release from our hard and brutal sins. In fact, Jesus now stands at the front door of our hearts and knocks. "Behold," he says, "I stand at the (front) door, and knock: if any man hear my voice, and open the door, I will come in to him, and will sup with him, and he with me" (Rev. 3:20).

In the very presence of Jesus, face to face, she confessed that she was the one who had touched him. ". . . She declared unto him before all the people for what cause she had touched him, and how she was healed immediately." This was the public confession that Jesus wanted from this woman. She had received a blessing from God, and now Jesus wanted her to make a public confession of that fact. The private confession of faith in Jesus is good. This must take place before a public confession is possible. Once the private confession is acknowledged, then we ought to tell what great things God has done. We are to be public-oriented. "Let the redeemed of the Lord say so" (Ps. 107:2).

"For the Lord is a sun and shield: the Lord will give grace and glory" (Ps. 84:11). "The Lord is merciful and gracious" (Ps. 103:8). "Call upon his name: make known his deeds among the people" (Ps. 105:1). "The Lord upholdeth all that fail, and raiseth up all those that be bowed down" (Ps. 145:14). "The Lord is nigh unto all them that call upon him, to all that call upon

166   HELP ME, SOMEBODY!

him in truth" (Ps. 145:18). "My mouth shall speak the praise of
the Lord: and let all flesh bless his holy name for ever and ever"
(Ps. 145:21). "I sought the Lord, and he heard me, and delivered
me from all my fears" (Ps. 34:4). "Wait on the Lord: be of good
courage, and he shall strengthen thine heart: wait, I say, on the
Lord" (Ps. 27:14).

When the woman made her confession, Jesus then said to
her tenderly, "Daughter, be of good comfort: thy faith hath
made thee whole; go in peace." The word *daughter* is a word of
respect, affection, and recognition. It was a word of respect
because men in those days did not treat women with the same
kind of respect they had for each other. Jesus showed a different, more tolerant attitude towards women than did most
religious teachers of antiquity. The rabbis were seldom seen in
public speaking to women. But Jesus spoke to them and treated
them with respect as human beings with divine claims on the
kingdom of grace and love and mercy. *Daughter* was also a word
of affection, as used by Jesus here. He used this word on several
occasions when talking to women. When the woman who was in
the temple needed healing, he called her "daughter of
Abraham." The term carries a personal feeling of affection. This
is especially true for those who have not known affection. Then,
this word is a word of recognition. This woman was from the
very loins of Jesus, the loins of Abraham. This placed her within
the covenant community. This community had been promised
the blessings of Almighty God. Jesus was the fulfillment of those
blessings and benedictions.

That is the true meaning of those words spoken to another
woman whom Jesus met at Jacob's well. Jesus told her, "God is a
Spirit: and they that worship him must worship him in spirit and
in truth." The woman responded to Jesus with these words: "I
know that Messias cometh, which is called Christ: when he is
come, he will tell us all things." Jesus then responded to her with
the most profound words ever spoken by a religious teacher in
Judaism: "I that speak unto thee am he" (John 4:24-26).

Jesus then went on to say to this woman who had been

Help Me, Somebody! 167

saved from wretchedness, weakness, and sickness, ". . . Be of good comfort." I think Jesus was saying several things to this woman. "Be happy, you are whole." "Rest assured you will not bleed anymore." "Go and live your life in the glory and honor of God." "Take time to taste of health and life." "Go home and sleep at night." "You do not have to go to doctors anymore." "You might use your money from this day onward to secure your old age." "Take your disability checks, return them to the temple, and return to your work." "Be of good cheer and comfort; your prayers and faith have been vindicated. In fact, daughter, thy faith hath made thee whole. Not your touching me, but the fact that you reached out in faith healed you. There is no magic in my garment. The power is in your faith. You have sustaining faith. You have whole faith. You have godly faith. You have determined faith. You have touching faith or reaching faith. You know how to stretch your hands to God. Somewhere along the line you have heard the song,

> Father, I stretch out my hands to Thee;
> No other help I know;
> If Thou withdraw Thyself from me
> Ah, whither shall I go?
> Author of faith, to Thee I lift
> My weary, longing eyes;
> O may I now receive that gift!
> My soul without it dies.
> —Charles Wesley

"Because you have walked the hard road of life for the past twelve years bleeding and crying and praying and seeking and knocking on the door of heaven, you have received the blessing of heaven. Heaven has come down and heard your cry. Go in peace. Go in peace, my daughter." This was and is the blessed benediction. It is a Semitic benediction! This is the same kind of blessing and benediction Eli gave to Hannah, Samuel's mother, when he discovered her divine wishes and desires. He said to her, "Go in peace: and the God of Israel grant thee thy petition that thou hast asked of him." This was the blessing and benediction which Achish, the Philistine, blessed David with when David wanted to go to battle with him, but the Philistine lords did not want him to go. Achish sent David back with these words: "Wherefore now rise up . . . and . . . depart."

"Go in peace, daughter—mental peace, spiritual peace, moral peace, physical peace, emotional peace, healing peace, healthy peace, loving peace, saving peace, divine peace, righteous peace, glorious peace, majestic peace, dynamic peace, wonderful peace, blessed peace, real peace, peace that passes all understanding. Go, daughter, go in peace! You are in my peace and my peace is in you. We are in each other. I have entered your life, and you have entered my life. Your life is mine, and my life is yours. We are one in the spirit, and we are one in the Lord. We are bound together forevermore. Your peace is my peace; my peace is your peace. We have merged heart and soul and mind. Thine is mine, and mine is thine. Glory to God. Amen and amen."

Help Is Needed in the Valley

Jesus casts an unclean spirit out of an epileptic child
Luke 9:37-43

Patient/Diagnosis:
    A child with an unclean spirit

Doctor:
    Jesus of Nazareth

Cure:
    "And Jesus rebuked the unclean spirit, and healed the child,
    and delivered him again to his father."

Comments:
    The Bible does not link epilepsy with demon possession,
    and even the description of the fits of the possessed boy . . .
    seem to indicate something more than epilepsy. The nature
    of epilepsy is still unknown, but it can be artificially induced
    in apparently normal people (W.G. Walter, *The Living Brain,*
    1953, pp. 60f.). Students of personality disorders know that
    it is often impossible to say just how these are triggered off.
                          The Illustrated Bible Dictionary, p. 382

Epileptic seizures may have many causes. They follow brain damage secondary to traumatic brain injury, drug sensitivity, brain tumor and infection, as well as other inherent neurologic diseases. A seizure secondary to a psychogenic disorder is almost unheard of.

Dr. Edwin W. Cocke, Jr.
Specialist in diseases of the ear,
nose, neck, and throat
Memphis, Tennessee

In this sermon we again see the ministry of healing as perfected by Jesus when he healed a suffering child and restored him to his father, whole and well. A father requested help then. Christian parents still request help in dealing with their children today.

The healing ministry was a valid form of ministry for our Lord. He also made it a vital part of the ministry of his disciples. This can be seen in Luke 9:1 and 2:

Then he called his twelve disciples together, and gave them power and authority over all devils, and to cure diseases.

And he sent them to preach the kingdom of God, and to heal the sick.

After our Lord rose from the grave, Mark says that Jesus sent his disciples forth with these words ringing in their ears:

Go ye into all the world, and preach the gospel to every creature. He that believeth and is baptized shall be saved; but he that believeth not shall be damned.

And these signs shall follow them that believe; In my name shall they cast out devils; they shall speak with new tongues;

They shall take up serpents; and if they drink any

Help Is Needed in the Valley

deadly thing, it shall not hurt them; they shall lay hands on the sick, and they shall recover (Mark 16:15-18).

The healing ministry became a part of the life and work of the early Christian community. Of course, Peter and John had the gift. Paul was given this extra gift of grace to use for the ministry of our Lord as he carried the gospel to the Gentile world. James gives some direction for the community when he says:

Is any sick among you? let him call for the elders of the church; and let them pray over him, anointing him with oil in the name of the Lord:
And the prayer of faith shall save the sick, and the Lord shall raise him up; and if he have committed sins, they shall be forgiven him (James 5:14, 15).

It is also James' contention that "the effectual fervent prayer of a righteous man availeth much."

It is my deep conviction that this vital ministry is a live option for the church of Jesus Christ today. God has given the gifts of grace to his church. Our earnest and fervent prayers are aids to healing. Our lives, when pure and holy, are channels of grace for those who are sick and those who are well. God works through us. He works in many ways. Jesus knew this, and thus gave this authority to his disciples to heal the sick, raise the dead, and preach the gospel of the kingdom. He sent them forth and gave them power to perform the work.

If we do not have the healing power, Jesus, our Lord, has the healing power. In our Scripture we see another demonstration of this unique power possessed by Jesus.

According to the account, Jesus and his disciples were coming down from the Mount of Transfiguration. On the top of that mountain three of his most trusted disciples saw the unique relationship of Jesus to divinity. Jesus went there to pray. While in the act of praying, a transformation took place in the being of Jesus. Luke and the other gospel writers recorded this incident: "And as he prayed, the fashion of his countenance was altered, and his raiment was white and glistering" (Luke 9:29).

His holy presence in prayer lifted Jesus beyond the ordinary mode of his existence. While in prayer Jesus became engulfed in that awefulness which is Godness, which was a part of his "being-ness." It was the intensity of his prayer which caused, perhaps, the celestial change. Or maybe this was the only way that Moses and Elijah could or would talk with Jesus. Just as they changed from an invisible to a visible presence, so Jesus was changed from an earthly presence to a spiritual presence which would allow the lines of communication to be fully opened. The Deep was calling to the Deep.

On the other hand, it might have been an experience which the disciples needed to fortify them for the task ahead. The more concrete information they had, the greater would be their belief and faith. Maybe this is why they could write books while some of the other disciples could not. Nevertheless, there was a divine reaction and transaction on that mountain.

While our Lord was praying on the mountain peak, there was trouble in the valley. Perhaps this is why Jesus would not listen to Peter when he suggested that they remain on the mountain. Peter wanted them to build three tabernacles: one for Jesus, one for Moses, and one for Elijah. Moses was the lawgiver, and Elijah represented the best in the prophetic tradition. And Jesus, our Lord, was recognized as priest, prophet, and king. Mountain-top experiences are always neutralized by valley problems, complexities, difficulties, and frustrations.

From our text we see that Jesus and his disciples stayed on that mountain a day and a night. Peter wanted to stay there, but Jesus knew that there was work to be done in the valley. There is always trouble in the valley when Jesus is absent. If we want to control the valley, we must have Jesus or the mighty Spirit of God in some form. If we don't have Jesus, we must have God's Spirit, God's might and God's power to tame the wild, woolly,

Help Is Needed in the Valley

wormy, wily, and worrisome valleys of life. We need power to deal with the valleys of life.

"And it came to pass," says verse 37, "that on the next day, when they were come down from the hill, much people met him." They went up one day and they came down the next. The greater portion of life is built around polarities—up and down, night and day, right and left, backward and forward, mountains and valleys. These polarities are essential to the whole of life. We must always try to see life in this light. This is what the Germans call "the gestalt," the notion that one must seek to see life and see it whole. However, we must remember that only God can see life and see it whole. There is in us, however, the deep desire to do this. Paul was right when he said, "We see through a glass, darkly." He then went on to say, "Now I know in part; but then shall I know even as also I am known."

I should think that this is a very good lesson for a Christian father to teach his son. "We see through a glass, darkly." We see in part; we don't know at all. So I suggest to all fathers to make a serious effort to inculcate this early into the thinking structure of their children. I feel that if we do not give them this bit of divine wisdom, time and experience and people will. All of them can be so much more brutal than a kind father who explains this to his child. Life might deal with them a little kinder further down the road. Tell them now! Life has its ups, and life has its downs! Life has its valleys, and life has its mountains! Life has life, and life has death! Tell them the truth, and the truth will make them free.

I like the way Luke states the next idea: "When they were come down from the hill." Jesus' life was filled with condescension. Coming from above, he came down from glory to help, heal, and hold us until the kingdoms of this world become the kingdoms of our Lord and of his Christ. "For God," says John, "sent not his Son into the world to condemn the world; but that the world through him might be saved" (John 3:17). John makes it clear to us again that Jesus came down. He says in John 3:13, "No man hath ascended up to heaven, but he that came down from heaven, even the Son of man which is in heaven."

The apostle Paul understood this condescending tendency in the mind of Jesus when he wrote to the Philippians:

> Let this mind be in you, which was also in Christ Jesus:
> Who, being in the form of God, thought it not robbery to be equal with God:
> But made himself of no reputation, and took upon him the form of a servant, and was made in the likeness of men:
> And being found in fashion as a man, he humbled himself, and became obedient unto death, even the death of the cross (Phil. 2:5-8).

Jesus was always bending low to help, heal, and hold those who needed him. He became our servant that we might first become his servants and then be raised to positions of glory and honor and praise. The glory and honor and praise come after we have borne our stewardship of suffering for the kingdom here on earth. And yet, our names are written on high the moment we believe, repent, and are baptized in the name of the Father, the Son and the Holy Spirit.

You remember in Luke's gospel when Jesus sent out the seventy disciples who became his servants and gave them power to cast out devils and to heal the sick. When they came back they were rejoicing at the fact that they had won some victories. They came back and told Jesus, "Lord, even the devils are subject unto us through thy name." Jesus, our blessed Lord, said to them,

> I beheld Satan as lightning fall from heaven.
> Behold, I give unto you power to tread on serpents and scorpions, and over all the power of the enemy: and nothing shall by any means hurt you.
> Notwithstanding in this rejoice not, that the spirits

Help Is Needed in the Valley

are subject unto you; but rather rejoice, because your names are written in heaven (Luke 10:18-20).

Fathers, remember that to help your sons and daughters you must bend low. There are times in your life when you won't feel like bending low to help your sons, but if you would save them, bend low. Bend down to them, and hear what they are saying. Bend down to them, and guide them. Bend down to them, and feed them. Bend down to them, and love them. Bend down to them, and nurture them. Bend down to them, and be with them—at home, at school, at play, at church.

God bent low to guide Jesus. When he was baptized, the Father bent low: "This is my beloved Son." When he was on the Mount of Transfiguration, the Father bent low: This is my beloved Son: hear him." When it was time for the Son to be glorified, the Father bent low: "I have . . . glorified [my name], and will glorify it again." When Jesus was in the Garden of Gethsemane, uncertain of the directions for his life, the Father sent an angel to give strength to His Son.

Bend low, fathers! Your sons are small; they need you to bend down and hear them. Remember the poem called "Introspection":

To get his goodnight kiss he stood
    Beside my chair one night
And raised an eager face to me,
    A face with love alight.

And as I gathered in my arms
    The son God gave to me,
I thanked the lad for being good,
    And hoped he'd always be.

His little arms crept 'round my neck,
    And then I heard him say

Four simple words I shan't forget—
Four words that made me pray.

They turned a mirror on my soul,
On secrets no one knew.
They startled me, I hear them yet;
He said, "I'll be like you."
—Herbert Parker

The words of the text move us onward. These words are recorded: ". . . much people met him." There was no way for Jesus to escape the crowds with all that he had to offer. They were sure to find him and seek his divine help. They might not have had a desire for discipleship, but they certainly had a desire for healing. I suppose they were like the vast majority of the peoples of this earth. They want wholeness, health, and peace, but they are not willing to become disciples of Jesus so that these things might become a reality. The people desired to use Jesus, but they did not want Jesus to use them. They wanted his healings, but not his teachings.

I suppose that this is what we find in most of our churches today. We want the blessings and benedictions of God, but we don't want God. We don't want Jesus. We don't want the Holy Spirit. For God, Jesus, and the Holy Spirit lay claim to all that we have, and we don't want to give up our so-called freedom from slavery to any being—human or divine. We demand the healing without the kneeling. We don't want to bow and submit.

Nevertheless, Jesus came down from the mountain with his heart committed to complete the task God gave him. That task was to help and hold and heal as many men and women as possible.

In that crowd that day was a man who had a son—an only child. The boy was afflicted with some malady. Luke says:

And, behold, a man of the company cried out, saying, Master, I beseech thee, look upon my son: for he is mine only child.

Help Is Needed in the Valley   177

There is no name given for the man. The record merely states that "a man of the company" attracted Jesus' attention. One could raise the question, "Was this an actual cry or just a plea to Jesus for the son?" Both cases are possible. This was his only son, and the affliction was more than the child could master or the father could stand. If he were a widower, I would be more inclined to believe that this was a real cry. The man did not want to see his only child afflicted night and day. If the man had to work, the boy was unable to take care of himself. Babysitters were not known in that day. Then, too, this child was his father's only link between himself and his tomorrow. Every Jewish father looked with favor on male children. Boys gave them a sense of pride and honor in the community. Boys could become warriors, defenders of the family name and property. They could also become rabbis or, possibly, the long-expected Messiah. So we can believe that the father's cry was real, that it was genuine.

The father said to Jesus, "Master, I beseech thee." The word "Master" was a word of respect and honor. It really means "teacher." It denotes one who has divine authority about divine things. Jesus possessed such authority and power, and on several occasions showed that he would use it for good. So the man was right on target when he addressed Jesus with such respect and honor. He came to the right place and source and person and time. This was the moment for healing and helping. Jesus was on his way to complete his ministry.

After addressing the man from Nazareth with respect and honor, the man said to him, ". . . look upon my son: for he is mine only child." The father wanted Jesus to observe the condition, to examine his son with divine skills and talent. "Watch him closely as you move along. There is something drastically wrong with him." The father went on to tell Jesus that not only was the child sick, but that he was his only child. He might have been trying to express the idea that this might not be his happy privilege again. "I am old and wifeless. Winter is on my head, but spring is still in my heart. There will be no tomorrow for me."

The man might also have been saying to Jesus, "Master, you know how much we Jewish men love our sons. You know to

178   HELP ME, SOMEBODY!

what great lengths we will go to protect them. You also know what we expect of them. I need you now to do something for my son, my *only* son. This is the last chance for me—and perhaps for him. The doctors have been unable to help us, but I believe you can."

In verse 39 the father describes the boy's condition: "And, lo, a spirit taketh him, and he suddenly crieth out; and it teareth him that he foameth again, and bruising him hardly departeth from him." It "taketh him"—the word *taketh* means "to lay hold of, so as to make one's own, to seize upon, take possession." The picture in the Word is that of seizing something and pulling it down. The word "katalepsy," from the Greek, is the word from which we get our word "epilepsy." Greek writers use it when speaking of fits.

"It teareth him"—the word *teareth* means to distort or convulse and was used of a demon causing convulsions in a possessed man. The man went on to say that the spirit "bruising him, hardly departeth from him." This was the final stage of the boy's attack. He had now become the victim of motionless stupor.

The father continues, "I besought thy disciples to cast him out; and they could not." This was one of the reasons Jesus came down from the mountain. The father was there with his only child, waiting, while the disciples were unable to do anything about the pitiable situation. Of course, Jesus would have some concerns for the boy who was a victim of frequent epileptic seizures. There was trouble in that valley. As I have stated before, there is always trouble when Jesus is not there.

The disciples were impotent in this situation. Yet Jesus had given them divine power and authority just before they all went upon the mountain to pray. Luke 9:1 states, "Then he called his twelve disciples together, and gave them power and authority over all devils, and to cure diseases." Jesus sent them out to preach the kingdom of God and to heal the sick. This was most disturbing to me before reading with keener insight into the chapter a little further. According to verse 28, this event took

Help Is Needed in the Valley 179

place eight days later. It could be that the disciples had the power and the gift, but they failed to keep in contact with the source of power. They failed to cultivate the gift, and hence, the power was low when they needed it most. At least, this is the indication when Jesus speaks to them about their impotence a few verses later.

You and I, if we are to be effective in our ministry, must remain close to the source of power. To stay close, we must practice prayer, meditation, reflection, study, and consecration. Worship is essential to power. Prayer is essential to power. Study is essential to power. Service is essential to power. Practice is essential to power. We cannot manufacture power. It is a gift from God, and we have to beseech God for it. We have to ask in faith that God will grant us power. Then we have to use that power for God's glory and not our own. God wants the glory. Jesus wants the glory. The Holy Spirit teaches us to give God the glory.

Jesus was upset with his disciples, the man, and the people. Listen to his words, "O faithless and perverse generation, how long shall I be with you, and suffer you? Bring thy son hither." He accused them of being faithless and perverse. They were not only lacking in faith, but they were also lacking in character. They were not the correct instruments for the power of God to flow through. Maybe that is our problem too. We don't have the content of character required to become the vessels through which the power of God and the grace of God can flow with healing and redemptive love.

He asks, "How long shall I be with you?—a question which lends itself to speculation that Jesus did not care to be much longer in the presence of such faithless people. There is a bit of disillusion with those who are unfit and unworthy to be in his presence. He was too holy and too pure to remain much longer with those who were faithless and perverse. Jesus was longing for his home, where no such actions and disbeliefs abide.

"Bring thy son hither." "Bring him from thither to hither, and let me see him. Let me look at his condition. Let me understand what happens to him. I want a close-up view of this boy's condition. Bring him hither! Bring him to the healer from Nazareth!"

The father was obedient. Fathers ought to be obedient today. Jesus is requesting your children. Hear him calling, "Bring them to me!" He does not want us to *send* them. He wants us to *bring* them. For if we bring them, there is the possibility of being saved and made whole ourselves. We need Jesus just as much as our children do. We need his grace and healing power. We need his love and mercy. We need his forgiveness and righteousness. We need his salvation and redemption. We need his compassion and pity. We need to learn about him and his wisdom. We need Jesus. "Bring him to me." I can hear him saying to fathers across the ages, "Bring them to me."

As the man was bringing his son, the devils became active in the child. "And as he was yet a coming," says Scripture, "the devil threw him down, and tare him. And Jesus rebuked the unclean spirit, and healed the child, and delivered him again to his father."

The devil became active again, just as the man was bringing his son to Jesus. This is the time when Satan is most busy. The moment we start Jesus-ward, the devil becomes destructive and disruptive. The father did not stop. He carried his son to Jesus. Don't stop, fathers, when Satan gets in your way. Fight to get your children to Jesus. You have to fight with all your might. Satan does not want our sons and daughters to get to Jesus. Jesus will salvage them from the satanic forces which seek to destroy them.

Satan threw the boy down and then made him have convulsions. This time there was someone there who could deal with the boy's condition. Jesus was there, and when Jesus is around, Satan has to run. He cannot stand in the presence of Jesus. He cannot match strength with Jesus. His power is powerful, but Jesus' power is all-powerful. So Jesus just spoke the word of healing. Luke says that he rebuked the unclean spirit, and healed the child. Jesus just spoke the word of health and wholeness. That is all Jesus had to do on this occasion. Jesus spoke the word of health.

Help Is Needed in the Valley 181

I am glad that my Savior has that kind of mysterious power. There have been times in my life when I have needed him, and he spoke the word of health and wholeness. Jesus is still speaking the Word in hospital rooms, operating rooms, nursing homes, mental institutions, rehabilitation units, and other institutions of custodial care.

Then Jesus gave the whole son back to his father. Jesus makes us happy by returning our children to us, whole and well. I am sure that this father went away thanking God for the blessing which had just come into his life. Jesus had blessed him and the boy. No blessing comes to our children which does not come to us. We are a part of our children and a part of what makes them healthy, wealthy, and wise. We are bound to our children. When they are sad, we are sad. When they are glad, we are glad. Jesus can make them happy. Jesus can make them whole. Jesus can make them live and active.

Finally, Luke placed these interesting words in his account: "And they were all amazed at the mighty power of God." Amazed at the power of God! They were—and yet they should not have been. God can do what seems impossible. Those things which are impossible with man are not so with God. He is a God who specializes in things which seem impossible. He can do what no other power can do. My God specializes. He specialized when He saved us and brought us from the wilderness. Our souls felt good when we came out of the wilderness.

We are not surprised at what God can do. Our God can do anything but fail. What about your God? What can He do? What will He do?

The Helper of the Dumb
Part I

Jesus casts out a demon from a dumb man
Luke 11:14-26

Patient/Diagnosis:
A demon-possessed man who was dumb

Doctor:
Jesus of Nazareth

Cure:
"And it came to pass, when the devil was gone out, the dumb spake. . . ."

Comments:
The individual in this instance was described as being *dumb*. This term is used to describe an individual who is mute, or one who lacks the power of speech. There is an array of medical conditions resulting in inability to speak. These may be anatomical, neurological or psychological derangements. The prognosis for the spontaneous appearance of speech is poor.

The Helper of the Dumb—Part I

Roger G. Smith, M.D.
Internal Medicine
Memphis, Tennessee

This passage in Luke further broadens our understanding of our Lord's healing ministry. His ministry was a holistic, healing one. No illnesses or abnormalities were too difficult for him; and he was able to heal and to help the least of God's children.

The first verse of the passage states, "And he was casting out a devil, and it was dumb." This devil had gained control over its victim, rendering him destitute of the power of speech. Verbal communication was unknown to him. In this silent world, turmoil, torment, and tension were his constant companions. He was forced by the devil within him to live a miserable existence, an existence compounded by frustration and sorrow. When Jesus confronted him, the divine physician was compelled to act. His compassionate nature forced him to use his unique healing power.

It is significant to remember that Jesus in this instance was dealing with more than just another physically handicapped person. Satan had invaded this man's life. And Satan here was not merely the devil or another demon, but the chief devil. This seems to suggest that Satan selects the most pathetic cases for his domination. In fact, he is insensitive to all who suffer and stand in need of God's healing power. He is not partial, but will attack all—the weak and the strong, the high and the low. Wherever he can find an entrance, there he enters and dwells with destructive force and finality.

But just as Satan is in the business of destroying, Jesus is in the business of helping and healing. Let us consider again Luke's description of this devil: ". . . it was dumb." The implication is that the man, not the demon, was dumb. Here we have the first indication of a potential clash between the satanic power of the demon and the divine power of Jesus Christ, the Son of God.

The next statement, "And it came to pass," brings to mind the myriad wonders that did come to pass as Jesus made his way to Calvary. Things happened. Minds were stimulated, spiritual insights were gained, new teachings were unfolded, lame bodies were made whole, blind eyes were made to see, deaf ears were unstopped, even dead bodies were restored to life as Jesus passed through the villages and the towns and the countrysides of ancient Palestine.

On this occasion a man unable to speak was miraculously healed by the Son of God. "When the devil was gone out, the dumb spake." Life was now given another outlet for this man, for he had been the recipient of divine power from Jesus Christ, the divine source of authority and power.

We do not know how long this man had been unable to speak, but we can draw the conclusion that he would use this new-found freedom, liberation, and deliverance from his handicap to glorify God the Father, for "God has made us," said Luther, "and our hearts are restless until they rest in Him." Our minds are restless until we learn to glorify Him, to magnify Him, and to sing His praises both night and day.

"The dumb spake." We do not know what he said, but we can imagine his first words were outbursts of thanksgiving and gratitude. All men who are helped by Jesus ought to speak kindly of him, to extol his virtues, to glorify his name, to give praise and honor for what he has done to make their lives more liveable, to make their lives more productive, to make their lives an inspiration for others.

The next statement turns our attention from the man to the people: ". . . and the people wondered." The people were in awe. The people were astounded. The people wondered. They wondered. They wondered about this lowly Galilean and his powers to remove this obstacle of dumbness, to loose the man's tongue, to give him freedom of speech. They wondered at the mysterious power encased in a nobody from the back-streets of Nazareth, who was born in a lowly stable of ordinary, poverty-stricken parents. Without formal, academic training,

The Helper of the Dumb—Part I   185

without medical knowledge, without having matriculated in any
of the medical centers of his day and time, this prophet from
Galilee had at his fingertips the authority and power to heal, to
help, and to relieve sickness and suffering and sorrow.

"And the people wondered." They still wonder. They are
still amazed. They are amazed at how God equips those whom
He sends forth with power and authority. We are today accustomed to institutionalized power and authority. Those who
have been trained in our medical centers are licensed to practice medicine. Those who have been trained in our legal centers
are authorized to practice law. Those who have been trained in
our educational centers are certified to teach in our schools and
colleges—and on and on we could go.

But there is a power beyond the institutionalized powers
created by man, and it is the power and authority which comes
from God. Man cannot institutionalize this power, nor can he lay
hold of it without God's approval. God dispenses this power
and authority in mysterious ways. Sometimes He endows
humble instruments with potentialities and possibilities which
allow them to function creatively, miraculously, and wonderfully
in His world.

Jesus had that authority and power, and with it he
demonstrated over and over again his unique, compassionate
nature, using it always for God's glory on man's behalf. He never
once violated this sacred gift from his Father. Never did he
misuse it for his own personal aggrandizement or recognition;
always did he use it for the advancement of his Father's
kingdom.

"And the people wondered." They still wonder. They are
still amazed. They are still startled when from the backwaters,
the backwoods, and the hellholes of our urban ghettos come
men and women, boys and girls with God-given powers to
shake the foundations of our society. Thus it was that a Martin
Luther King, Jr. could change the course of history with his exceptional and persuasive power of speech. Thus it was that a
Fannie Lou Hamer could rock the state of Mississippi, inspiring

multitudes to see its racist undersides. Thus it was that descendants of American slaves could start a movement in Greensboro, N.C., that was destined to move this nation into another era of brotherhood and goodwill. It has often been the case that God chooses the lowly, the underdog, the despised of this earth to do His will. They become His channels for moving toward the final consummation, when all of the kingdoms of this world will become the kingdoms of our Lord and of his Christ.

"And the people wondered." In the midst of that wondering, however, we find in verse 15 that there were those who wondered and yet misconstrued the facts. They said, "He casteth out devils through Beelzebub the chief of devils"—a sad commentary on the kind of mentality that manifested itself at a time when Jesus was relieving one of their fellowmen of a serious handicap.

Despite all of the positive deeds of Jesus, there were those who felt that he was in league with the devil, a representative of satanic forces. They were acknowledging the fact of Satan's power; and it is biblically sound, for the Bible, over and over again, shows Satan using his powers to thwart God's kingdom on earth.

Although they were wise enough to understand that Satan had great power, they were naive enough to believe that he could overpower Jesus. And so they accused Jesus of performing his miracles through Beelzebub, the chief devil, the arch devil, the head devil, the ultimate cause of all demonic activity on earth. They ascribed to Jesus a compact with this demonic force. They could not see beyond the kingdom of darkness to the kingdom of light. They could not raise their horizons from the kingdom of Satan to the kingdom of God. And they wanted more.

But notice that they did not want another healing. They did not desire that someone else be made whole. They wanted a sign from heaven. They wanted the stars to dance; they wanted the sun to cry; they wanted the clouds to disappear suddenly. They sought some spectacular cosmic event to delight their idle curiosity.

The Helper of the Dumb—Part I

"But [Jesus], knowing their thoughts, said unto them, Every kingdom divided against itself is brought to desolation; and a house divided against a house falleth." Here is the final clash that will take place at Calvary, the clash between Satan and his kingdom of darkness and Jesus and his kingdom of light. Wherever this confrontation exists, we find weakness and divisiveness, not only in our black ghettoes here in America but all over this nation and across our world.

Jesus, knowing that he was not in league with Satan, confidently told them, "Every kingdom divided against itself is brought to desolation; and a house divided against a house falleth." This brings to mind another revelation of Jesus. In John's gospel he says, "I and my Father are one." "He that hath seen me hath seen the Father." The Father, the Son, and the Holy Spirit all work together. There is unity. There is harmony. There is oneness. $1 + 1 + 1 = 1$ is the best theological thinking about the doctrine of the Trinity. They have power. They have authority. They have control of the kingdom of light.

Don't you want to enter this kingdom of light? It is an invincible kingdom that no one can ever overthrow, overpower, or destroy. Once in it you are safe from the fury without, even from Beelzebub and his dastardly demons of darkness.

Come into the kingdom of light! Come in today. Come in to stay. Come into this kingdom of light! Amen and amen.

The Helper of the Dumb
Part II

Continuing with the healing miracle of Jesus as recorded in Luke 11, we begin with verse 18. Jesus here continues to question his adversaries, those who accused him of consorting with the devil. He asks, "If Satan also be divided against himself, how shall his kingdom stand?" Jesus was saying to them that it was Satan that had the man's tongue immobilized so that he could not speak. It was never the intention of God that any kind of physical illness or handicap should inflict humankind, for God made Adam a perfect man, and they could walk and talk together in the beautiful Garden of Eden. But when Adam sinned, when he rebelled, sin entered into the world and brought with it decay, destruction, disease, and all kinds of maladies—and ultimately death. Paul put it succinctly: "The wages of sin is death." Sin promises us rewards that are beautiful, marvelous, everlasting; but eventually sin leads to death.

Jesus knew that Satan is not divided. He is together. He is as one. Isaiah 14 tells us that Satan was created an angel of light, but his overriding, selfish ambition caused him to exalt himself above God Almighty. This led to his expulsion from God's

The Helper of the Dumb—Part II

189

heaven; and ever since he and his angels were kicked out of heaven, there has been a clash between the kingdoms of light and darkness. It was Satan who made the suggestion in the garden to Eve that the fruit was good to eat. He, therefore, antedates Adam and Eve. And Satan is today alive, real, and active on planet Earth, still in the business of causing destruction, disease, decay, and death.

Jesus questioned the people further, "If I by Beelzebub cast out devils, by whom do your sons cast them out?" He seemed to be referring to others of his day who were also able to perform miracles and cast out devils.

In fact, at one time one of Jesus' disciples came across a man who was casting out demons, and this man was not a follower of Jesus. The disciple wanted to know if he should intervene. Jesus, in essence, said, "No, for he that is not against us is for us" (Luke 9:49, 50). He acknowledged that there were others outside of his ministry who were also endowed by God to use God's powers and God's authority miraculously. However, the people had not attributed to these men demonic and satanic motives—but they accused Jesus of them.

It is baffling how we react to the unknown, to the lowly, to the unlettered, to those outside the structures of organized religion. "Therefore," said Jesus, "shall they be your judges." "These people who have this power," he seemed to be saying, "shall sit in judgment on you, for they recognize that their authorities come from God. They do not attribute their gifts to Satan, but to God Almighty."

We, too, are prone to believe that those who are unusually endowed with gifts receive those gifts from some source other than God. We are often reluctant to recognize people to whom God has bequeathed exceptional gifts and talents. And if we do recognize them, we want to attribute the gift to an accident, not to divine choice. Yet God knows when, where, and to whom He wishes to bestow His gifts. He requires only that His name be glorified. "Therefore shall they be your judges." "They shall be your judges because you are not able to discern that the kingdom of God moves like the wind, whithersoever God wills it."

In verse 21 we read, "When a strong man armed keepeth his palace, his goods are in peace." They are safe; they are secure; a weak man cannot take them. In verse 22 comes the clincher, "But when a stronger than he shall come upon him, and overcome him, he taketh from him all his armour wherein he trusted, and divideth his spoils."

Note how Jesus used this earthly analogy to evoke the conflict that is occurring in the spiritual realm between Satan and God, between darkness and light, between Jesus on earth and the demons of sin. Jesus makes crystal clear his awareness that there is a war being waged. And he wants to assure us that his strength is able to keep the demons away. God has power, and He uses it to defeat the purposes of Satan. If God would allow it, Satan would usurp all of the power that God has. He would take it and divide it as soldiers do the spoils of war. He would ration it out among his many demons—his lieutenants, his sergeants, his corporals, his buck privates. Let us not be deceived: Satan has his army. Satan has his forces, and they are armed with weapons of violence and destruction. But thank God, God also has His weapons! Remember how He led His children out of Egypt, not with chariots and horses and soldiers, but with the elements and the obstacles He created—the frogs and the lice, the hail, the storms, a death angel and a stretched-out rod over the Red Sea.

Jesus went on to say in verse 23, "He that is not with me is against me: and he that gathereth not with me scattereth." Jesus knew that many people of his time were not with him, were not for him, did not follow him, did not want to become his disciples. He was well aware of this. And this is still true. There are anti-Jesus forces right now. There are ideologies that are alien to the thoughts of Jesus. There are isms that are alien to the thoughts of Jesus. There are religions that are actively seeking to destroy the Christian church and the influence and impact of Jesus Christ. They are arrayed against our Lord today, even as they were then.

The Helper of the Dumb—Part II

"He that is not with me is against me." For judgment he came into the world, and we stand judged when we do not acknowledge him as the Son of God. We stand condemned when we do not accept him as the Lord of our lives. He sits in judgment upon every heart that is stubborn, rebellious, hard, cold, and indifferent to his teachings, to his concept of love—love for all men of all colors, all races, and all classes. We are against him when we refuse to support him and his principles.

"He that gathereth not with me scattereth." Are we gathered here this day in his name? Are we singing in his name? Have we gathered to pray in his name? Have we gathered to teach in his name? Have we gathered to hear preaching in his name? Have we gathered to plead for the lost in his name? Have we gathered as one body in his name?

If we are not here this day in his name, we are scattered. Jesus is saying that we are useless for the kingdom if we have come because of form and fashion, full of sound and fury, signifying nothing. Why are you here? What is your motive? How answereth thou? O God, O God, let our motives be pure as we gather together in your name.

And so he moved on rapidly, for Jesus did not have much time. "When the unclean spirit," he said in verse 24, "is gone out of a man, he walketh through dry places, seeking rest; and finding none, he saith, I will return unto my house whence I came out." The speaker is Satan, the chief of demons, Beelzebub, the adversary, the evil one, the cruel one, the wicked one, the rotten one, the damnable one. He's unclean; he's untidy; he's unwholesome; he's profane; he's unkind to man's and woman's well-being.

How does he get into us? He's born in us. We are conceived in iniquity. We are congenitally more prone to evil than to good—to think evil, to act evil, to do evil, rather than to be good, to be kind, to be just. Jesus says that after God frees us, liberates us, disentangles us from Satan, Satan then leaves us and walks through dry places. He walks around looking for places to stay, lives to enter into, houses to dwell in, spirits to inhabit, souls to malign, minds to upset, eyes to blind, limbs to paralyze, legs to cripple, bodies to make miserable. He's seeking rest, looking for a place that is conducive to his style of thinking, his style of wickedness and rottenness and meanness, his style of devastation. He's seeking rest; he's seeking a hiding place.

And we are prone to accommodate him, to offer him the hiding place he's looking for, for we, too, sometimes love darkness more than light. All around us we see the awesome aura of darkness—in homes, schools, government, even in churches. We see the dying members of darkness engulfing our young men and women, the tragic plague of all kinds of dope and mind-altering drugs, unbridled sex, and filth peddled by those who walk in darkness along the streets of America on both sides of the tracks.

The great Reformation leader, Martin Luther, commented on the bondage of the human will. He said that man is either in bondage to God or in bondage to sin—that there is no middle ground. And yet we believe that somehow we can walk the middle ground between darkness and light. But it is either/or, either darkness or light. We are for God, or we are against Him.

Jesus said in verse 23, "He that is not with me is against me: and he that gathereth not with me scattereth." There it is! How can we gather with him? Here's how: Fill your life with good. Fill your life with beauty. Fill your life with righteousness. Fill your life with love. Fill your life with peace. Fill your life with the things of God. Fill your life with life—divine life. Fill your life with Jesus. Let him become an obsession. Go to sleep with Jesus on your mind. Wake up at the midnight hour with Jesus on your mind. Wake up early in the morning with Jesus on your mind. For he said, "I am the way, the truth, and the life." If our lives are filled with him, we have an inner, air-tight, burglar-proof insulation that Satan cannot penetrate.

"Greater is he that is in [us] than he that is in the world." Jesus drives out Satan. He drives him out, for the holy seed implanted in us at our conversion will not let the claims of God be

The Helper of the Dumb—Part II

destroyed, for that seed is holy and it grows in us mysteriously and wonderfully until we are wholly, totally sealed and delivered through the kingdom that is here in presence and one day will be here in power.

Our Lord continued in verse 25 with these words, "And when he cometh, he findeth it swept and garnished." He is saying that if Satan finds our house swept and garnished and bearing a "Not Welcome" sign for him, he is not deterred—he keeps coming and coming and coming again. He came to Jesus in the wilderness and for forty days and forty nights hounded our Lord. He tested Jesus; he tried Jesus in hopes of triumphing over Jesus, but Jesus had filled his life with fasting and prayer, with holy principles, and with God's will. Therefore, Satan could not enter into his house. He kept knocking and knocking and knocking, but there was no response, no entrance, no opportunity to come in.

And the Bible says, "He departed from him for a season." Satan flees momentarily, but he'll always come back. He fled from our Lord for a season, not permanently, and he did come back. But again he was defeated, for the divine hedge his Father had put around Jesus was still there, and Satan could not get in.

In verse 26 we read, "Then goeth he, and taketh to him seven other spirits more wicked than himself; and they enter in, and dwell there: and the last state of that man is worse than the first."

When Satan leaves one victim, he may return to him later or he may go to another. It seems as though he is not satisfied with entering a man and causing all kinds of chaos in his life, but "he taketh to him seven other spirits more wicked than himself." And when Satan releases these other, more damnable, spirits, they become uncontrollable like cancer cells and wreak havoc in the lives of their victims. Watch how the dope addict becomes a gambler, a robber, a murderer, a thief, a liar, a cheat. He begins at one level and ends at another, sometimes more tragic than the first. You can see it in the eyes of the demon-possessed. You can hear it in their quivering voices and see it in their shaking bodies, their wild, starry eyes, and their snorting noses. We see it as we walk through the institutions of mental illness. We see what Satan can do.

This agony, this pain, this misery is not God's will. It is the work of alien and unclean spirits that are taking possession of the lives of men and women. And when they enter in, they dwell there—morning, noon, and night. People get up—they dwell there; people lie down—they dwell there; people try to sleep—they dwell there; people try to eat—they dwell there. If we are not careful—and prayerful—our last state will be worse than the first!

I am glad the helper is here to help you and to help me. He is our Lord. He has come to set the captives free. This man's tongue was captive, but Jesus cut the tongue strings and gave to this man the ability to speak, gave to the man the means of human communication. He cast out the devil and let him go.

Go, man, and live! Go, man, and speak! Shout and sing! Lift your new voice in thanks and praise to your deliverer! Tell of his goodness to you. Speak in his name! Tell others what the Lord has done for you!

The Helper
Helps the Helpless

Jesus heals a "crooked woman" on the Sabbath
Luke 13:10-17

Patient/Diagnosis:
    A woman who was bent over, unable to straighten herself

Doctor:
    Jesus of Nazareth

Cure:
    "And when Jesus saw her, he called her to him, and said
    unto her, Woman, thou art loosed from thine infirmity. And
    he laid his hands on her: and immediately she was made
    straight, and glorified God."

Comments:
    This type of problem is seen today in two forms: There is a
    disorder of the spine called *kyphoscoliosis*, in which the patient
    is bent both to the side and forward. It is a chronic disorder,
    with no effective treatment. Also, paralyzed patients can
    develop gradually progressive contractures of muscles,
    causing the body or extremities to bend severely. Again it is

extremely difficult to correct this after this length of time (18 years).

> Dr. Joseph Blythe
> Pulmonary specialist
> Memphis, Tennessee

This exposition will center around a portion of Scripture found only in Luke's gospel—Luke 13:10-17. Its subject is "The Helper Helps the Helpless." The focus is on one of the many healing miracles of Jesus.

Luke begins the episode this way: "And he was teaching in one of the synagogues on the sabbath." We are not told where this synagogue was. There were many synagogues in Palestine; they were scattered about everywhere. And in these synagogues on every sabbath prayers were offered, and the Old Testament was read and interpreted by men of God. We find numerous biblical references to this practice. Alfred Edersheim tells us that the holy men of Jesus' day took seriously their responsibility to read the Scriptures and to hear those Scriptures expounded upon by other holy men.[1]

"And, behold, there was a woman which had a spirit of infirmity eighteen years, and was bowed together, and could in no wise lift up herself." We are not told that she was born this way nor do we know her age, but we do know that she had been a victim of this physical abnormality for eighteen years. There she was—a helpless, crippled woman; and there was Jesus, standing in the synagogue noticing her. Jesus, the helper, called her to him, initiating the healing process without the woman's asking for his help.

The woman's spinal curvature had caused her to bow, and it rendered her unable to lift herself up. None of us is able to lift ourselves by ourselves. We must all go to God and pray for His

---

1. Alfred Edersheim, *The Life and Times of Jesus the Messiah*, Book III (Grand Rapids, MI: Eerdmans Publishing Company, 1979), p. 432.

The Helper Helps the Helpless 197

capacity to lift us from whatever physical, mental, spiritual, and moral problems we face. We are helpless in our sinning; and sinful in our helplessness. We cannot lift ourselves. We need doctors when we are physically ill, and psychiatrists when we are mentally sick. We also need our lawyers, our teachers, and our dentists. We need all of those who are in the helping professions to lift us. But above all, we need the lifting power and authority of Jesus Christ.

This woman could not lift herself up. She could not stand erect. How she would have loved to stand straight and whole, healthy and sound and solid in the midst of the throng in the synagogue! She needed the helper who helps the helpless. And fortunately she was in his presence. Like many who are infirm, ill, or handicapped in some way, she did not cease coming to the Lord's house, for she remembered his promise to come with healing in his wings. Because she was in the synagogue, there is reason to believe that she had great belief in the sovereign power of God and faith that He would in His own time provide relief from her ailment.

And thus Jesus saw her. To be seen by Jesus, to be noticed by Jesus, to be observed by his keen, trained, powerful, glorious, healing eye is for all of us evidence of the great beneficent love of God. *He saw her.* No doubt there were others present with physical handicaps, but Jesus often singled out the most helpless and hopeless cases and selected them for the spotlight. So today this bent-over woman was the glaring example whom Jesus chose to experience his healing power and authority.

Then, ". . . he called her to him." Oh, to be summoned by Jesus! To be called into his divine presence! Why this woman was chosen we do not know, and Luke does not say, but the significant point is that she was chosen by him. Why? I think her being chosen by God is best left in the hands of God, and it is best that we do not ponder it or question it.

God in His freedom selects and elects those who will play a special role in His work, in His salvific enterprise. This woman had been called; she had been chosen by Jesus; and in this healing miracle we see his divine power, his holy power, his sovereign power at work. This power substantiates; it corroborates his resurrection claim: "All power is given unto me in heaven and in earth."

At the moment of this blessed confrontation, Jesus merely spoke the words, "Woman, thou art loosed from thine infirmity." There was no telling the woman to go wash in the Pool of Siloam, no making of a poultice from spittle and mud—only the spoken word of the Master Healer, "Woman, thou art loosed from thine infirmity." Divine power in action!

"And immediately she was made straight." After Jesus laid his hands on her and gave the command, the divine energy, the divine power, the divine healing current that flowed through his body from God his Father in heaven effectuated the cure. The touch of the Master's hands completed the cure.

Today, when he touches us, we can appreciate this beautiful piece of music that expresses fulfillment and joy:

> He touched me,
> Oh, he touched me,
> And oh, the joy that floods my soul;
> Something happened—
> And now I know,
> He touched me
> And made me whole.
> —William J. Gaither

We are told that the woman "glorified God" after she was made straight. This woman was not ashamed to praise God, to glorify God, to thank God. The psalmist admonishes us over and over again to praise God. In Psalm 147 he says, "Praise ye the Lord: for it is good to sing praises unto our God." Psalm 148 says, "Praise ye the Lord. Praise ye the Lord from the heavens: praise him in the heights." In Psalm 149 he says, "Praise ye the Lord. Sing unto the Lord a new song, and his praise in the congregation of saints."

The Helper Helps the Helpless

And this is exactly what this woman was doing, praising her God for His wonderful, personal, healing attention. Far too many people who have experienced God's healing and helping power in their lives are mute, fearful to praise Him, ashamed to say, "Amen," to thank God, to magnify His name. But not this woman—she glorified God; she thanked God; she praised God; she magnified the name of God. For her nights had been miserable; her days had been wretched. She had been looked upon in pity and sometimes in scorn. Every hour had been a miserable hour; every minute had been a miserable minute. But now, God had brought relief after eighteen years.

Let us now turn our attention to the onlookers, the spectators who had gathered there in the synagogue. Luke records that, "The ruler of the synagogue answered with indignation, because that Jesus had healed on the sabbath day, and said unto the people, There are six days in which men ought to work: in them, therefore come and be healed, and not on the sabbath day."

This was a challenge directed to Jesus, for he had effectuated this cure on the sabbath day. The synagogue ruler was attempting to uphold the judicial law given to Moses at Sinai: "Remember the sabbath day, to keep it holy." The interpretation of that law held that no work of any kind was to be performed on the sabbath, and the ruler felt that this healing miracle was an act of work. Thus, his indignation that the sacred institution of the sabbath had been violated.

Listen, now, to Jesus' response: "Thou hypocrite, doth not each one of you on the sabbath loose his ox or his ass from the stall, and lead him away to watering?" Jesus' response was an attempt to help the ruler and all of the religious leaders of that day to understand that the sabbath is like any other day *if* we help the helpless and provide assistance for anyone who needs it. Kindly deeds of helping sisters and brothers in need are acceptable to God on any day.

Nevertheless the ruler of the synagogue was dead serious when he explained that there were six days on which one could heal. "Come on one of those days," he said, "But not on the sabbath. Not on this holy day. Not on this glorious day. Do not come to be healed, to be helped on this day."

Jesus then referred to him as a "hypocrite," and put his question to them all: "Doth not each one of you on the sabbath loose his ox or his ass from the stall, and lead him away to watering?" In other words, they could attend to the needs of their beasts, but he could not help this poor woman on the sabbath.

Jesus was raising the level of human evaluation, which is far too often forgotten in our culture. Human life has been devaluated in our day and time all over the world. To raise the level of man's humanity to his fellowman is exactly what God sent Jesus into our world to do.

Jesus obediently carried out his Father's command. He dealt with lonely men and women in isolated places, one at a time in many instances, to show them that we are all our heavenly Father's children, and He loves us one and all. Once it was a lonely widow whose only son had died. Another time it was a lonely rich man up a tree, a tax collector named Zacchaeus. On another occasion an adulteress was forgiven of her sin. One night an inquisitive, brilliant rabbi named Nicodemus came at nightfall to inquire about Jesus' plan of salvation for his soul. And at other times, vast multitudes sat on mountaintops waiting to be taught, while others waited on the sides of hills as Jesus ministered unto them.

Jesus lifted the evaluation of our humanity. It would behoove our culture and society to hear again the value placed on us, regardless of and in spite of all our man-made barriers, by the penetrating question of Jesus, "Doth not each one of you on the sabbath loose his ox or his ass from the stall, and lead him away to watering?" Then Jesus delivers the punch line, "And ought not this woman, being a daughter of Abraham, whom Satan hath bound, lo, these eighteen years, be loosed from this bond on the sabbath day?"

If you can water your asses and your oxen on the Sabbath,

The Helper Helps the Helpless

isn't there a moral obligation where humanity is concerned? This woman is a daughter of Abraham, the father of the faithful. She is not an outsider. She is not a foreigner. She is not a stranger. She is a part of the household of Abraham. She has status and dignity in the eyes of God.

Then Jesus reveals the cause of the woman's infirmity: "... whom Satan hath bound." Many of us believe that Satan is not real, but biblical records abound with the fact of his existence. It was he who, in the form of a serpent, tempted Eve in the garden. In the Book of Job, one of the oldest books in the Bible, we find Satan present when the sons of God came together. Satan is there, throughout the pages of holy writ, though we may not be willing to accept the actuality of Satan. He is real and has to be dealt with.

The apostle Paul knew that there is something drastically wrong in our world and in our lives—that there is a power beyond us with which we cannot successfully cope unless we are armed with divine power. In Ephesians 6:12 Paul states, "For we wrestle not against flesh and blood, but against principalities, against powers, against the rulers of the darkness of this world, against spiritual wickedness in high places." There are powers of wickedness in high places that are more powerful than we are, more potent and more capable of causing human misery and anguish and agony. Paul was also personally aware of it. Remember his confession in Romans 7:24: "O wretched man that I am! Who shall deliver me from the body of this death?" "... when I would do good, evil is present with me" (Rom. 7:21). "For the good that I would I do not: but the evil which I would not, that I do" (Rom. 7:19).

Those who think that evil, Satan, and demons are not real are not honestly facing the evil in their own hearts, minds, and spirits. For there are times in our own lives when we too are like Dr. Jekyll and Mr. Hyde.

In this particular confrontation with the Pharisees, Jesus is stressing the point that institutional structures, rules, and laws cannot hinder the penetrating presence of goodness, the invasion of divinity, the intrusion of healing power and helping power into the lives of men and women, boys and girls. No corporate bodies, however sacred, are of more importance than human personalities.

In this healing incident Jesus lifts womanhood to its supreme status. "Ought not this woman . . . ?" "Ought not this black woman, white woman, Chinese woman, Japanese woman, Indian woman, Korean woman, Filipino woman, African woman—ought not she be the recipient of the highest and best that God offers, even on the Sabbath Day? Ought any block her? Ought any stop her? Ought any stand in the way? She is a daughter of Abraham and therefore has freedom of access to all of the blessings promised to Abraham's seed. I am that Promised Seed. I am that Eternal Seed."

"And when he had said these things, all his adversaries were ashamed: and all the people rejoiced for all the glorious things that were done by him." Jesus embarrassed the Pharisees, the ruler of the synagogue, and the other religious leaders who were there. They were ashamed, for they could not deal with Jesus. He was too wise for them. His interpretation of the law took a new turn. He came, as he said, not to destroy the law but to fulfill it. One man has said, "He came to fill it full."

I would like to say he came to expand the law. He came to push back the frontiers that had been encrusted with rabbinical hair-splitting, for there were more than 600 additional rules and regulations attached to the original Ten Commandments. Life at that time had become entangled with rules and regulations. They had forgotten that above the tables of the law that were placed in the ark were the cherubim; and above these was the mercy seat, indicating that God ultimately placed mercy over law.

Law is good. Law is necessary. But law must never take the place of mercy. God has said, "I desired mercy, and not sacrifice" (Hos. 6:6). So they were ashamed. Jesus had again outthought them. He had not only outthought them, but Jesus had outperformed them. They had the structures, but Jesus had ac-

The Helper Helps the Helpless

cess to the Source of the structures.

While his adversaries were ashamed, the people that were in the synagogue that day rejoiced. These worshipers gave God the glory. These worshipers reached beyond the structures, outside the normal processes of organized worship and gave to God the glory for what they had seen and heard. They had seen our Lord in action. They had seen our Lord perform, and they gave God the glory for the wonderful things that were done by His Son through Him.

The deliverer, the liberator, the Savior, the holy Christ, the healing physician had performed. He had done that for which he was sent into the world—to serve as a sign, as a symbol, as a source of God's power, never for himself, but always pouring out, giving out, and going out unselfishly on behalf of others. He performed miracles, and that is one way to be assured of followers. For as the old saying goes, "The saint who works no miracles has few pilgrims."

As Christ moved toward his appointment with death, he gathered pilgrims in ever-increasing numbers. They had seen him cast out demons, open blind eyes, unstop deaf ears, give life to paralyzed bodies, multiply bread, walk on water, stop bleeding bodies, and call back the dead. He is a miracle worker, I tell you! He is a miracle worker. He came to seek and to save that which was lost.

Here is the helper who helps the helpless. He is available to you this day. He is available to me. If we ask in faith, he will act. But beyond that, he acts in our lives each and every day. There are miracles all around us. Look! See! Hear! Feel!

Amen and amen.

Is It Legal to Heal and Help on the Sabbath?

Jesus heals a man with dropsy on the Sabbath
Luke 14:1-6

Patient/Diagnosis:
    A certain man with dropsy

Doctor:
    Jesus of Nazareth

Cure:
    "And he took him, and healed him, and let him go."

Comments:
    Greek, *hydropikos*, full of water.
                                    The Illustrated Bible Dictionary

If we can relate the term *dropsy* to modern medical terminology, we should recognize this patient as being in heart failure. Dropsy refers to swelling of feet, ankles, and legs. No doubt his abdomen protruded from accumulation of fluid in his abdominal cavity. His face also was probably puffy with discoloration of skin, sclera of eyes, and shortness of breath.

This could have originated from high blood pressure, kidney disease, etc. This patient appears to have advanced disease, and I doubt, even with modern therapy, he could have been saved.

Dr. Edwin W. Cocke, Jr.
Specialist in diseases of the ear,
nose, neck, and throat
Memphis, Tennessee

Dropsy is a term derived from the Greek word *hydor*, meaning water. Dropsy means an abnormal accumulation of fluid in the body, and has multiple causes including malnutrition and failure of a vital organ, such as the liver, heart or kidneys, to function properly. In modern times the condition may respond to medication to strengthen organ function or to powerful diuretics. Spontaneous cure of this type of malady would have been extremely unlikely.

Dr. Joseph Blythe
Pulmonary specialist
Memphis, Tennessee

Jesus, our divine Redeemer and divine physician, comes to grips with our problems. One of the most disturbing human problems is the problem of disease, sickness, and prolonged illness. So as we journey with him through the Gospel of Luke, we want to take special note of the instances in which Jesus used his divine power and divine authority to heal the bodies of men and women.

Jesus was the grand physician in every way. No disease was too devastating, and no illness was too slight for him. Jesus was willing and able to heal and help those who came to him in faith, hope, trust, and love. He responded with unshakable confidence in the God who sent him and the God he claimed as Father and Creator of the whole cosmic order. The Father and Creator claimed him as the Blessed One, the Son of God and the

Messiah of Israel. To him he gave authority and power to effect cures and healings and salvation for the whole world.

The case in point is a case which only Luke records. It is found in Luke 14:1-6. None of the other Gospel writers records this particular healing incident. Luke adds another story to this phase of our Lord's ministry. We are most thankful to Luke for giving us this brief but fascinating account. It focuses on the clash between Jesus and the Pharisees and Jesus' alleged disrespect for the sabbath. The sabbath was one of the basic institutions in Judaism. Jesus by his actions violated the canons of sabbath observance.

Let us look then at this passage with a keen analysis.

The story begins with this verse: "And it came to pass, as he went into the house of one of the chief Pharisees to eat bread on the sabbath day, that they watched him."

This passage is filled with much food for thought. Jesus was not accustomed to eating with Pharisees as houseguests. Pharisees were socially above Jesus, and they very seldom associated with the common people in Galilee. So there must have been some ulterior motive that prompted the invitation in the first place. They would not, under normal circumstances, have associated with Jesus.

Then, too, note that he was the guest of one of the chief Pharisees. This was no ordinary Pharisee who had invited Jesus to dinner; this was one of the leading men in the Jewish community. He was foremost among those who held the community together and on the right course. The right course, that is, as interpreted by rabbinic law and tradition. The host's influence was felt far and wide. Few in the community would question his authority and leadership.

There were about 6,000 Pharisees in the Jewish community in the time of Jesus. The object of this select body was twofold: to observe in the strictest manner and according to traditional law all of the ordinances concerning levitical purity, and to be extremely punctilious in those laws pertaining to religious dues—tithes and all other dues. Special requirements were laid

Is It Legal to Heal and Help on the Sabbath?   207

down for a man who would become a Pharisee, and not many were included in this elite group.

The man who invited Jesus to his house was one of the leading Pharisees. He had committed himself and his family to the principles of tithing and levitical purity. Such men were known as "traditionalists."

In light of this we can better understand why he invited Jesus to dinner on the sabbath. The Pharisees placed great stress on the sabbath observance. They sought to secure, negatively, absolute rest from all labor and, positively, to make the sabbath a delightful day.

Among some of the sabbath violations of the rabbis was sabbath desecration, which was considered one of the most heinous crimes and for which a violator could be stoned. They sought to make, by a series of complicated rules, a breach of the sabbath rest impossible.

On the other hand, they sought to make the sabbath a delight. Two of the special pleasures of the sabbath included special dress, the best that could be procured, and the choicest food, even though a man had to work for it all week.[1]

There was to be no tinkering with the sabbath. Any other day could be violated, even the great Day of Atonement, but not the sabbath. It was around this great day that the Pharisees rallied to justify their condemnation of Jesus. They felt that he was going too far and needed to be dealt with. Thus, Luke's interesting observation: ". . . they watched him." They were closely observing Jesus to see what he would do.

They were there, not so much for conversation as for controversy; not so much for cordiality as for contention; not as disciples, but as disrupters of the plans, purposes, and promises of God; not as companions, but as critics. They watched him closely. They had one hand on the table and the other hand under the table. They were there for mean and devious pur-

1. Alfred Edersheim, *The Life and Times of Jesus the Messiah*, Book III (Grand Rapids, MI: Eerdmans Publishing Company, 1979), p. 52.

poses. Jesus had said and done too much that was beyond their spiritual comprehension. This they did not like, and they were determined to get rid of him one way or another, by fair means or foul. Our Lord had to live his life under the glare of earthly critics, but he had the glow of heavenly approval. Ultimately this is what his life was all about.

While at the home of this Pharisee, Luke records that the Master was presented with a sick person. This time it was a man. "And, behold, there was a certain man before him which had the dropsy." Perhaps he was deliberately brought there to trap Jesus. The Pharisees were desperate. They wanted to see what Jesus would do on the most holy day in Judaism, the sabbath. Like a doctor, Luke gives us a diagnosis of the man's illness. He was a victim of what was once called dropsy, but today is referred to as *edema*. The term means that water has accumulated in the tissues of a person's arms or legs, blowing them up like balloons. This swelling is common to many sicknesses, often beginning at the ankles. In time it could bring death.

Luke does not indicate how the man got there. He does not tell us whether the man was standing or sitting, and these details are really not important. He just says, "There was a certain man before him which had the dropsy." This man was in the presence of Jesus. He was also in the presence of the Pharisees. The man was in a peculiar position, one which posed a dilemma for both him and Jesus. If Jesus healed the man, he would be guilty of violating the sabbath law, and the man would be guilty of accepting. Both would be trapped. But we must remember that the critics were not dealing with just another Palestinian preacher. They were face to face with the divine Son of God, the divine healer.

Jesus did not speak to the sick man first. Instead he turned to the lawyers and Pharisees and asked, "Is it lawful to heal on the sabbath day?" This was the same question the Pharisees asked Jesus in Matthew 12:10, "Is it lawful to heal on the sabbath days?" To this Matthew adds, "that they might accuse him."

Jesus did not ask this question to accuse them. He wanted to

Is It Legal to Heal and Help on the Sabbath? 209

get an answer from these religious leaders—an answer in keeping with their standing in the religious community of Israel. He raised a fundamental question with those who should have known the answer. "Is it lawful to heal on the sabbath day?" "Is it legal to heal on the sabbath day? Is it morally right to heal on the sabbath day? Is it permissible to heal and help on the sabbath? What say ye?"

Their answer was complete silence. Not one of these leaders of Israel said a word. "And they held their peace." Luke includes all who were at that dinner in order to trap Jesus. "And they held their peace." They would not say anything because they were determined to force the hand of Jesus. They wanted the evidence so that they could say they saw it with their own eyes. They wanted to make sure that they were not trapped in their own snare. So they held their peace. They did not want to get caught in the horns of a dilemma. This had happened several times to other shrewd men who had sought to trap Jesus.

There are many today who seek to trap Jesus in their little nets of silence and indifference. I would warn those who seek to trap Jesus. You, too, might find yourselves in the horns of a dilemma, for Jesus is untrappable and unstoppable. There are no man-made traps intricate enough to trap Jesus. You and I don't have the wisdom to trap Jesus. It would be better for us to have faith, trust, and hope in Jesus than to seek to trap Jesus and his church.

While they remained silent, Jesus took the man, healed him, and let him go. We are not told how Jesus healed the man. Luke does not share those intimate details with us. I wish he had.

One can accurately say that Jesus did not prescribe complete bedrest for the man. Neither did he prescribe a salt-free diet. Jesus possessed no dehydration pills to give the man. Whatever the problem, Jesus took care of it. Luke says, "he took him, and healed him, and let him go." Is this to say that the man was forced there against his will? I don't believe this to be the case.

When Jesus gets through with you, you can go. When Jesus

fixes you, you have been fixed. When Jesus completes the job, the job is well done. They said of him, "He doeth all things well." That is why Jesus said, "Come unto me, all ye that labour and are heavy laden, and I will give you rest."

Jesus gave this man rest from the painful swelling; rest from the long nights and hard days; rest from the burden of sickness; rest from the trials of pain; rest from the tribulations of misery; rest from loneliness and self-pity; and rest from the threat of death. Jesus let him go! Go back and live again! Go back and begin life over! Go back and pick up the pieces of your life! Go back and thrill at the rising of the morning sun! Go back and enjoy the golden sunset! Go back and worship in truth and in spirit! Go back! Go back! Go back!

After sending the man back into life and living, Jesus turned to his tormentors and detractors and said, "Which of you shall have an ass or an ox fallen into a pit, and will not straightway pull him out on the sabbath day?"

Jesus made a case for the saving of an ass or an ox. In Luke 13:15 he said, "Thou hypocrite, doth not each one of you on the sabbath loose his ox or his ass from the stall, and lead him away to watering?"

Exodus 23:4 stipulated, "If thou meet thine enemy's ox or his ass going astray, thou shalt surely bring it back to him again."

It is apparent from this passage that Jesus, the healer, saw the "rightness" of saving an ox on the sabbath. From a deeper perspective Jesus made a case for this act of mercy. In the thoughts of Jesus, persons have more dignity with God than barnyard stock. Therefore, Jesus placed his acts of healing above the institution of the sabbath. Thus, we can sing this glorious day and every day:

> Jesus loves me! This I know,
> For the Bible tells me so.

Jesus, Master, Help Us!

Jesus heals ten lepers
Luke 17:11-19

Patient/Diagnosis:
Ten men that were lepers

Doctor:
Jesus of Nazareth

Cure:
"And when he saw them, he said unto them, Go shew yourselves unto the priests. And it came to pass, that, as they went, they were cleansed."

Comments:
Leprosy is a bacterial infection caused by the organism *mycobacteria leprae*. The infection varies in severity from person to person. Without specific therapy the prognosis would be poor although some persons gradually lose signs of infection over time. Even with modern medical science, the instant cure described by Luke would be impossible.

Roger G. Smith, M.D.
Internal Medicine
Memphis, Tennessee

We have stated before, and we state again, that we must see Jesus as he saw himself. He saw himself as a divine physician: "They that are whole need not a physician: but they that are sick. I came not to call the righteous, but sinners to repentance" (Matt. 9:9-13; Mark 2:14-17; Luke 5:27-32). In these verses Jesus identifies himself as the Divine Physician who came into the world to cure the ills of men. He is able to cure the bodies and save the souls of men. He is a complete Savior.

In the mind of Jesus there was a close connection between the coming of the kingdom of God and the defeat of suffering, disease, pain, and even death. Because he was the herald of the kingdom of God, he was also the great healer of men, both of their bodies and their souls.

William Barclay has an interesting comment:

In the New Testament *soteria* is the word for salvation, and it is interesting and significant to remember that *soteria* was not originally a theological or specially religious word, but meant health, safety, and security in general.

In the private letter of the papyri we constantly find people writing to enquire about the *soteria*, the health and the welfare, of their friends and their loved ones. We find Epicurus using the word *soteria*, or welfare and security, quite generally. "The first measure of *soteria*," he says, "is to watch over one's youth and to guard against what makes havoc of all by means of pestering desires." The history of the word *soteria* makes it clear that the supreme bringer of it must be physician both of the bodies and the souls of men. Herophilus, one of the great Greek physicians, says:

Jesus, Master, Help Us! 213

"Science and art have equally nothing to show, strength is incapable of effort, wealth is useless, and eloquence is powerless, if health is wanting! True Christian salvation is salvation of body and soul alike."[1]

The healing miracles of Jesus played a vital part in his ministry. He was able to heal the mind as well as the body. All of his miracles were a part of that blessedness which he brought from his Father in glory.

Jesus was convinced that he was sent by God with special blessings and benedictions for men and woman. He said to the Jews in John's gospel, "Ye are from beneath; I am from above: ye are of this world; I am not of this world" (John 8:23). He proceeds to say to them further, "The works that I do in my Father's name, they bear witness of me" (John 10:25). He wants the Jews to believe in him, so he says to them with an almost desperate necessity, "If I do not the works of my Father, believe me not. But if I do, though ye believe not me, believe the works: that ye may know, and believe, that the Father is in me, and I in him" (John 10:37-38).

The works of God were manifest in the mighty deeds of Jesus in behalf of the sick, the lame, the mentally deranged, the blind, the deaf, and even the dead. He was and is a mighty worker of miracles—a miracle worker with might, skill, and power.

This should be remembered as we examine the works of Jesus as evidenced in the Gospels. Luke the beloved physician, was aware of the healing power in Jesus. He thus takes the time to record the details of those incidents as they were given to him and others.

Luke opens this incident with Jesus set on going to Jerusalem. He has Jerusalem on his mind. This was his goal. He

1. William Barclay, Jesus As They Saw Him (New York: Harper & Row, 1962), pp. 205-6.

would not be back in this area any more. Jerusalem was the place of his crucifixion and was also to be the place of his resurrection. Luke says, "And it came to pass, as he went to Jerusalem. . . ."

Most of us would not have gone to Jerusalem, had we known, as Jesus did, that it would be the place of our dying and death. We would have purposefully avoided Jerusalem. We don't want to face our dying ground. Somehow we prefer to get around those places where pain is in the offing. Not so with Jesus. Jesus' face was set like flint. "And it came to pass, when the time was come that he should be received up, he stedfastly set his face to go to Jerusalem" (Luke 9:51). The disciples could not stop him. He was marching to the beat of a distant drummer. The will of that drummer was foremost in the mind of Jesus.

> Behold, we go up to Jerusalem; and the Son of man shall be delivered unto the chief priests, and unto the scribes; and they shall condemn him to death, and shall deliver him to the Gentiles:
> And they shall mock him, and shall scourge him, and shall spit upon him, and shall kill him: and the third day he shall rise again (Mark 10:33, 34).

Most authorities say that the next phrase should be "passed along the frontier," instead of "through the midst of Samaria and Galilee." I concur with this idea, for it lends more credence to the fact that he was on the outer limits of the city of Samaria, and it is inconceivable that lepers would be quartered in the city. It is more likely that a leper colony would be located outside, rather than in the middle of, the city.

Verse 12 states, "And . . . he entered into a certain village." This seems to support the notion that Jesus was not in the middle of the province of Samaria, but on the edge or frontier of the province. It is important to locate Jesus at this particular time, for this illuminates what Luke seeks to do. He is attempting to give

Jesus, Master, Help Us!

us some details about the ministry of Jesus which will substantiate the universalism Luke sees in his healing and helping ministry. Luke's gospel has this universal emphasis. Therefore, to place Jesus in this area and to show that Jesus was willing to help those in Samaria would support the major theses of Luke's gospel. Jesus, for Luke, was to be "a light to lighten the Gentiles, and the glory of . . . Israel" (2:32).

As Jesus entered this village, "there met him ten men that were lepers, which stood afar off." This is very interesting. This is the first time we see ten persons of any sex, afflicted with any disease, approaching Jesus. Luke takes pains to say that there were ten men. Some scholars think that Luke enlarged upon the number given in Matthew 8:1-4, but there is no hard evidence to support this belief. However, one would suspect this, as Luke does use Matthew and Mark for other material.

Luke records that there were ten men who met Jesus. In the light of Jesus' concern for men, it is remarkable that so few men are willing to give Jesus first place in their hearts. This is noticeable in the Black community. Other religions and cults—old and new—are playing havoc with large numbers of Black men who once belonged to the community of faith. Consequently, the Black church has lost tremendous power as the direct result of the church's inability to appeal to a host of Black men.

Many reasons may be given, and some may be justified, but I suspect that this exodus from the traditional Black church calls men to a high commitment which demands total sacrifice, suffering, and service—a commitment that does not sanction weapons of force and violence. Our age glories in sensationalism, force, and power. For this sole reason, it is my contention that Jesus has lost his appeal to the masses of Black men. They prefer to take the road of violence, force, and destruction.

As Jesus entered the village, "there met him ten men that were lepers." These men must have been in a common leper colony, for theirs was a most devastating disease.

Hebrew laws held certain strict regulations concerning this

216   HELP ME, SOMEBODY!

dreadful disease. The law covering this malady is found in Leviticus 13 and 14. Deuteronomy 24:8 states: "Take heed in the plague of leprosy, that thou observe diligently, and do according to all that the priests the Levites shall teach you: as I commanded them, so ye shall observe to do." This affliction was very common in Palestine. The rabbis usually regarded it as a direct punishment for various sins, and though the law presupposes that it was curable, they said that its healing was as difficult as the raising of the dead. Lepers were shunned because they rendered the people of Israel unclean (Lev. 13:45, 46). It is believed that biblical leprosy included several skin diseases variously identified as contagious ringworm, psoriasis, leucoderma, and vitiligo (see Lev. 13:30). Also, this disease was thought to attack clothing and the walls of buildings, which indicates that it might have been due to a fungus (Lev. 13:47; 14:34).[2]

At any rate, it was a dread disease, and most people avoided those who were stricken with it. Lepers were isolated from community life and they lived a miserable and pathetic existence. Life was a living hell for them. Thus we can understand Luke's statement, "[they] stood afar off."

The lepers stood some distance away for three reasons: They were embarrassed because of their condition; they were horrible to look upon; and they were compelled by law to remain several paces from other human beings and cry, "Unclean! Unclean!"

Since it is believed that lepers were ineligible for forgiveness and forbidden to receive kindness, their only joy was to anticipate death! It is also possible that many people were extremely unkind to lepers, and so they feared exposing themselves to those who could inflict mental pain to accompany their physical pain. They were indeed a pathetic lot. Leviticus 13:46 states emphatically: "All the days wherein the plague shall be in him he shall be defiled; he is unclean: he shall dwell alone;

___

2. *The Interpreter's Bible*, Vol. VII, Matthew-Mark (Nashville: Abingdon Press, 1951), p. 338.

Jesus, Master, Help Us!

without the camp shall his habitation be."

There were others who stood afar off from Jesus, but because of spiritual leprosy. They were blinded by the most tragic disease of all. They saw—and did not see. They heard—and did not hear. They did not—and would not—accept the teachings of Jesus. Thus they stood afar off. Even some of his disciples stood afar off. They were not able to comprehend the lofty thoughts which Jesus came to bring to the minds and hearts of men. It was not until after the resurrection that they were finally convinced that Jesus was the Christ, the Son of the living God. After their baptism in the Holy Spirit, they went forth with new strength and new power, as flaming evangelists for their resurrected Lord.

Likewise, in our own day there are thousands who stand afar off. They will not come to Jesus and believe in his saving power and might. They refuse to surrender to the Jesus of history and the Christ of faith. They travel at a far distance from Jesus and his church. Thus, they are against him and his cause and crucify him anew in our day.

On the other hand, there are thousands who have accepted the way of Christ Jesus. They have decided to follow Jesus, and they will "never turn back no more." Hence, they sacrifice, suffer, and serve in the blessed name of Jesus. They are willing to be counted in that number who have already bowed the knee to him who is King of kings and Lord of lords. I count it a joy and privilege to be among that number. Ultimately, every Christian knows, or should know, that God will some day bring in that blessed moment when the kingdoms of this world shall become the kingdom of our Lord and of his Christ because,

> God also hath highly exalted him, and given him a name which is above every name: That at the name of Jesus every knee should bow, of things in heaven, and things in earth, and things under the earth; And that every tongue should confess that Jesus Christ is Lord, to the glory of God the Father (Phil. 2:9-11).

The men who were in misery must have heard about Jesus. They spoke with one voice. Theirs was a collective pain and misery. Therefore, they spoke with one voice. Luke says, "And they lifted up their voices, and said, Jesus, Master, have mercy on us." They lifted up their voices as brothers in pain. They sought a common solution for their problem. Their lives were polluted, and they needed a solution. They lifted their voices in pain and misery to the one who could relieve them of their wretched condition. Only Jesus could and would have the answer for their problem. They lifted up their voices to him.

The psalmist long ago knew that there are times in our lives when we must take our cases to God. He is our sure physician. He heals and helps those who are down and out. He heals the bodies of the least of the children of this earth. We must remember with the psalmist: "I will lift up mine eyes unto the hills, from whence cometh my help" (Ps. 121:1).

The psalmist, however, knew that it was not wise to look to the hills alone. There is no help in the hills *per se*. He is saying more than, "Look to the hills." He agrees with Jeremiah, "Truly in vain is salvation hoped for from the hills, and from the multitude of mountains: truly in the Lord our God is the salvation of Israel" (Jer. 3:23).

So the psalmist continues in the next verse, "My help cometh from the Lord, which made heaven and earth" (Ps. 121:2).

These ten men lifted their voices to Jesus, "Jesus, Master, have mercy on us." They used the word *Master* to address Jesus. Only in Luke's account is this word used. *Master* denotes a chief, a commander, an overseer. It is used by the disciples in addressing the Lord, in recognition of his authority rather than his instruction.

The name *Jesus* means Savior, deliverer, liberator, holy Redeemer. This was the name given to Joseph before Jesus was born. "And thou shalt call his name *Jesus*: for he shall save his people from their sins."

So when the ten men cried out, "Jesus, Master" they were asking for relief from one who had the power and the authority

Jesus, Master, Help Us!

from heaven to grant them relief. They had cried from the depths of their being to one who would and could hear their cry. Their cry sprang from a collective need in a desperate situation. So they cried, "Have mercy on us."

It is interesting to notice that they did not say, "Have mercy on *me*." They said, "Have mercy on *us*." Their common pain had driven them to want common wholeness. They knew the agony of that pain and did not want a single man to remain in that condition a day longer. If there was to be relief, that relief must be collective. They were brothers in pain. Now they wanted to be brothers in gain with healing and help from the God-man, Jesus.

It may be that God our Father would do more for us if our cries were for the whole world. It may be that our cries are too narrow and personal to gain much healing and help from God. God wants to help us all, and for the most part our prayers are self-centered and narrow and small. Hence, the God of heaven and earth is deaf to many of our pleas.

It may be that we should persist in prayer until we universalize our prayers. Our prayers must have cosmic dimensions before they can really move heaven and earth.

These men asked for mercy. Mercy is the outward manifestation of pity; it assumes need on the part of him who receives it, and provides resources adequate to meet the need on the part of him who shows it. These men needed mercy. They felt that Jesus had the resources to deal with their problem.

Jesus, as God's ambassador, was rich in mercy. He was like his Father. Paul says in Ephesians 2:4, "But God, who is rich in mercy, for his great love wherewith he loved us." Our God does not merely love us, but He loves us one and all. In Romans 10:12 Paul tells us, "For there is no difference between the Jew and the Greek: for the same Lord over all is rich unto all that call upon him."

The lepers called on the name of Jesus. They called him *Jesus*. Then they called him *Master*. They had said more than they really knew. This is also the case with us. When we speak the name of Jesus, we are really saying more than we know. His name is not just another name; it is the name which is above every name. It has power, and it carries weight with God and the angels in glory. It will carry authority and power and dominion until he delivers the kingdom to God our Father. One blessed day Jesus Christ will deliver the kingdom to God our Father. This is what Paul meant when he wrote:

> For as in Adam all die, even so in Christ shall all be made alive. But every man in his own order: Christ the firstfruits; afterward they are Christ's at his coming. Then cometh the end, when he shall have delivered up the kingdom to God, even the Father; when he shall have put down all rule and all authority and power. For he must reign, till he put all enemies under his feet. The last enemy that shall be destroyed is death (1 Cor. 15:22-26).

We might get more mileage out of a collective call than from an individual call. For when these ten men called Jesus, he saw them. Jesus took time from the journey to Jerusalem to hear their cry. He saw them. He saw their pain and misery and felt their agony. He heard the pathos in their voices. He heard from decaying bodies, rotting flesh, paralyzed hands, eyes which could no longer focus, limbs which were no longer mobile, and life which was hell.

Jesus heard them all. He still finds the time to hear us. The us-ness of our religion keeps us moving close to God-ness. Our us-ness gives us courage to move closer to the God-ness in him and love-ness in his bosom.

We love Jesus for his love-ness and God-ness. Jesus heard them and said to them, "Go shew yourselves unto the priests." Jesus said this, for only the priests could declare lepers clean. "This shall be the law of the leper in the day of his cleansing: He shall be brought unto the priest" (Lev. 14:2). Even though the highest priest was with them, he wanted them to obey the law of Moses. This would in no way contradict what Jesus did on other

Jesus, Master, Help Us!

occasions when the priests and Pharisees and Saduccees were against him. They needed to be certified as being healed, and only the priest could do this. He wanted them back in society. So he sent them to the priest.

Jesus also wanted to see if they would obey his command. He did not touch them. He did not say the healing word. He just told them to go show themselves to the priests. That was an act of authority which Jesus wanted them to obey. Obedience is still better than sacrifice. We, too, must learn to obey the word of Jesus.

"And it came to pass, that, as they went, they were cleansed." In obedience they found healing and help. They found something which they had been looking for for a long time. Now that blessed day had arrived. As they went, they were cleansed. They were made whole. They were healed. They were well. They were new men. They were new spirits. They were new souls. They were new hearts. They were new minds.

There must have been joy on that road. I know there was joy on that road. Ten men had been made whole. Ten men had a new lease on life. Ten men could enter the city with new vigor, purpose, and determination, as well as with new physical bodies.

This statement, "As they went, they were cleansed," suggests something deeper to me. It suggests that initial action is necessary for deeper meaning and deeper faith. The venture of faith grows as we go in the name of Jesus. Jesus sustains our growth and development as we obey him and do the will of his Father. I believe that this is what Jesus had in mind when he said in John's gospel, "If any man will do his will, he shall know of the doctrine, whether it be of God, or whether I speak of myself" (7:17).

Those men willingly obeyed the commands of Jesus and found on the way the road to healing, health, and new strength. The more we obey him, the more he reveals to us the Father's power and might. By doing what Jesus suggested, they became whole, healthy, well, healed. As we go in his name and at his word, more faith is possible, more love is assured, more grace is available, more power is ours, more hope opens up, more love develops, and the more God directs us. By going with Jesus, we become faithful, hopeful, and loving.

Moses did not know the power in the rod until he got to Pharaoh's court. David did not know the power in his sling until he met Goliath. Elijah did not know the power on Mount Carmel until he got there. Ezekiel did not know the power in the word until he preached in the valley of dry bones. Manasseh did not know the power of prayer until he became sick and prayed. The disciples of Jesus did not know the power in his authority until they returned from their first missionary journey. They were able to cast out demons and were unharmed by serpents and scorpions. The venture of faith requires that we first venture; then comes the power.

Now comes the hard part of this passage. As we read it, some disturbing thoughts arise in our minds. Nonetheless, we press on with the exposition. We trust and pray that God will give us some light along the way. We have come this far trusting only in what He gives. We are sure that He will illuminate the darkness.

Luke then tells us this: "And one of them, when he saw that he was healed, turned back, and with a loud voice glorified God."

This man did not forget the source from whence his healing came. The others were not ungrateful; they were doing exactly what Jesus told them to do. He sent them to the priests. But one returned to give thanks and glorify God. I believe that the others gave thanks, but they rejoiced as they went toward the temple. They were preoccupied with temple worship, not realizing that someone greater than the temple was in their midst. Jesus was greater then the temple; and while he never solicited gratitude from those he helped, he was prompted in this case to say something because of one who came back.

I suspect that all the rest were Jews; the one who came back was a Samaritan. In fact, Luke makes this plain: ". . . and he was

Jesus, Master, Help Us! 223

a Samaritan." This in itself was an achievement. Leprosy had driven Jew and Samaritan together into the company of misery. Normally, they would not have had any relationships with one another. Misery loves company! They had been driven together by their common misery, and therefore, all artificial boundaries and barriers were forgotten.

In times of great community stress people forget who they are and deal with each other on a more humane basis. It is sad that this is true; but frequently this is the case. We are more humane in times of stress and strain than in times of peace and tranquility.

When Jesus saw what had happened, he said, "Were there not ten cleansed? but where are the nine? There are not found that returned to give glory to God, save this stranger."

Jesus' question seems to suggest that he expected the others to return and give thanks. They had been together for a long time in misery. Now in their moment of joy, why did they divide themselves? Could there have been a division on the way which prompted the split? It is possible that this was the case. Racial pride and racial inclusiveness resurfaced as they went along the way. The Jews rushed to get to the temple, and the Samaritan, remembering that he would not be welcome, turned back to Jesus.

We do know that this can happen—that many people in times of crisis will act with kindness toward other racial groups. As soon as the turbulence subsides, they return to their old biases and traits and doctrines. This can be seen in the rise of hate groups in America. As long as things were at a high level of economic prosperity, racial feelings were muffled. Now that things are in a decline, old animosities are reviving themselves. Vernon Jordan is shot down by bigots in the night. Two young black men are ambushed and slain because they are jogging with two young white girls. Little men and little women are putting on white sheets and parading around with a great show of hate and ill-will.

The nine might have forced this man out of the fellowship by their attitudes. He returned to Jesus because he knew that there was understanding, compassion, and fellowship. He returned to Jesus to give thanks for his healing and help. Ingratitude is inbred and cannot flourish where it is watered by refreshing streams of gratitude. The nine might have believed that they merited God's blessing. The Samaritan might have felt that whatever Jesus did for him was a gracious act on the part of God. The Jews might have felt that they were supposed to receive healing power from God. Not so with this man. He knew that God had blessed his life, and he felt a keen need to say thanks to Jesus for what he had done for him. He counted this a special blessing which he would never forget.

We ought to count our blessings. God does bless us each and everyday. We ought to develop the habit of giving thanks to God for the many blessings which He sends into our lives. There is more mercy in God than there is thanksgiving in us. A grateful heart is hard to find. For gratitude grows out of an attitude which reaches upward daily. Our altitude determines our attitude. Jesus said to this one man as he fell to the ground in thanksgiving, "Arise, go thy way: they faith hath made thee whole."

The man's way from that moment on was the Lord's way. He would never turn around from that day onward. Jesus had pointed him heavenward, and the man would grow God-ward. The man had entered the way of the Lord Jesus Christ, and this way was the eternal way of wholeness and health. He had been delivered from the death pains of hell. He had been saved from the agony of earthly misery. He had been freed from the pains of constant bodily torture. He was in the way of the Lord. The Lord will "keep him in perfect peace, whose mind is stayed on thee." God will take care of His own.

Jesus also said to this man, ". . . thy faith hath made thee whole." Jesus came that we might have life and have it more abundantly. He came to create the climate in which we may have our faith activated. Our faith is dormant until Jesus comes into our lives and creates the spiritual soil in which faith can abide. It becomes activated when we repent, believe, and have faith in the Lord Jesus Christ.

Paul stated the case of faith in Jesus when he wrote to the Romans:

> The word is nigh thee, even in thy mouth, and in thy heart: that is, the word of faith, which we preach;
> That if thou shalt confess with thy mouth the Lord Jesus, and shalt believe in thine heart that God hath raised him from the dead, thou shalt be saved (Rom. 10:8, 9).

Paul further says to those who are confessors of Jesus Christ as Savior:

> For with the heart man believeth unto righteousness; and with the mouth confession is made unto salvation (Rom. 10:10).

This man, along with the others, called Jesus *Master*. That was the element in their cry which perhaps motivated Jesus to move with compassion on them. Theirs was an open cry of faith, hope, and trust. They saw the possibility of wholeness in Jesus, and that is all God desires. Their faint cry was enough to move Jesus and to move heaven. They came to Jesus in faith, and Jesus responded in love. In like manner men and women have always responded to Jesus in faith. A gifted songwriter composed with clear intent what motivates every believer:

> My faith looks up to Thee,
> Thou Lamb of Calvary,
> Savior divine!
> Now hear me while I pray,
> Take all my guilt away;
> O let me from this day
> Be wholly thine.
>
> May Thy rich grace impart
> Strength to my fainting heart;

My zeal inspire;
As Thou hast died for me,
O may my love to Thee
Pure, warm, and changeless be,
A living fire.

While life's dark maze I tread,
And griefs around me spread,
Be Thou my guide;
Bid darkness turn to day,
Wipe sorrow's tears away,
Nor let me ever stray
From Thee aside.

When ends life's transient dream,
When death's cold, sullen stream
Shall o'er me roll,
Blest Savior, then, in love,
Fear and distress remove;
O bear me safe above,
A ransomed soul. Amen.

—Ray Palmer

Jesus, Son of David, Help Me!

Jesus restores a blind man's sight on the way to Jericho
Luke 18:35-43

Patient/Diagnosis:
A man who was blind

Doctor:
Jesus of Nazareth

Cure:
"And Jesus stood, and commanded him to be brought unto him: and when he was come near, he asked him, saying What wilt thou that I shall do unto thee? And he said, Lord, that I may receive my sight. And Jesus said unto him, Receive thy sight: thy faith hath saved thee."

Comments:
Blindness was common throughout the Middle East in biblical times. It is probable that several different diseases were responsible. Trachoma may have been common then, as it still is in some parts, causing blindness in infancy.

Gonorrhea in the mother can affect the eyes of the children during their birth and lead to blindness.

The Illustrated Bible Dictionary, p. 617

We have seen the divine physician at work as we have followed him through the Gospel of Luke. We have seen him use his healing powers on more than one occasion for those who needed his help. He was willing and ready to help those who sought wholeness.

We have witnessed our Lord master some of the most difficult cases known to his day and time. None proved too baffling for Jesus. He was master of every condition and situation. He was, as I have said before, a general practitioner who specialized in changing things which seemed impossible. The impossible became possible in his hands. The possible became realized as wholeness, health and restoration were given to those who were blessed to come into the presence of his glory and power.

We have sought to base our case on the fact that there is a sound basis for Christian healing in the life of Jesus our Lord and thus in our world today. We believe that the supernatural invaded the natural in Jesus of Nazareth. He brought with him all the powers of heaven for healing and helping the sick, the lame, the blind, and the maimed. Jesus' first exposition of Scripture in the Gospel of Luke bears testimony to this fact: "He hath sent me to heal the brokenhearted." There is nothing in life which breaks the heart of man more sorely than an unhealthy body.

The healing miracles of Jesus were not mythological as some would contend. They were a part of that great, grand, and glorious ministry of our Lord designed by God before the foundation of the world. They manifested the power of God's might and God's glory.

Now we come to a healing miracle in the Gospel of Luke that is filled with the mystery of God's ways in His world for the benefit of men and women.

Jesus, Son of David, Help Me!

Luke records this miracle by beginning with a familiar introduction, "And it came to pass." He indicates that a period of time had elapsed between the time of this incident and a previous happening in the life of Jesus. He is unable to give us the exact time period. He uses this formula over and over again.

It should be noted that in the lives of each of us time passes, and we seldom realize that time is passing. This is why it is so difficult for us to commit ourselves to work while it is still day. We are prone to believe that we have an unlimited amount of time. We cannot believe in the mortality of our beings.

This was not the case with Jesus. He was aware of the fact that his time was limited. This fact can be borne out by the incident noted in the early accounts of his life. In the temple at age twelve, he was conscious of time and its meaning for his life and work. He did not let time use him; he used the time and used it wisely for the lifting of men and women from the quagmires of sin and degradation.

Luke goes on to tell us the place of this miracle, which helps in our understanding of the movements of Jesus as he journeyed towards Jerusalem. Luke says, ". . . that as he was come nigh unto Jericho." This ancient city was known as the "city of palm trees" (Deut. 34:3; Judges 1:16; 3:13). The word means "place of fragrance."

Jesus apparently had passed this way many times and had known about this city. Some believe that the temptations of Jesus might have taken place in the forbidding mountains above this city. To reach the reputed place of his baptism, he must have passed through the streets and villas of this town. Jericho had a long and illustrious history. It was the first city captured by Jesus' people from the Canaanites many centuries before.

Just as Jesus came near this city, Luke records that, ". . . a certain blind man sat by the way side begging." Matthew says that there were two men, one of whom was called Bartimaeus. Mark states that there was one blind man and that Jesus healed the man on the way out of the city. Luke does not give the man a name; he implies that Jesus was just entering the city. But we must not quibble over details. All we need to know is that Jesus healed a man—or men—who was begging.

The world is bad enough when seen with good eyesight. To live without sight is worse than most of us can imagine. Blindness is a living prison. Milton said of his blindness, "That one Talent which is death to hide, Lodg'd with me useless. . . ."

Most of us who have sight cannot imagine what is is like to be unable to awaken and see the brilliance of the shining sun. Nor are we aware of what it is like to live and not see stars dancing across a black velvet sky, red and white roses blooming in May, falling petals of snow, and little children at play. We have two shining jewels, bequeathed to us by God. We have two eyes, and we can see. Not so with this man on the Jericho road. He could not see, and he was a beggar.

Nothing is more demoralizing to the human spirit than to spend one's days begging. But this was all the blind man could do. He could not work, and therefore, sat on the roadside begging for a handout. Those who have to live this way are never the men and women they might be. For no sane man or woman wants to be a beggar. We like to feel that we can earn our bread, as the Bible says, "by the sweat of our brows." This adds dignity to our efforts and pride to our undertakings.

This might be the point where we have gone astray in our efforts to help people. Our welfare systems do not speak to the heart of the problem of the poor. Our systems should be designed to get them on their feet so that they can walk tall like men and women—not crawl and grovel like animals. Our systems rob men and women of their right to exist as human beings with potentials and possibilities as contributing citizens in gainful employment. Any system which stifles human aspirations is dead and ineffective.

This blind man sat there begging, and in the midst of his begging he heard a noise. He actually heard the thunderous feet of desperate men and women who were following Jesus. Luke states the case this way, "And hearing the multitude pass by, he asked what it meant."

Throughout the Gospel records, we find Jesus frequently beseiged by the multitude. There were times when he had to retire from the crowds in order to renew himself and teach his disciples. But we can understand the motives of the crowd. Jesus had everything they needed. There was no need to look further. However, most of them did not understand that Jesus was not just another miracle worker sent by God to give demonstrations of healings. That was merely one part of his work. The greater part of his work was designed to bring men and women into the kingdom of God.

Although the blind man could not see, he was not deaf. He could hear the tramp, tramp, tramp of marching feet. Some say that when one of the five senses is taken away, the others increase in efficiency. This man *heard* the crowd though he could not *see* it. At least he could hear. There were, and still are, those who could see yet not see, and those who could hear yet not hear. But the cause of Christ goes marching on. Will *you hear?* Do *you see?*

The blind man not only heard what was going on, he wanted to know what the noise meant. His day had been interrupted by an unusual amount of noise, more than the normal level for him. Unaccustomed to this amount of noise, he naturally wanted to know what it meant. Little did he know that by raising this question, he was laying the groundwork for his recovery and healing.

Sometimes it is good to raise questions. Questions often help physicians and others in the healing professions to understand our problems better and to alleviate them more quickly.

When the blind man asked, "What does this mean? Why all this noise?" he was told, "Jesus of Nazareth passeth by." Their answer was the key to his problem, the solution to his midnights that had become blighted and blurred. They gave to him the key which was to unlock the door of God's redeeming power.

God is a hearing God. "Ask, and it shall be given you; seek, and ye shall find; knock, and it shall be opened unto you: For every one that asketh receiveth; and he that seeketh findeth; and to him that knocketh it shall be opened" (Matt. 7:7, 8).

Just as those in that crowd told the man that Jesus was passing by, we in our day should tell this good news to those who do not know that Jesus is still passing by. He is still on the move in our world and in our lives. "Lo, I am with you alway, even unto the end of the world." Jesus is with his church. Jesus is with those who have confessed him as Lord and Savior. He is still passing by, seeking souls in distress, hearts that are broken, and lives that are desperate. Jesus was passing by *then*; Jesus is passing by *now*.

Have you ever told anyone in a desperate condition that Jesus is still on the move and doing great things for the kingdom which is here, there, and everywhere? Have you shared the good news about him with a hungry soul in search of salvation, redemption, and release? Have you tried to win someone for the man from Galilee? Have you been a witness in your home, school, factory, office, community, or church? If you have not, you have denied the man who was sent into the world with this bold and liberating message:

> The Spirit of the Lord is upon me, because he hath anointed me to preach the gospel to the poor; he hath sent me to heal the brokenhearted, to preach deliverance to the captives, and recovering of sight to the blind, to set at liberty them that are bruised,
> To preach the acceptable year of the Lord (Luke 4:18, 19).

If you tell someone that Jesus is passing by, you have done your work. That is all you can do. You and I cannot force people to love Jesus and to accept what he has to offer. One has to respond on his or her own free will. Jesus is the gospel, and the gospel is Jesus. He *is* what he was, and he *was* what he is. He combines the dimensions in his being, bringing with him both salvation and condemnation, judgment and justification, inclusion and fellowship, exclusion and separation. John expressed it beautifully:

Jesus, Son of David, Help Me!

> For God so loved the world, that he gave his only begotten Son, that whosoever believeth in him should not perish, but have everlasting life.
>
> For God sent not his Son into the world to condemn the world; but that the world through him might be saved.
>
> He that believeth on him is not condemned: but he that believeth not is condemned already, because he hath not believed in the name of the only begotten Son of God.
>
> And this is the condemnation, that light is come into the world, and men loved darkness rather than light, because their deeds were evil (John 3:16-19).

After hearing that Jesus was passing by, it was up to the blind man to follow through on the information that he had been given. He could not see, but he could hear. We are not able to see salvation. "Salvation," says Paul, "comes by faith."

You can be blind yet have faith. Faith comes by hearing the Word of God. In Romans 10:17 Paul tells us, "So then faith cometh by hearing, and hearing by the word of God." The Word of God is none other than Jesus of Nazareth. John focuses our attention on this profound idea with these majestic words: "In the beginning was the Word, and the Word was with God, and the Word was God" (1:1). Referring to Jesus as the Word, John continues, "and the Word was made flesh, and dwelt among us, (and we beheld his glory, the glory as of the only begotten of the Father,) full of grace and truth" (1:14).

The blind man heard, and his faith surged forth in melodious tones like the ones set to music by Fannie J. Crosby:

> Pass me not, O gentle Savior,
> Hear my humble cry,
> While on others Thou art calling,
> Do not pass me by.

Savior, Savior, Hear my humble cry;
While on others Thou art calling,
Do not pass me by.

Let me at the throne of mercy,
Find a sweet relief;
Kneeling there in deep contrition,
Help my unbelief.

Trusting only in thy merit,
Would I see thy face;
Heal my wounded, broken spirit,
Save me by thy grace.

Thou the spring of all my comfort,
More than life to me,
Whom on earth have I beside thee?
Whom in heav'n but thee?

That was the surge within. For faith begins from within. It is an inward journey which leads to an outward expression of action and commitment. The blind man cried out loud, "Jesus, thou son of David, have mercy on me."

The lepers, as you recall, called Jesus "Master." The blind man called him "son of David." This is very interesting. This idea had a long history in the traditions, customs, and expectations of the Jewish people. It was to David that God made this promise: "Thine house and thy kingdom shall be established for ever before thee: thy throne shall be established for ever" (2 Sam. 7:16). It was on the mind of every Jew that God would one day restore to his people a blessed age like the one in the time of David. The most persistent idea was that one day God would send the Messiah from the house of David, restore the kingdom, deliver his people, and lead them to national power and prominence. This was their dream. This was their hope. This was their great expectation.

Jesus, Son of David, Help Me!

This idea can be found in the works of some of Israel's most prolific writers. Isaiah says:

> Of the increase of his government and peace there shall be no end, upon the throne of David, and upon his kingdom, to order it, and to establish it with judgment and with justice from henceforth even for ever (9:7).

Jeremiah had the dream:

> Behold, the days come, saith the Lord, that I will raise unto David a righteous Branch, and a King shall reign and prosper, and shall execute judgment and justice in the earth (23:5).

Amos writes with a similar hope:

> In that day will I raise up the tabernacle of David that is fallen, and close up the breaches thereof; and I will raise up his ruins, and I will build it as in the days of old (9:11).

It was also the dream of Ezekiel:

> I will set up one shepherd over them, and he shall feed them, even my servant David; he shall feed them, and he shall be their shepherd.
> And I the Lord will be their God, and my servant David a prince among them (34:23, 24).

Time changed the thinking of those who felt that this dream would not come true. They projected their hopes to one who was superhuman, or they looked toward the day when God would intervene on behalf of His people. Thus, the idea took on apocalyptic tendencies. But in the popular mind, the people looked forward to a descendant of David, who would save them from their oppression.

In the New Testament, Jesus is referred to as the Son of David. At the very beginning of his Gospel, Matthew says, "The book of the generation of Jesus Christ, the son of David" (1:1). The angel's promise to Mary in Luke's gospel is that the Lord God will give to the child she will bear "the throne of his father David" (1:32). Paul speaks of Jesus as one "which was made of the seed of David according to the flesh" (Rom. 1:3).

The masses of the people were waiting for the Messiah, who was the Son of David. John 7:42 asks, "Hath not the scripture said, That Christ cometh of the seed of David, and out of the town of Bethlehem, where David was?" In many other passages in the Gospels Jesus is addressed as the Son of David. He was so called by two blind men (Matt. 9:27); by the masses when he healed the blind and dumb demoniac (Matt. 12:23); by the Syro-Phoenician woman (Matt. 15:22); by the blind man in the current text (Luke 18:38); in other references to blind men (Matt. 20:30, 31; Mark 10:47, 48); by the crowds in the streets of Jerusalem (Matt. 21:9); and by the children in the temple courts (Matt. 21:15).

However, it should be noted that on one occasion, Jesus took exception to that title. It is my belief that the title was not enough to explain Jesus or to interpret who he was, is or will be. Jesus was more than that title or any title man could give him. He was the Son of David by physical descent and by the fact that all Messianic hopes and promises were fulfilled in him. But Jesus accepted that title and all other titles which people conferred on him and transcended them all. He gave to every title a new dimension which had more potentiality and more possibility than ever conceived by the mind of man.

This blind man's appeal was for an act of mercy on the part of Jesus. He pleaded, "Have mercy on me." This was a sincere and private concern. His blindness had numbed him to the needs of others. He was determined to get help from the helper of helpers. He cried, "Have mercy on *me*." He was not re-

Jesus, Son of David, Help Me!

questing help for others. He saw and knew only his own personal and private need. His blindness was more than he could bear. He wanted to see again. One might argue from both points of view, but it does not matter: the man was blind and wanted to see. He was sick and wanted to be well. He was broken by blindness and wanted to be whole. He was handicapped and wanted to overcome his handicap. He was disabled and wanted to defeat his disability. He was defeated, deflated, and depressed. So the man cried, "Have mercy on me."

Now the sad part of this passage comes to us like a bolt out of the blue. The people going up to Jerusalem with Jesus were very unkind to this blind man. They tried to stop him from calling on the name of Jesus. They had their sight; they could walk; and they were experiencing the joy of making the pilgrimage to Jerusalem at the Passover season. Luke is very blunt. He says, "And they which went before rebuked him, that he should hold his peace." They did not want the afflicted man to interrupt the agenda of Jesus as they went toward the city of Zion, the city of David. They wanted peace so that they might hear, and hear well, the word of the Master.

This was well, very well indeed; but they forgot one important thing: Jesus came to save the sick and the lost. They forgot that they could not put a fence around Jesus and keep this man from the healing resources of Jesus. They forgot that they had no monopoly on the mercy, pity, compassion, and love of Jesus. They forgot that Jesus was not theirs to have and to hold for themselves alone.

Jesus came for the whole world. He came to all men and all women. We cannot and dare not think that we have a special corner in the heart of Jesus. We must never make the mistake of thinking that we have somehow fenced Jesus in with our narrow minds and little hearts. Jesus is never too busy to hear a sincere prayer. He is never too tied up to answer an earnest plea. He is never too committed to instruction and teaching that he cannot stop to answer the pathetic cry of one of the children of God, "Have mercy on me."

I am grateful that Luke recorded the fact that this helpless blind man paid no attention to those who told him to hold his peace, "but he cried so much the more, Thou son of David, have mercy on me."

Ebonsen is the word used in verse 38; it denotes an intelligent cry for help. In verse 39 the Greek word *Ekrazeh* is used. The classical Greek word, *Krazo*, is often an instinctive cry or scream, a loud expression of strong emotion, sometimes used to refer to the cries of animals.

There are always folks who think that our call to God must be highly intelligent, that our verbs and words must be in perfect order before God will hear us. But God can hear your cry, even if you don't know a verb from an adjective or a noun from a pronoun. What God wants is a clean heart and a sincere, humble, contrite spirit. He wants not only our heads but our hearts as well.

Then there are folks who want to keep other folks quiet when they are speaking to or hearing from Jesus. They don't want too much noise around them, yet they live in the midst of noise each and every day. When they come to church, they become confused when folks say, "Amen!" "Preach the word!" "Tell the truth!" "Help yourself!" "Yes! Yes!" or "Glory! Glory!"

If you want a hearing from the Lord, keep asking! Keep on seeking! Keep on knocking! God is not deaf to your earnest plea. Call His name, and tell Him about your trials and tribulations. Call on the name of the Lord!

The blind man screamed in a loud voice, "Thou son of David, have mercy on me." "Thou son of David, have mercy on me." "Thou son of David, have mercy on me." Each time he cried, "Have mercy on me" his scream could be heard above the tramp, tramp, tramp of dusty feet along the Jericho road. His voice went from a low bass black to a white treble clef. His desperate cry shook the palm trees and the olive trees and bombarded the ears of those who walked with Jesus. "Son of David, have mercy on me."

The desperation in his voice was enough to stop the lowly

Jesus, Son of David, Help Me! 239

Galilean. Jesus was on his way to the cross, but he was not yet there. This cry he heard was desperate and worthy of an immediate response. So Luke gives to us a vivid account of what Jesus did next: "And Jesus stood, and commanded him to be brought unto him: and when he was come near, he asked him. . . ." When Luke says, "And Jesus stood," he is really saying that Jesus *stopped.* Jesus was walking with the multitude on the road that led to Jerusalem. Jesus stopped. When Jesus stops, something wonderful happens to those who call on his name. When Jesus stopped, he commanded that the man be brought to him—a most blessed response to the man's cries and pleas. Jesus was willing to stop what he was doing to hear what this man had to say. Jesus had heard that awful, howling, pathetic cry. It spoke to the very depths of his being. Jesus detected in that plea a serious and sincere desire to be made whole and healthy. The man's persistence was evidence enough that he wanted to be made well. He did not let the people stop him from appealing to Jesus, the Savior of men. The crowd wanted him to be silent, but he wanted to be heard.

The people spoke negatively to him, but he acted positively to the faith in himself and Jesus. The crowd is always wrong when it comes to Jesus. They will put us down, but Jesus will pick us up. They do not know. Jesus knows all the answers and has the answer to our problem. The crowd is filled with crowd psychology, thinking logic, and rationalizations. Jesus, on the other hand, is filled with faith, hope, and love. Jesus stands in lonely opposition to the crowd and says, "Follow me!" He calls us to knock in the dark. He calls us to ask without seeing. He calls us to seek, not knowing what we will find. He calls us to ask, believing that it will be given to us. He calls us to hear the words of healing, wholeness, and wellness. He calls us to activate the faith dormant in our hearts. The hymnist wrote with holy insight:

> Jesus calls us; o'er the tumult
> Of our life's wild, restless sea,

Day by day His sweet voice soundeth,
Saying, "Christian, follow me."

Jesus calls us from the worship
Of the vain world's golden store,
From each idol that would keep us,
Saying, "Christian, love Me more."

In our joys and in our sorrows,
Days of toil and hours of ease,
Still He calls, in cares and pleasures
"Christian, love Me more than these."
—Mrs. Cecil F. Alexander

So they brought the man to Jesus. This was the best place to be on that road on that day, for Jesus is the real source of healing and wholeness. Health is found in his presence. There we can find strength for the day and light for the journey. They brought him to Jesus. They brought the man so far, and then it seemed as though the man went the rest of the way by himself. For it says in the passage, ". . . and when he was come near. . . ."

There is just so much that others can do for us. The Christian religion is personal and private in conviction, commitment and consecration. We have to come to Jesus for ourselves. Others might bring us to the church, but we have to enter the church ourselves. We can be in the church and never *really* be in the church. We can have our minds stayed on other things. We can be in the presence of Jesus and never know the joy of his saving power and grace. Jesus said, "And ye will not come to me, that ye might have life" (John 5:40).

The closer we get to Jesus, the more clearly we can hear his sweet voice. I believe this is why John stayed close to Jesus' breast. John could write five books when most of the other disciples could write only one or two; some wrote nothing. John stayed close to Jesus. Jesus poured into his head, mind, and heart deep and eternal truths which John was able to pass on to the next generation. We today benefit from John's closeness with Jesus. We ought to stay close to Jesus. This is why I love to sing:

> O, for a closer walk with God,
> A calm and heavenly frame,
> A light to shine upon the road
> That leads me to the Lamb!
> —William Cowper

Every now and then, I love to raise my voice with another writer who said:

> O Master, let me walk with Thee
> In lowly paths of service free;
> Tell me Thy secret; help me bear
> The strain of toil, the fret of care.

> Help me the slow of heart to move
> By some clear, winning word of love;
> Teach me the wayward feet to stay,
> And guide them in the homeward way.

Teach me Thy patience! still with Thee
In closer, dearer company,
In work that keeps faith sweet and strong,
In trust that triumphs over wrong.
> —W. Gladden

The man came near to Jesus. Then Jesus asked him, "What wilt thou that I shall do unto thee?" The man had called Jesus. Now Jesus wanted to know what he most desired. Jesus was actually extending an open account to this man. He had unlimited credit with the healing doctor from glory. "What do you want? What is your desire? What can I give you? What do you want from the storehouse of God? What is your deepest and most earnest wish? Do I have something you want? Do I have what you are looking for? Am I able to help you? What is your wish, blind man? You have called on the Son of David, and so I am. Now that I am with you, and you with me, what do you want? Name it and claim it!"

This blind man had been sitting at this wayside for many years begging. He had to think, because if he asked for sight, it would mean a drastic change in his lifestyle. He could no longer beg for a living. He would have to get a job and work. This was a crucial question that Jesus asked of this man. What would it be? Thanks be to God, the man was ready with a sound and solid answer: "Lord, that I may receive my sight."

"I want to see the golden sunrise and sunset! I want to see the fullness of the moon! I want to see the twinkling of a thousand stars! I want to see the blue of the sky! I want to see the green grass of the meadows! I want to see the cattle on a thousand hills! I want to see sheep by still waters! I want to see the lilies of the valley! I want to see the palm trees of Jericho! I want to see wild olive trees! I want to see little children playing ring-around-the-roses! I want to see the City of David! I want to see the daughters of Abraham! I want to see men cultivating the uplands! I want to see the tomb of David! I want to see the temple in Jerusalem! I want to see the employment office! I want to see the pilgrims walking with you!

"Son of David, I want to see! Son of David, have mercy on me! Let me see! Help me! Cure my blindness! Lord Jesus, I want to see your face and behold the beauty of your countenance. I know that some sing, 'All I want up in glory is just to behold his face!' but I want to see your blessed face right now. Let me see your face and gaze on those holy eyes which can sympathize with the lame, broken, maimed, crooked, brow-beaten, and bereft. Yes, let me see your blessed face!"

The man's request was within the realm of possibility. He believed that Jesus could cure him, and Jesus knew that he could cure him. What is impossible with man is possible with God.

Jesus, Son of David, Help Me!

Jesus is the God-man and thus has that divine capacity to heal, help, and provide hope for the hopeless. When one is reaching upward and God is coming downward, a climate for healing is made possible by faith. Jesus then said to the man, "Receive thy sight: thy faith hath saved thee."

The blind man's faith had been his trust factor all his life. It had been his trust in the dark. He could not make himself whole, but he could and did call for wholeness when it came near. He called in a loud and desperate voice. And Jesus heard that cry. Now Jesus had answered that cry and given him light and a new lease on life. "Receive thy sight: thy faith hath saved thee."

Luke is very clear at this point in the account. He gives us the results of the divine healer's powers and the blind man's confidence in those powers. "And immediately he received his sight." There was no delay in the healing process. The man received his sight immediately.

It was not enough for him to receive his sight. He got up from his old lifestyle of begging and followed Jesus. He became a follower of the master healer. He did not ask Jesus if he could go with him; he took it upon himself to follow this man who had done so much for him. Not only was he following God, but Luke says he was "glorifying God." The man must have been saying to himself and to all who would hear him, "I once was blind, but now I see." Or maybe the man might have been saying, "Where he leads me, I will follow. Where he leads me, I will follow. I'll go with him, with him, all the way."

The man might not have known where Jesus was really going. Jesus was going to Jerusalem to die for the sins of the world. He was on his way to Calvary. Luke states Jesus' goal and destiny:

> Then he took unto him the twelve, and said unto them, Behold, we go up to Jerusalem, and all things that are written by the prophets concerning the Son of man shall be accomplished.
> For he shall be delivered unto the Gentiles, and

shall be mocked, and spitefully entreated, and spitted on:

And they shall scourge him, and put him to death: and the third day he shall rise again (Luke 18:31-33).

Jesus knew where he was going, but I don't believe the blind man knew where Jesus was going. Neither did the disciples nor that vast throng of people who were following Jesus. You and I might not know where we are going when we follow Jesus. Jesus leads us along strange and difficult pathways. But he does get us home.

Because this one man was glorifying God, he motivated the others in that crowd to do likewise. You and I ought to sing the Lord's praises. We don't know whose faith we might strengthen by thanking God and glorifying God and praising the name of God and His Son, Jesus Christ.

If God has done something for you, praise His name!

If God has given you a new beginning, praise His name!

If God has lifted you up, praise His name!

If God has healed you, praise His name!

If God has given you a good wife, praise His name!

If God has give you a good husband, praise His name!

If God has brought you from a long way, praise His name!

If God has strengthened your faith, praise His name!

If God has opened doors for you, praise His name!

If God has given you healthy children, praise His name!

If God has given you spiritual insight, praise His name!

If God has given you unusual intelligence, praise His name!

If God has given you a sound, solid body, praise His name!

If God has forgiven you, praise His name!

If God has had mercy on you, praise His name!

If God has had compassion on you, praise His name!

If God has blessed your pantry, praise His name!

If God has given you a good job, praise His name!

If God has brought you out of trouble, praise His name!

If God has broken bad habits in your life, praise His name!

Jesus, Son of David, Help Me!

If God has moved mountains in your life, praise His name!

If God has given you health and wealth, praise His name!

If God has stood over your body in a dying hour and brought you from the door of death, praise His name!

If God has given you obedient children, praise His name!

If God has brought you through storms and vociferous winds, praise His name!

If God has relieved you of stress and strain, praise His name!

If God has given you emotional control, praise His name!

If God has taught you how to give to kingdom work, praise His name!

If God has put running in your feet and clapping in your hands, praise His name!

If God has given you a new song to sing, praise His name!

If God has filled your midnights with day, praise His name!

If God has made a way when no way was there, praise His name!

If God has straightened your back so that you can walk like a man or woman, praise His name!

If God has filled your life with the power of the Holy Ghost, praise His name!

If God has filled your life with Jesus, praise His name!

If God has filled your life with Himself, praise His name!

Praise God! Praise God! Praise God!

The man decided to follow Jesus and praise God. Like this man, I have decided to praise God and follow Jesus.

Jesus says to each one of us, "Learn of me." "Believe in me." "Have faith in me." "Abide in me." "Follow me."

Amen and amen.

The Healer
Helps the Earless

Jesus restores the severed ear of Malchus,
the high priest's servant
Luke 22:47-51

Patient/Diagnosis:
> The servant of the high priest whose ear was severed

Doctor:
> Jesus of Nazareth

Cure:
> "He touched his ear, and healed him."

Comments:
> In modern times it is not unheard of for an ear to have been avulsed from the head, replaced with stitches, and expected to survive. Today other organs are being successfully transplanted. Could the ear have been only lacerated and not completely severed from the head? Again it seems like another miracle.
> > Dr. Edwin W. Cocke, Jr.
> > Specialist in diseases of the ear,
> >   nose, neck, and throat
> > Memphis, Tennessee

The Healer Helps the Earless   247

This miracle is found in the Gospel of Luke, the 22nd chapter; and for our expository purposes we want to look at verses 47 through 51. This is the final miracle of healing for our Lord before the miracle of Calvary. It takes place in the vicinity of the garden known as Gethsemane. Luke does not mention the Garden of Gethsemane, but he does say that Jesus was in the vicinity of the Mount of Olives. The Garden of Gethsemane was at the foot of the Mount of Olives. And it was there that Jesus had gone on previous occasions with his disciples. All four evangelists record a prayer period before Calvary, and each of them—with the exception of Luke—mention the Garden of Gethsemane.

Jesus had completed an intense period of prayer. In that prayer period Jesus submitted to the final demand of his Father. His Father's will was that he would go to Calvary. He was to be the sacrificial Lamb of God. It was in that garden that he said "yes" to Calvary. He had made the request in verse 42: "Father, if thou be willing, remove this cup from me; nevertheless not my will, but thine, be done." The other evangelists say that he made this request three times. Luke mentions the request only once. "Nevertheless not my will, but thine, be done."

Jesus left that prayer period in the inner confines of the garden, regathered his disciples, and started to leave. As he started to leave the garden, something happened that was to help Jesus fulfill his destiny. It is beautifully stated by Luke when he says, "And while he yet spake, behold a multitude, and he that was called Judas, one of the twelve, went before them." This was to be the last time Jesus was to speak to his disciples as a free teacher of the Word. From that point on, he would be imprisoned, illegally tried by the officials, and ultimately condemned to death. In a sense, these final words would be his last as Jesus, the man, to his disciples. His next words to them would come after his crucifixion and resurrection.

"And while he yet spake." He had said so much in a short period of time. He had taught so profoundly, spoken so authoritatively, given such explicit directions concerning man's spiritual well-being, man's understanding of his relationship to his Father in heaven, and the sacredness of human personality. Jesus had spoken well in a short period of three years. He had given to humankind the complete plan of salvation. He had revealed to us the very heart of our Father who is in heaven.

"And while he yet spake." This seems to me to be so final, that Jesus spoke and never spoke again, for his word is an eternal word. He is like others whose words still live. Jesus spoke a relevant word for his own day, but his word still speaks. His word still guides the lives of men and women in our own day and time. His words are timely and timeless, because they are eternal words from the Father.

John could say of him in the magnificient prologue to his gospel, "In the beginning was the Word, and the Word was with God, and the Word was God" (John 1:1). His word is yet alive.

As we continue to examine these passages for our growth, our insight and our foresight for living, we find Luke saying, "Behold, a multitude." One might wonder why so many came to arrest one man. Why a host of people to bring to Roman justice one man? Why a mob? Why a crowd? Why armed soldiers to arrest a harmless, peripatetic proclaimer of divine truth? Yet this is always a problem, for evil has to have a multitude to do its bidding. Evil is never satisfied with having just a few people to do its bidding. Jesus had to be confronted by the might of the Roman Empire as a single individual. He had to confront all of the forces of evil. This was the beginning of that constant antagonism between Jesus, representing the forces of righteousness, and the multitude, representing the forces of evil. This clash continues throughout history. Sometimes a lonely figure stands tall for the forces of righteousness against a multitude of the forces of evil and wickedness and sinfulness. The greater evil in this passage, however, was that there was one man in that multitude who should not have been there.

As Luke goes on to tell the story, he says, "And he that was called Judas, one of the twelve, went before them." This was Judas, the son of perdition. Judas should not have been there in that multitude. But there he was, on the side of evil.

The Healer Helps the Earless   249

There are speculations galore as to why Judas betrayed
Christ, why Judas would lead that host of rabble-rousers, Roman
soldiers, and officials from the high priest to the beautiful
garden of prayer where his Lord and his Savior was wrestling
with the destiny of mankind. Why was Judas there? Judas was
there, according to the Scriptures, because Satan entered into
Judas and won control over Judas' thinking, mental equilibrium,
loyalty, and fidelity. As much as we would like to blame Satan
for Judas' collapse, one must examine the many passages which
point to Judas as the villain. Could this have been a deliberate
plot on the part of the other disciples who sought to paint Judas
a different color as they looked back on the ministry of their
Lord and Savior many, many years later?

There are those who believe that this is the case—that they
tried to portray Judas as a demonic, corrupt, treacherous,
money-loving disciple. Luke sums it up when he says, "Then
entered Satan into Judas surnamed Iscariot, being of the number
of the twelve. And he went his way, and communed with the
chief priests and captains, how he might betray him unto them.
And they were glad, and covenanted to give him money" (Luke
22:3-5). The deed of Judas becomes grotesque when we consider what he does after leading the people to Jesus. I think that
the disciples, especially Luke, tried to give some reason beyond
Judas for Judas' evil deed. We have to blame someone. So the
disciple Luke blamed Judas' deed on Satan. It seems to me that
Judas betrayed his Lord for money. This was a willful decision
on the part of Judas. He loved money. And as Paul said, "The
love of money is the root of all evil." Money is not evil in itself; it
is the love of money that makes men commit evil deeds. The
deed of Judas, however, becomes more grotesque when we
consider what he does after leading the people to Jesus.

Luke says, "And [he] drew near unto Jesus to kiss him." That
was the kiss of death. Judas helped to crucify Jesus by delivering
him to his enemies. The fact that he was a trusted disciple of our
Lord makes his deed one of the most infamous in the history of
mankind. He had been granted the sacred privilege of being a

disciple of Jesus Christ. The miracles Jesus performed should have convinced Judas that he was the Son of God. The authoritative teachings of Jesus should have convinced Judas that Jesus was more than another teacher of the Law of Moses. The tender love and compassion shown by Jesus should have been sufficient evidence for Judas that he was walking with the Anointed of the Lord God Almighty. And yet the cumulative evidence of who Jesus was was not enough to prevent the betrayal by Judas. Jesus had not done enough. And so Judas betrayed him with a kiss.

There are some Greek authorities who say that Judas kissed Jesus repeatedly—over and over again. There are those who believe that this kissing episode was designed to make sure that the officials arrested the right man, for this was—and still is—a custom in parts of the East. When men meet one another they kiss and embrace. A repeated kiss by Judas singled Jesus out as the one that was to be arrested by that multitude.

"And [Judas] drew near unto Jesus to kiss him." Jesus raises a fundamental question with Judas. "Judas, betrayest thou the Son of man with a kiss?" "Would you finger me as the one they are looking to kill? Would you be the one who would betray your calling, betray your inner best man? Would you betray your divinely-given destiny? Would you, Judas, utilize the time-old tradition of greeting one another with a kiss? Would you deliberately remove me as the center of man's chance for redemption? How cold, Judas! How callous! How indifferent! How unaware and unconscious you are, Judas, of the implications of this act! Your name will go down in history as one of the names that men will curse and damn from this day forward."

And for what purpose? Thirty pieces of silver. "Judas, betrayest thou the Son of man with a kiss?" Jesus was also saying to Judas, "I am among you as a man among men. I have exemplified for you the ultimate frontiers of human development. I have shown you what a man should be and can be. I have revealed to you man's capacity to grow and develop spiritually, morally, and physically. And in my manhood you have seen me

The Healer Helps the Earless   251

come to grips with human frailty, human feebleness, and human
weakness and conquer all of man's inadequacies. I have been
victorious over the temptations of evil with the naked spirit of
Almighty God. This gift is available to all men who would follow
the commands and demands of the Father in heaven. Man's
capacity to grow is unlimited, Judas.

"I have given you the role model which, if followed, would
help you and millions more, but you have betrayed the perfect
Son of God. Nevertheless, you are blind and have not seen."

Then Luke continues with this final experience in the Garden
of Gethsemane. In verse 49 he says, "When they which were
about him saw what would follow, they said unto him, Lord,
shall we smite with the sword?" The disciples of Jesus now
sought to take matters into their own hands. They had been with
Jesus. They had walked behind the lowly Galilean for almost
three years. They had been in that prayer period with
Jesus—some at the entrance of the garden, some in the middle
of the Garden—all of them, with the exception of Judas, had
been there. And now they sought to rally their little forces
together for a great conflict.

"They said unto him, Lord, shall we smite with the sword?"
As Luke tells the story, one can recognize that the story is told
from the perspective of looking back, for Luke uses the word
Lord here. In Christ's day and time, it is believed that the
disciples did not call him Lord. That word was not used with
reference to Jesus until after his resurrection experience. The
Greek word kurios (Lord) is the ultimate name given to Jesus by
his followers. It is the name that is above all names. It is the
name that singles Jesus out as the person to be worshipped. It is
the translation of Jehovah in the Old Testament (Gen. 2:4-22) and
Adonai (Exod. 4:10). The word lord could have been used to
designate a husband, as in Genesis 18:12. Men also used it to
designate other men as sir, as in Matthew 21:30. It also was used
as master, as in Genesis 24:14-27. Luke uses it for Christ (Luke
6:46), and again it was applied to God, as in Genesis 3:1-23.

William Barclay takes the position that the name Lord was

never applied to Christ until after his resurrection. As applied to Christ, *kurios* indicates identity with Jehovah. It indicates a confession of Christ's lordship in Joel 2:32, it refers to Jesus as Lord in Romans 10:9, and it indicates his absolute lordship in Philippians 2:11.

"Lord," they said to Jesus, "shall we smite with the sword?" They wanted to use the sword. They wanted to use violence. They wanted to use weapons of destruction to defend their Lord and their God.

This was not the first time the disciples of Jesus had wanted to use violence as a working hypothesis to get done what they felt was the Master's will. James and John on one occasion wanted to bring down thunder and lightning upon a village in order to destroy it. There were other occasions when his disciples wanted to resort to violence to defend their Lord. But Jesus never wanted to use violence; he never sought to use weapons of destruction to defend himself, his disciples or the community of believers who were to be developed after his resurrection. His weapons were weapons of the Spirit. "All they that take the sword," he said, "shall perish with the sword" (Matt. 26:52).

"Lord," they said, "shall we smite with the sword? And one of them smote the servant of the high priest, and cut off his right ear." Before Jesus could answer, one of his disciples acted. Luke does not tell us which one of the disciples it was. Tradition has it that it was Peter. If we were to examine the Gospel accounts, we would be fairly justified in making this kind of judgment. Peter was always impetuous, prone to speak when he should have been silent, prone to step ahead of his Lord, and prone to make independent judgments. A good case could be made that this was an act on the part of Peter.

"And one of them smote the servant of the high priest, and cut off his right ear." There are those who say that only a medical doctor could have noticed that this was the right ear. Being a medical doctor, Luke would perhaps be more observant

The Healer Helps the Earless

about where the wound was on the victim. "He cut off his right ear."

Jesus answered and said after the incident, "Suffer ye thus far." In other words, Jesus was saying, "This is enough of this violence. This is enough of this use of the sword. Bloodshed is not what is needed. My role is not the role of a conquering warrior with a sword. My kingdom, remember, is not of this world. My kingdom deals with the spirit. It is not by might, nor by power, but by my spirit. Gentleness, mercy, benignity are my powerful, victorious weapons. Alas, Peter, thou hast used the sword for the last time. This is not my way. This is Rome's way. This is the world's way. A continued escalation of violence will only lead to open conflict with death, destruction, and desolation. But my way is the way of sacrificial love, and it suffers long and is kind. It is everlasting and durable. And it is upon this spiritual basis that I will build my church, and the gates of hell shall not prevail against it."

"Suffer ye thus far." Then Jesus used his touching power, his touching capacity, and touched the servant of the high priest's ear with healing. "And he touched his ear, and healed him." Over and over again in the miracles of Jesus we see his capacity for healing by touching.

We should notice that Jesus volunteered to heal the man's ear. This was a part of the nature of Jesus. He willingly and sacrificially performed his works of healing voluntarily. "I will to do His will. And it is the Father's will that men be whole, that men be healthy, that men be strong. It is the will of the Father." The touch of Jesus meant much to many people in his day. His touch is still vital. His touch is still necessary. His touch is still available to his people who believe and to those who do not believe.

There is no indication in this passage that this servant of the high priest was a believer in Jesus. It is Jesus' faith in his God-given powers to heal, to make whole, to make sound those who are afflicted that heals. He heals those whom he desires to heal.

He touches those whom he desires to touch. He selects and elects those to whom it is his divine choice to make whole. It is not the Father's will that any should suffer. And so, here is a man outside of the stream of Jesus' ministry who receives help from within that stream.

I am here reminded of the Syro-Phoenician woman's daughter. She was not of the household of Israel, but Jesus gave her her wish. He healed her daughter. And so it is always true, and always will be true, that his touch embraces all men and women who need healing and help. The touch of the Master's hand is the thing we need desperately in our day. He touched the servant's right ear. He touched his ear and made it whole. He did not want this servant to move into history earless, with the possibility of a hearing defect. Jesus did not like unsoundness. Jesus did not like bodies that were not whole, minds that were not mended, souls that were not saved. He touched his ear and healed him.

"Then Jesus said unto the chief priests, and captains of the temple, and the elders, which were come to him. . . ." Note here who is in this multitude. Late at night, when they all should have been sleeping, here they were plotting and planning the destruction of the Son of God. "The chief priests," plural, indicates there was more than just one priest in this group. A group of them had gathered together. As well, there was more than one captain and more than one elder of the community. A multitude came to do evil. A number of people came, including high officials of the Sanhedrin Court and official guards of the temple. And the elders came—these solid, sound, serious religious leaders who had been given their exalted state by the multitude, the people who should have known better, the people who should have been willing to listen to what this young prophet had done, the people who should have appreciated his ministry of healing, helping, teaching, preaching, and revealing the will of God. These people who were entombed in the past closed their eyes to the Son of God. These people were blinded by their frozen position; these people were stubborn. These people,

The Healer Helps the Earless   255

hard and mean, were cruel to those who were not of the high, priestly class. The captains of the temple and the elders of the community were gathered together to plot Jesus' destruction. And so Jesus asks them, "Be ye come out, as against a thief, with swords and staves?"

In Matthew's gospel we read, "Are ye come out as against a thief with swords and staves for to take me? I sat daily with you teaching in the temple, and ye laid no hold on me" (Matt. 26:55). Here they were, with swords and staves and clubs, as if Jesus was a notorious criminal. They had their weapons. They had their swords and clubs. In our day, we have our guns, rifles, planes, tanks, bombs, poison gas, and biological germs. This is the way of the state—to maintain law and order. To implement the demands of government, we need weapons of violence. But not so in the kingdom of God. Jesus raises fundamental questions: Can weapons of violence save us? Can arsenals bring us peace? Is there more security as we develop our weapons of destruction and proclaim peace? There can be no peace when we see our government expending more for weapons of violence than for weapons of the Spirit, for education and medical care and other civic responsibilities which will lift the spirit of man, instead of those which will depress the spirit of man.

Men still believe that weapons of violence will buy us security, and that there is no threat when we have weapons of violence. Men will not learn from the lessons of history. Our weapons of violence will not save us; they will not bring peace on earth and good will among men.

What, then, will save us? It is the attitude of Jesus. It will take the sword of his spirit to bring us peace. Paul was right when he said to the church at Ephesus,

> Finally, my brethren, be strong in the Lord, and in the power of his might.
> Put on the whole armour of God, that ye may be able to stand against the wiles of the devil.

For we wrestle not against flesh and blood, but against principalities, against powers, against the rulers of the darkness of this world, against spiritual wickedness in high places.

Wherefore take unto you the whole armour of God, that ye may be able to withstand in the evil day, and having done all, to stand.

Stand therefore, having your loins girt about with truth, and having on the breastplate of righteousness;

And your feet shod with the preparation of the gospel of peace;

Above all, taking the shield of faith, wherewith ye shall be able to quench all the fiery darts of the wicked.

And take the helmet of salvation, and the sword of the Spirit, which is the word of God:

Praying always with all prayer and supplication in the Spirit, and watching thereunto with all perseverance and supplication for all saints;

And for me, that utterance may be given unto me, that I may open my mouth boldly, to make known the mystery of the gospel,

For which I am an ambassador in bonds: that therein I may speak boldly, as I ought to speak (Eph. 6:10-20).

There is our solution! We are to put on the whole armor of God, in order that we may be able to stand against the wiles of the devil. And putting on the armor of God, that we may be able to stand in that evil day, and having done all, to stand. This was an evil day in the life of Jesus. And there he stood, one lonely witness to truth. There he stood, surrounded by enemies—the chief priests, the captains of the temple, the elders, and the soldiers. There he stood, a lonely witness to God's eternal Word. A lonely witness to God's eternal Spirit. A lonely witness to God's eternal being. A lonely witness to the proposition that

The Healer Helps the Earless

might does not make right. A lonely witness, declaring to those who take the sword that they will perish by the sword. A lonely witness to the galvanizing thrust in human history that goodness will ultimately overcome.

Jesus went on to say, "When I was daily with you in the temple, ye stretched forth no hands against me: but this is your hour, and the power of darkness." "When I was daily with you. . . ." Could he be alluding to the devious method they had used to arrest him? They arrested him at night, not in the day. They did not have the courage to arrest him in the day, for had they arrested him by day, the officials knew that the people would not have allowed them to do so without a fight. There would have been turmoil in Jerusalem had they attempted this dastardly deed in the day. They had worked their plan to perfection. Evil always examines the options; and many times evil uses the options that are open to it to have its way with the least amount of bloodshed. They came at night to arrest our Lord, for they feared the people—the common people who loved him dearly and heard him gladly.

It is still true that the minorities who are poor love to hear of the Lord Jesus Christ. It is still true that the minorities who are poor are not disturbed about spending time in worship, about making a sacrificial commitment, about doing the little works, the little things around the church. It is still true that the minorities who are poor find a great deal of satisfaction in being true and faithful to the lowly Galilean.

Jesus continues: "Ye stretched forth no hands against me." "You did not raise your voices against me in the temple. You did not debate with me in the temple, which is really your prerogative. You did not deny the Scriptures I quoted to you in the synagogue when I said, 'The Spirit of the Lord is upon me, because he hath anointed me to preach the gospel to the poor.' You did not dispute with any degree of consistency the divine proclamations I have taught for the last three years. You laid no hands on me."

And then Jesus closes by saying, "But this is your hour, and the power of darkness." There are two "hours" here. Jesus is saying to the chief priests, the captains of the temple, and the elders of the people, "This is your hour. This is the moment of victory for you. This is the moment of joy for you. This is the moment of happiness for you. This is the moment of delight. You have your pound of flesh. You have plotted and planned with Judas. You have, at this moment, the prize. You will be rejoicing in that you will remove from your view one who is the embodiment of God's eternal truth, which you believe conflicts with the law of Moses. It does not conflict with the law of Moses but fills it fuller, enlarges it, expands it, and extends its horizons. But you cannot see that, for you are victims of the *status quo*. 'Come weal or come woe, your status is quo.' This is your moment. Rejoice, for it will be your last!"

Jesus also seems to be saying something to the others who were there—all of those who represented the power of darkness. This was the moment of darkness. Evil was personnified here in the form of the captains, the chief priests, the soldiers, the elders, and all of those around him—representatives of the kingdom of darkness.

We must not fool ourselves. Darkness has power, but God has all power. Darkness has might, but God has all might. Darkness seeks to exert itself, but the kingdom of God will extend its exerting power ultimately over darkness. The kingdom of darkness wins victories, but God will win the ultimate victory. The kingdom of darkness seems to reign on this earth, but God will one day transform this earth. This earth will become a new earth. But darkness reigns now. Darkness controls now. "This is your hour, and the power of darkness." There is a light being deposited in the midst of the darkness. And the darkness will not overcome it.

Darkness was all around him, yet in the midst of the darkness that enveloped our Lord, he found the time to heal a man. So must we all in the midst of the darkness shine as his lights to give light to those who have no light. For he has said of us, "Ye are the light of the world. A city that is set on an hill can-

The Healer Helps the Earless

not be hid. Neither do men light a candle, and put it under a bushel, but on a candlestick; and it giveth light unto all that are in the house. Let your light so shine before men, that they may see your good works, and glorify your Father which is in heaven" (Matt. 5:14-16).

We are lights, and when the darkness of our Gethsemanes envelops us, we are to shine as lights. Let your light shine. We are engulfed by darkness. Let your light shine in order that you might help and heal.

> This little light of mine,
> I'm going to let it shine,
> This little light of mine,
> I'm going to let it shine,
> Let it shine, let it shine, let it shine.
>
> Ev-rywhere I go, I'm going to let it shine. . . .
>
> All in my home, I'm going to let it shine. . . .
>
> Out in the dark, I'm going to let it shine. . . .
> —Traditional

Amen and amen.

Epilogue

This sermon series, *Help Me, Somebody!* was delivered to the congregation of Metropolitan Missionary Baptist Church in Memphis, Tennessee, during the years 1980-84. The sermons evolved from my intense and ardent fascination with the healing miracles of Jesus as recorded in the Gospel of Luke. Luke's accounts so humbled and inspired me as I read, taught, and lectured on them that I felt compelled to try to convey these emotions to my people from the pulpit. So after preaching these narratives over this four-year period, I proceeded to set them down on paper, hoping that a wider audience could eventually be reached and brought into the aura of this phase of Jesus' ministry. Thus, this collection of the healing miracles in Luke, wherein I have tried to highlight the amazing transformation of the biblical personalities who were recipients of Jesus' astounding gift.

I was also impressed with Jesus' unselfish spirit in regard to his gift of healing wounded souls and minds and bodies. He passed it on to his early disciples: Peter had the gift; John had the gift; and Paul, the great apostle to the Gentiles, also had the gift. I believe that Jesus also gave it to his church, that through its ambassadors, spiritual, mental, and physical renewal and restoration might be given to the sick and suffering, the bereaved and distressed.

In retrospect, I now believe that I had accepted these healing miracles in a personally detached, though caring, way. For I was more or less a theoretician, an onlooker, an empathizer who saw and felt suffering—in Scripture and in my own life experiences—and then moved on. In reality, these were the slings and arrows that pierced the bodies and souls of others, not me. My wife and I had fortunately been blessed with reasonably good health. We had been able to function as fairly normal physical beings and had entered the middle years with minimal physical distress.

Then came the summer of 1984, when the cry, "Help me, somebody!" leaped from the pages of the sermon manuscripts and pierced the very crevices of my own soul, blatantly exposing its fragility and reminding me that I, too, am a vulnerable child of God. What was once a cry heard only theoretically became at once a deeply moving personal experience, not unlike many I had shared and prayed over with countless others during the years of my pastoral ministry. What was once *their* cross now became *my* cross—*our* cross. For my beloved, devoted spouse had been informed by doctors that her future health depended upon the outcome of two massive and difficult operations which needed to be performed immediately.

This was not my initial confrontation with personal pain, grief, and anguish, for other dear family members had fallen seriously ill: my own sweet mother had succumbed to death, and I had been close at hand during other family crises. But to know that Dorothy, my loyal, consecrated, dedicated, and gentle companion, was about to face hospitalization and surgery of a most delicate and serious nature was a devastating thought. How like Job I felt! I had read and preached from his life over and over—then with my head, now with my heart. And I knew that as I struggled with faith in this vineyard of experience, only a healing miracle from God could bring comfort and peace to us again.

Epilogue   263

So in the year of 1984, we entered into a period of utter mental agony and spiritual anguish, aware that only the God who created us could raise our spirits from the depths. In spite of the amazing progress that modern research and technology have made, in spite of the reassuring words of the doctors with their tremendous medical skills and knowledge, in spite of the comforting, kindly words and gracious deeds from family and friends, we knew that only God Almighty could mend our shattered spirits and heal our broken hearts.

"Why? Why? Why?" I asked myself repeatedly. Why did this life-threatening illness fall upon this beautiful child of God, this born-again Christian, this madonna, this Christlike lady, this humble, unsophisticated, small-town girl who has grasped the eternal truth that the way into the kingdom is through humility and tender trust in God? Why does God allow the beautiful people to suffer? How often I had tried to answer this profound question to others; and now I myself was asking it!

Having earlier read Elizabeth Kubler Ross' book, *On Death and Dying*, in an effort to gain some fresh insights on this perennial human condition, I now returned to it, this time to place the information closer to my heart. As I reread the successive stages that the sufferer experiences, I could totally and completely identify.

First, says Dr. Ross, there is the stage of denial and isolation. I wanted to deny that this was happening to my wife. I tried to think of her illness as something unpleasant that, like a child, she would outgrow; that it would magically disappear, never to surface again. I could not face the fact that so lovely a person should be faced, within the space of six months, with two tremendous surgical operations. I wanted to doubt the physicians' diagnoses, even while making sure that her doctors were men of skill and integrity. We had our moments of denial.

And then there was the stage of isolation. We felt torn apart from our mutual friends, my ministerial associates, the members of our congregation, the office staff, her family, my family, and the many, many others who love and respect her. We were alone, in a sense two against the world, unable at that time to bare our grief and share our frustrations even with our dearest friends. Like patients housed in an isolation ward, though separate, we shared our pain, often silently, often with groping, tear-stained words.

Just as God had isolated her for the glorious moment of redemption when she became His child, He had isolated her for this period of pain and suffering, just as He did His own dear Son, so that she could become a "servant" of the kingdom.

Admittedly, I had never before been angry with God and had silently scoffed at those who had. Anger, I felt, was inappropriate and unchristlike when it is directed toward a wise and omniscient God. But before long this self-defeating, ugly emotion had overtaken me too. I was angry with God, angry with Jesus, angry with others who enjoyed good health, angry with television and other media healers, even while ironically considering presenting the situation to them. The anger that Dr. Ross so objectively described had now pervaded my soul. I was angry with my wife and angry with myself. I was angry for being angry! The bitterness and perversity became so intense at one point during this spiritual journey that I actually felt the need to shake my fist in the face of God! Now I could see what drowning in the hinterlands of despair can do for one, even a committed disciple and proclaimer of the Word.

Dorothy's gentle and trusting nature would not allow this dire emotion to surface, although at times I felt that she, too, was unconsciously and helplessly stifling the temptation. However, we both held tenaciously to each other and to our faith; and despite my anger and what I presumed to be hers, we concluded, like Job, that "though He slay us, yet will we trust in Him."

The next stage in the emotional process described by Elizabeth Ross is that of bargaining, trying to devise a treaty with God, saying to Him, "If You do this, I'll do that." We then found ourselves characteristically involved in this phase of the grief pattern. "God, if You would show us a miracle like You did for

Epilogue 265

the demon-possessed man of Gadara, the woman with the crooked spine, the widow of Nain, all the others; if You would only remove our bitter cup, we will hereafter commit ourselves to You and live as Christians at a higher level and with a deeper commitment."

I dared to make a personal, secret commitment to God, promising Him that if He would heal her, I would be a perfect model of what I felt a preacher and teacher and leader ought to be. If He would lengthen her days and strengthen her body, I would forsake my comfortable pulpit and loving congregation and go out into the highways and hedges and proclaim Him to sinners across the length and breadth of America.

But God is not a bargaining agent, and though He knows our weaknesses and selfish inclinations, He will not accept from us an invitation to the bargaining table.

So when I consciously realized what I already knew—that I cannot compromise with God, I found myself again facing this monstrous problem again. It was still there with the same unpleasant circumambience, seemingly waiting for me to come back to it again.

In desperation, we realized that our cross was still before us, haunting us and challenging us. We were forced to face it and decide for ourselves whether this moment of lamentation would be a source of renewal and restoration or a catalyst that would plunge us deeper into the dark abyss of depression.

And at times it did. Sometimes it seemed that depression had enveloped her, then me, then both of us together. Familiar and now personally meaningful utterances and questions from the psalmists sprang from my soul: "Where is God?" "How long, O Lord, how long?" "Why art thou cast down, O my soul?" "Why art thou disquieted within me?"

And it emerged in other negative ways too. I did not want to preach. I avoided old friends. I neglected Bible reading, sharing with others, all the old habits that had so interested and delighted me. I simply wanted to be left alone. I longed for a spot "way down yonder by myself."

I thank God for that period of loneliness and desolation! For during that time a ray of light appeared, and with it came divine illumination like I had never felt before. I caught hold of a spiritual reality that became a living reality for me. The words of Hebrews 5:7 and 8 took on new light and endowed me with fresh insights:

> In the days of his flesh, when he had offered up prayers and supplications with strong crying and tears unto him that was able to save him from death, and was heard in that he feared; Though he were a Son, yet learned he obedience by the things which he suffered.

That verse was my light in darkness. It was the key that unlocked the door to my depression. If Jesus, strong Son of God, learned obedience by the things he suffered while here on earth, surely I, Fred Lofton, frail servant of God, could emerge from this shattering experience with the firm belief that God could miraculously save my wife. He could free her, relieve her, deliver her from her pain.

And God heard me. He heard us. And like Jesus, we have learned obedience from our suffering. We were then able to move to another level—that of acceptance, recognizing that her condition, her problem, could be the will of God for her life. We had prayed so many times, "Thy will be done," but really meaning *my* will be done through You. But to really accept His will, we must lose our wills in His.

There subsequently came upon me a renewed sense of sheer commitment to the ministry of prayer, of preaching, of teaching, of helping, of healing, and above all, of praise and adoration. For we began to understand that he whom the Lord loves, the Lord chastises. As He chastised His only begotten Son, He will chastise adopted sons and daughters. Then came the discovery that if our plight was not God's will, it was Satan's attempt to turn a child of God against God. Remember how

Epilogue   267

Satan tried to persuade Job to curse God and die? If this perhaps was a confrontation with Satan, we were able to withstand his wiles and say with an even greater determination and conviction, "Though He slay us, yet will we trust in Him." So our trust portion has increased; we are now trusting completely and obediently in Him. Whether the pain diminishes or disappears, whether the anguish goes away or the agony ceases, we have learned how to trust in Him. And in the midst of our trusting, the doctors have made some remarkable progress, helping us to cope with more confidence in our situation.

We have now experienced, separately and together, in varying degrees, the stages that Dr. Ross delineates so accurately in her book—denial, isolation, anger, bargaining, and finally, acceptance. But we do not stop here. We submit to you, our readers, that there is another better, bigger, and brighter plateau: it is the state of glorious hope.

It is a hope that has been given to us by innovative technology and startling scientific discoveries. And most importantly, it is the hope that we have in Christ Jesus. It is earthly hope, but it has eschatological implications. It is the hope that transcends the tragic moments in our lives. And in this hope, says Paul in Romans 6, we are saved.

The past months have taught us much about our relationship to God and to each other, and God has answered our sincere cries for guidance and help. We believe He is still working in us and through us, in response to our prayers and those of our many friends.

Whatever the outcome, we are grateful that we know the Lord and, like Paul, are sure "that neither death, nor life, nor angels, nor principalities, nor powers, nor things present, nor things to come, nor height, nor depth, nor any other creature shall be able to separate us from the love of God."

Bibliography

Buttrick, George Arthur, et. al., eds. *The Interpreter's Bible*. Vol. VII, Matthew-Mark. Nashville: Abingdon Press, 1951-57.
_____. Vol. VIII, Luke-John. Nashville: Abingdon Press, 1951-57.
Barclay, William. *The Gospel of Luke*. Philadelphia: Westminster Press, 1975.
_____. *Jesus As They Saw Him*. New York: Harper & Row, 1962.
Edersheim, Alfred. *The Life and Times of Jesus the Messiah*. Grand Rapids, MI: Eerdmans Publishing Company, 1979.
Frazier, Claude A. *Healing and Religious Faith*. Philadelphia: Pilgrim Press, 1974.
Hobart, William Kirk. *The Medical Language of St. Luke*. Grand Rapids, MI: Baker Book House, 1954.
Miller, Madeleine S. and J. Lane. *Harper's Bible Dictionary*. New York: Harper & Row, 1961.
Pherigo, Lindsey P. *The Great Physician: The Healing Stories in Luke and Their Meaning for Today*. New York: The Education and Cultivation Division of the Women's Division, General Board of Global Ministries, The United Methodist Church, 1983.

Plummer, Rev. Alfred. *The International Critical Commentary—The Gospel According to St. Luke*. Edinburgh: T & T Clark, Ltd., 1975.

Redding, David A. *The Miracles of Christ*. Westwood, NJ: Fleming H. Revell Company, 1964.

Spence, H. D. M. and Joseph S. Exell, eds. *The Pulpit Commentary*. Grand Rapids, MI: Wm. B. Eerdmans Publishing Company, 1962.

Weatherhead, Leslie D. *Psychology, Religion and Healing*. New York: Abingdon-Cokesbury Press, 1951.